Books for You

Committee on the Senior High School Booklist

Shirley Wurth, Chair, Raytown Public Schools, Missouri
King Anderson, Truman High School, Independence, Missouri
Ina Butler, Pattonville Senior High School, Maryland Heights, Missouri
Laurel Ellingson, Truman High School, Independence, Missouri
Janet Ferguson, William Chrisman High School, Independence, Missouri
Clara Fisher, Raytown South High School, Missouri
Nancy H. Flamank, Raytown South High School, Missouri (retired)
Jean Gelsinger, Hickman Mills C-1 School District, Kansas City, Missouri
Linda Griffith, Truman High School, Independence, Missouri
Diane Hunter, Second Presbyterian Church, Kansas City, Missouri
Delores Lunceford, University of Missouri–Kansas City
Myrna McCain, Bridger Junior High School, Independence, Missouri
Paula Neale, Ingels Elementary School, Hickman Mills, Missouri
Doris E. Negaard, William Chrisman High School, Independence, Missouri
Joyce Pettus, Holman Middle School, St. Ann, Missouri
Dorothy E. Staley, Truman High School, Independence, Missouri (retired)
Alyse Stoll, Raytown South Middle School, Missouri (retired)
Janet Sturgess, Ruskin High School, Hickman Mills C-1 School District, Kansas City, Missouri
Sharon Thompson, Truman High School, Independence, Missouri
Lucinda Wilkinson, Houston, Texas
Carole A. Williams, Executive Committee Liaison, Mehlville School District, St. Louis, Missouri
Michael Spooner, NCTE Staff Liaison

NCTE Bibliography Series

Books for You

A Booklist for Senior High Students

Eleventh Edition

Shirley Wurth, Editor,
and the Committee on the Senior High School Booklist
of the National Council of Teachers of English

National Council of Teachers of English
1111 Kenyon Road, Urbana, Illinois 61801

Manuscript Editors: Michael Ryan and Marya Ryan

Production Editor: Rona S. Smith

Cover Design: R. Maul

Cover Illustration: Lisha A. Banks

Interior Design: Tom Kovacs for TGK Design

NCTE Stock Number 03650-3050

It is the policy of NCTE in its journals and other publications to provide a forum for the open discussion of ideas concerning the content and the teaching of English and the language arts. Publicity accorded to any particular point of view does not imply endorsement by the Executive Committee, the Board of Directors, or the membership at large, except in announcements of policy, where such endorsement is clearly specified.

Library of Congress Cataloging-in-Publication Data

Books for You: a booklist for senior high students/Shirley Wurth, editor, and the Committee on the Senior High School Booklist of the National Council of Teachers of English. —11th ed.

p. cm. —(NCTE bibliography series, ISSN 1051-4740)

Includes index.

Summary: An annotated bibliography of fiction and nonfiction books of interest to high school students. Includes author, title, and subject indexes.

ISBN 0-8141-0365-0

1. Young adult literature—Bibliography. 2. High School students—Books and reading. 3. High school libraries—Book lists. 4. Bibliography—Best books—Young adult literature. [1. Bibliography—Best books.] I. Wurth, Shirley. II. National Council of Teachers of English. Committee on the Senior High School Booklist. III. Series.

Z1037.B724 1992
[PN1009.A1]
011.62'5—dc20 92-26206

CIP

AC

Contents

Acknowledgments

One icy, wintry afternoon, three educators braved the nearly impassable streets to gather in my book-dominated basement for the first meeting to organize for the revision of *Books for You.* That was the initial indication of the devotion Nancy Flamank, Jean Gelsinger, and Dorothy Staley brought to this project. For their assistance in reading and encouraging their colleagues to volunteer, I am grateful, because much of this book is the result of their cooperative efforts.

The other readers, many of whom were English teachers loaded with papers and lesson plans, were faithful to the project because they themselves had used previous editions of *Books for You.* Now it was their turn to pass on information about books for reading enjoyment and knowledge to students, teachers, and librarians. They gave their time, talent, and energy in just one more way to help young people and their profession.

The NCTE staff, especially Michael Spooner, remained constant in giving assistance and even provided additional help in reading and annotating as the deadline neared. Without them, the book would not be as complete as it is.

The publishers regularly sent books as requested by the NCTE staff in Urbana. They, too, are interested in encouraging reading in a time when it is not always a number-one priority with young people. For their materials, we send them our appreciation for the gifts of books.

Without the authors, we would not have had the opportunity to compile this book. From those of us who are avid readers, we recognize and thank contemporary writers for continuing the history of good writing for good reading.

Shirley Wurth

Foreword

The National Council of Teachers of English is proud to publish four different booklists, renewed on a regular rotation, in its bibliography series. The four are *Adventuring with Books* (pre-K through grade 6), *Your Reading* (middle school/ junior high), *Books for You* (senior high), and *High Interest—Easy Reading* (junior/senior high reluctant readers). Conceived as resources for teachers and students alike, these volumes reference thousands of the most recent children's and young adults' trade books. The works listed cover a wide range of topics, from preschool ABC books to science fiction novels for high school seniors; from wordless picture books to nonfiction works on family stresses, computers, and mass media.

Each edition of an NCTE booklist is compiled by a group of teachers and librarians, under leadership appointed by the NCTE Executive Committee. Working for most of three or four years with new books submitted regularly by publishers, the committee members review, select, and annotate the hundreds of works to be listed in their new edition. The members of the committee that compiled this volume are listed on one of the first pages.

Of course, no single book is right for everyone or every purpose, so inclusion of a work in this booklist is not necessarily an endorsement from NCTE. However, it is an indication that, in the view of the professionals who make up the booklist committee, the work in question is worthy of teachers' and students' attention, perhaps for its informative, perhaps its aesthetic qualities. On the other hand, exclusion from an NCTE booklist is not necessarily a judgment on the quality of a given book or publisher. Many factors—space, time, availability of certain books, publisher participation—may influence the final shape of the list.

We hope that you will find this booklist useful and that you will collect the other booklists in the NCTE series. We feel that these volumes contribute substantially to our mission of helping to improve instruction in English and the language arts. We think you will agree.

Michael Spooner
NCTE Senior Editor for Publications

Introduction for the Student

When we want to share our latest telephone call from that special person or our winning goal, we usually go to our best friends. Oftentimes, those friends are our oldest friends. Other times, they are our latest acquaintances.

That is the way it is with books. We feel comfortable with old favorites, but the same diet becomes stale if we don't try new dishes to stimulate our appetites. We, as the *Books for You* committee, think that is the way it is with you, for whom we have gathered these titles. We want you to continue to read and enjoy your old favorites, but we realize the need to look at the thoughts and writings of contemporary authors. Books can bring you to a new discovery about yourself, your family, your world. Books can lead you to new hobbies, societies, thoughts, solutions, and beliefs.

You are in an ever-changing world which demands creative answers to countless questions. One of the ways to do this is to read and think about what you have read. Your interactions with the characters and the facts of a book are your own; the images come from within yourself, not a television or video producer. Your ability to synthesize what you are reading improves and broadens your outlook on life. Books, then, are one means of growing and learning.

There is another side to books. Books are for pure enjoyment, too. They take you places you have never gone; they push you into daredevil tricks you are hesitant to try; they drop you into situations which hold mystery and are filled with fantasy; they carry you to relationships which are better than any dream; they provide you with escapes from everyday problems. They become friends who stretch, tease, tantalize, and even terrorize you. They comfort you; they make you chuckle; they charm you; they play games with you. Most of all, they entertain you.

Since a reference book is as good as its organization, we have tried to make this issue of *Books for You* easy to use by organizing the titles into categories which hold special interest for you, a teenager. Under these categories, the books are arranged alphabetically according to the author's or editor's last name. The title, appearing in bold type, precedes the annotation, which gives the flavor of the book's content. This annotation, then, is the key to your discovering the right books for you.

If you have a special author who appeals to you, look for his or her name in the Author Index, located at the end of the listings, to find his or her latest book.

If you know the title, look in the Title Index, which conveniently lists all entries alphabetically.

What if you have just heard about a new book and cannot find it? We know that we have not been able to include all the latest volumes because we did not have access to all books in print. Book publishers were cooperative in sending their titles for the years 1988–1991, but some companies sent more than others. We relied on their sources for this issue of *Books for You.* You will notice that there are some reprints of old standbys. We found good reasons for including them, but we do not want you to think that these are the only earlier published works worth reading. We trust that you have access to earlier editions of *Books for You* to look up classics and other books published before 1988.

We have tried to make this book a helpful reference for all of you. Varying reading skills, different interests, and time for reading are major considerations when choosing a book. There are books just right for you. Glance through the topics, find titles, skim the annotations, take the book off the shelf, and settle in with a new friend.

1 Adventure and Survival

1.1 Anderson, Scott. **Distant Fires.** Illustrated by Les C. Kouba. Pfeifer-Hamilton, 1990. 156 pp. ISBN 0-938586-33-5. Nonfiction.

Crashing onto the rocky shore of Lake Superior on their second day out was not in the plan Scott Anderson and his friend Steve had made for their canoeing trip. But despite this less-than-glorious beginning, the two adventurers manage to make the 1,700-mile trip from Duluth, Minnesota, to York Factory on the shores of Hudson Bay. Scott Anderson chronicles the three-month trip, managing to convey his deep respect for the wilderness and the importance of preserving it, while using humor to make the narrative readable.

1.2 Bell, Clare. **Ratha and Thistle-chaser.** Margaret K. McElderry Books, 1990. 232 pp. ISBN 0-689-50462-4. Fiction.

In a world free of humans, a clan leader faces physical and emotional hardships during a time of drought. Ratha, leader of a clan of intelligent, speaking cats, faces some hard decisions as she moves her clan across the plains to the shore. During the trip, they encounter some "unnamed" cats, those not of the clan. It is accepted that unnamed cats are lesser beings, as they cannot talk and do not show intelligence. But Ratha's prejudices are challenged in a dramatic and life-threatening way when her own past rears its head, and she must face the one thing she has done that she truly regrets.

1.3 Bell, William. **Forbidden City.** Bantam/Starfire Books, 1990. 199 pp. ISBN 0-553-28864-4. Fiction.

Tiananmen Square comes alive in this novel when a young American would-be reporter finds himself staring with horrified eyes at mass murder. Young Alex Jackson is eyewitness to China's heartbreaking tragedy, and he shares that story with you.

1.4 Blake, Michael. **Dances with Wolves.** Fawcett/Gold Medal Books, 1988. 313 pp. ISBN 0-449-13448-2. Fiction.

In 1863, Lt. John Dunbar is the only man left alive at Fort Sedgewick. With his steadfast horse Cisco and a wolf that befriends him, Lt.

Dunbar roams the vast prairie until encountering a young Comanche widow who is near death. After returning her to her people, Lt. Dunbar gradually finds a new life with the Comanches and learns the startling secret of the young woman's identity. Mature language and situations.

1.5 Brinkley, William. **The Last Ship.** Viking, 1988. 616 pp. ISBN 0-670-80981-0. Fiction.

The U.S. destroyer *Nathan James* is possibly the last ship left in the world. After the nuclear holocaust, the world as we know it is in ruins, and the *Nathan James* heads for the South Pacific to avoid the deadly radiation that has spread over the rest of the planet. After surviving four months at sea and a mutiny staged by a third of the crew, the remaining crew of 152 men and 27 women settle on a lush tropical island. Dissension slowly begins to mount as the women, despite being in the minority, begin to gain in power. But then several of the women are murdered, raising great doubts as to whether this small band of men and women will be able to perpetuate the human race.

1.6 Camp, John. **The Fool's Run.** Henry Holt, 1989. 254 pp. ISBN 0-8050-0990-6. Fiction.

Kidd, the tarot-reading painter, finds himself involved in computer counterespionage on the corporate scene, along with sidekicks Luellen, a cat burglar; Dace, a down-and-out journalist; and Maggie Kahn, their ruthless contact with the corporation. Kidd stays ahead of the rival corporation, federal agents, and other impediments by using his brains, brawn, and tarot cards.

1.7 Charles, Kevin. **Shooters in Tech High School.** Turman, 1990. 87 pp. ISBN 0-89872-306-X. Fiction.

Two gangs, the Crips and the Bloods, keep the halls of Technical High School in constant turmoil. If Principal Jefferson does not want a repeat of last year's lunchroom killing, he must keep control of the situation at all times.

1.8 Curran, Jim. **K2, Triumph and Tragedy.** Photographs by Jim Curran. Hodder and Stoughton, 1987. 219 pp. ISBN 0-340-41526-6. Nonfiction.

K2, standing some 28,250 feet, is considered the second highest peak in the world and may prove to be even taller than Mt. Everest. It is recognized as the hardest and steepest mountain to climb. British photographer and climber Jim Curran spent the summer of 1986 in the K2 base camp as climbers from nearly a dozen countries attempted to climb this peak in the Karakoram range in northern Pakistan at its border with China. Nine expeditions attempted the climb, and twenty-seven climbers reached the summit. But there were thirteen climbers who died on K2 that summer, seven of them after making it to the top. Curran describes both the triumphs and the tragedies of the men and women who climbed K2. Color photographs, appendixes, bibliography, index.

1.9 French, Michael. **Circle of Revenge.** Bantam/Starfire Books, 1988. 151 pp. ISBN 0-553-05495-3. Fiction.

Sixteen-year-old Robbie Cavanaugh is thrilled to land a job as a subject in a psychological experiment at Western Pacific University. All he has to do is watch films, and he gets paid. His girlfriend Samantha, however, begins to question Robbie's behavior changes and the secrecy of the project. Defensive at first, Robbie eventually realizes that he has become a pawn in a deadly political game involving the doctor running the project and the doctor's rich friend, Carlos Montano.

1.10 Holland, Isabelle. **The Journey Home.** Scholastic, 1990. 212 pp. ISBN 0-590-43110-2. Fiction.

Maggie is twelve and Annie seven when they are orphaned in the slums of New York. But before her death, their mother arranged for them to be taken west with a group of other orphans, to find a new home. Almost immediately, Annie accepts their new life on the Kansas prairie with their new family, the Russells. Maggie, however, cannot let go of the past, especially since she doesn't fit into the present. She can't milk cows, she can't read, and she does not get along with animals. What will it take for Maggie to accept her new home? Easy reading.

1.11 Hudson, Jan. **Dawn Rider.** Philomel Books, 1990. 173 pp. ISBN 0-399-22178-6. Fiction.

Sixteen-year-old Kit Fox is a Blackfoot girl in the 1700s. As a middle child, she feels unappreciated and unexceptional. She finds an interest and identity when her people capture a horse from their rivals, but she must sneak around to learn to ride it. Together, girl and horse are given the chance to prove themselves to the tradition-bound and suspicious Blackfoot tribe when a raid leaves them devastated and some of the people are taken hostage.

1.12 Jenkins, Lyll Becerra de. **The Honorable Prison.** Lodestar Books, 1988. 199 pp. ISBN 0-525-67238-9. Fiction.

When Marta Maldonado's journalist father, Miguel, began criticizing the dictator of their Latin American country, the government closed down his newspaper, forcing Miguel and his friends to go underground to print and circulate the paper. Now Miguel fears for his family's safety, so he makes plans for them to sneak across the border and reach safety in Costa Rica. But just hours before their scheduled departure, army officers rush in and take Marta, her brother, and her parents to an isolated military base in the Andes—their honorable prison. Their safety and Miguel's declining health are constant concerns, and when their money is depleted, staying alive becomes an obsession. Is there no one to turn to for help?

1.13 Kingsolver, Barbara. **The Bean Trees.** Harper and Row/Perennial Library, 1989. 232 pp. ISBN 0-06-091554-4. Fiction.

Pittman County, Kentucky, is not the place that Missy Greer wants to spend the rest of her life. After she finishes high school, she works long enough to buy an old car, and then she heads west. Along the way, she changes her first name to Taylor. When she stops to eat in Oklahoma near a reservation, a woman abandons a child in her car. Taylor now has a little girl to take care of, but she has no home, no job, and no particular destination.

1.14 Laird, Christa. **Shadow of the Wall.** Greenwillow Books, 1990. 138 pp. ISBN 0-688-09336-1. Fiction.

Misha, along with his two sisters, is taken into an orphanage when times get hard for his widowed mother in Nazi-occupied Warsaw. Foraging and begging food to keep his mother alive, he loses out on a normal life as a teenager. The orphanage director, Dr. Janusz Korczak, becomes Misha's role model as Misha experiences feelings of hope, despair, anger, fear, and disgust with what is happening to the Jews in Poland. The character of Dr. Korczak is based on a real Polish hero, Henryk Goldszmit, who ran an orphanage in Warsaw.

1.15 Lasky, Kathryn. **The Bone Wars.** Morrow Junior Books, 1988. 378 pp. ISBN 0-688-07433-2. Fiction.

Thad Longsworth, an orphan, and his friend Julian, the son of a world-famous paleontologist, team up to excavate a dinosaur for the world to see, not for the scientists to hide away to study. Amidst intriguing characters, the boys experience adventures trying to outwit unscrupulous paleontology teams, everyone trying to unearth the ancient bones. Who would imagine that paleontology during the 1870s would be a thrilling activity?

1.16 Lisson, Deborah. **The Devil's Own.** Holiday House, 1990. 169 pp. ISBN 0-8234-0871-X. Fiction.

Fifteen-year-old Julie Dykstra does not want to leave Australia and travel with her family on a trip aboard their yacht, but she finds excitement when she is mysteriously transported into the seventeenth century. The *Batavia,* a Dutch ship, has been shipwrecked because of a mutiny, and Julie is tossed into a world of soldiers against soldiers, where plots of murder and revenge are commonplace. A loving relationship with Dirk, another teenager, makes this time travel tale even more memorable and worthwhile.

1.17 McFann, Jane. **No Time for Rabbits.** Avon/Flare Books, 1991. 165 pp. ISBN 0-380-76085-1. Fiction.

Bethany and Starling are working late on a history project with their teacher, Mr. Baldwin, when an ice storm forces them to remain in the school all night. Three other students are trapped there, too: Rocco, a giant weight lifter; Jyl, the beautiful Honor Society president; and Herbert, a ninety-five-pound wimp. Conditions worsen as the telephone service and power go out. Then, when Mr. Baldwin has a heart attack, all five students must work together to get help. Through these trials, Bethany learns that Starling is more than just a good friend.

1.18 Nelson, Pèter. **Night of Fire.** Archway Paperbacks, 1991. 180 pp. ISBN 0-671-70583-0. Fiction

Sylvia Smith-Smith, a volunteer teacher in a burned-out ghetto in New York City, spends a memorable Fourth of July weekend with young students from the projects and suburbs. Although only a high school student herself, Sylvia finds herself in charge, along with two other high school students acting as counselors. No adults are anywhere near when members of the Blue Radio gang break in for revenge over an earlier encounter with Steve, one of the counselors. Sylvia assembles a group to fight the gang, as she knows the police won't help. Ingenuity and skills learned in other situations pay off for the ragtag group as they combat the gang's terror.

1.19 Paulsen, Gary. **Canyons.** Delacorte Press, 1990. 184 pp. ISBN 0-385-30153-7. Fiction.

When fifteen-year-old Brennan Cole finds a skull while camping near Dog Canyon, his adventure begins. He feels compelled to discover the skull's background. As his research unravels the mystery, he learns it's that of an Apache boy named Coyote Runs, who was killed by soldiers in 1864. Sensing a strong link to Coyote Runs, Brennan feels he must return the skull to the Apaches' sacred burial place. Will he succeed?

1.20 Paulsen, Gary. **The River.** Map by Neil Waldman. Delacorte Press, 1991. 132 pp. ISBN 0-385-30388-2. Fiction.

In *Hatchet,* Brian Robeson survived the wilderness for fifty-four days with nothing more than his hatchet and common sense. When he is asked to do it again, this time for science and humankind in researching survival techniques, he finds it difficult to make a decision. It is the first of many decisions he must make as he decides to try the trip again, this time with psychologist, Derek Holtzer, who will record what happens. But complications set in when Derek is injured in an accident, and Brian must once again rely on his skills to save them both. Nature is just as formidable as it was the first time around, but Brian finds inner strength to help him cope.

1.21 Peck, Robert Newton. **Hallapoosa.** Walker and Company, 1988. 215 pp. ISBN 0-8027-1016-6. Fiction.

It is a hot, muggy August day in 1931 when Justice of the Peace Hiram MacHugh receives word that his younger brother, Bobby, and Bobby's wife have been killed in an automobile accident. Their children, twelve-year-old Thane and seven-year-old Alma Lee, are to come live with Hiram in Hallapoosa, Florida, or be placed in an orphanage. Hiram immediately asks for the children, although at fifty-two, he questions whether he'll have the stamina for two active children. Hiram also knows that he'll have to end his one pleasure in life—the Saturday night visits from Glory Callister, a young "Cricker" woman, so named because her family lives on the swampy island where the "crick" divides. What follows is a story of suspense involving a murder, a dead man's secret, and a lost child.

1.22 Popham, Melinda Worth. **Skywater.** Graywolf Press, 1990. 206 pp. ISBN 1-55597-127-X. Fiction.

When Albert and Hallie Ryder discover that there are poisons seeping into the groundwater of the Sonora desert where they live, they are forced to foul their cistern so the unsuspecting animals won't drink it. One enterprising and gutsy coyote, dubbed Brand X by the Ryders, sets off on a quest to find the legendary skywater before all of them, people and animals, die of thirst. Much to his dismay, Brand X immediately becomes a hero and acquires a band of two- and four-legged companions on his journey.

1.23 Roskelley, John. **Nanda Devi: The Tragic Expedition.** Avon Books, 1988. 214 pp. ISBN 0-380-70568-0. Nonfiction.

John Roskelley, one of the world's foremost mountain climbers, tells the tragic story of his 1976 ascent of Nanda Devi, a 25,645-foot peak in the Himalayas of Northern India. His group of eleven men and women faced avalanches, snowstorms, physical exhaustion, and even death. Despite conquering the mountain, the climbers were burdened with strong emotions, powerful egos, and conflicting ambitions—all putting a damper on the memory of their mountain-climbing triumph.

1.24 Strasser, Todd. **Beyond the Reef.** Illustrated by Debbe Heller. Delacorte Press, 1989. 243 pp. ISBN 0-385-29782-3. Fiction.

Problems begin almost at once when Chris and his folks pull up stakes in New York state and move to Key West, Florida, to begin a new life. Chris's father, an ex-school teacher, takes on the appearance and the life of a poor treasure-hunter. His mother, after working as a waitress for a few years, just can't take the hard life anymore and returns to New York. When a good friend, Bobby Clark, is killed in a diving accident, Chris's father gives up and starts drinking heavily. Chris and his best friend Shannon team up to find a way to bring Chris's father out of his alcoholism and begin treasure hunting again.

1.25 Talbert, Marc. **Rabbit in the Rock.** Dial Books for Young Readers, 1989. 216 pp. ISBN 0-8037-0693-6. Fiction.

Sixteen-year-old Bernie wanders the canyons around her home, bored and restless during the summer vacation. One day, she stumbles upon a young man camping alone. He is obviously not from the area and is inept at survival in the canyons. She befriends him, and as they grow closer, Sean tells her that he is a rock star who has run away from a tour and from his domineering father. Although she is not sure if she believes him, Bernie agrees to help Sean pretend that he has been kidnapped. Things go well until the FBI is called in, and both Bernie and Sean realize that they have gotten in way over their heads!

1.26 Taylor, Theodore. **The Hostage.** Dell/Laurel-Leaf Books, 1991. 158 pp. ISBN 0-440-20923-4. Fiction.

Jamie Tidd and his father are celebrating their feat of cornering a whale in a cove and planning what they will do with the money they will have. Then along come many people who are against their killing the whale. Jamie and his dad believe in saving wildlife of all kinds, but this is money and achievement lost if they agree to do what members of the press and environmental groups want them to do. Their struggles with what's right and what's wrong cause problems for them and their family and friends. Eventually, the whale becomes a "friend" in their adventure.

1.27 Vander Els, Betty. **Leaving Point.** Farrar, Straus and Giroux, 1987. 212 pp. ISBN 0-374-34376-4. Fiction.

Ruth has been looking forward to leaving her boarding school in eastern China and rejoining her missionary family in Chengtu. But the police think that her two younger brothers are spies, and they will not be allowed to return to school. Worse, she and her family are going to have to find a way to get out of China. This is not going to be an easy thing for Ruth: her home is filled with strangers waiting to gain exit permits, she cannot get along with her once-trustworthy brother Simeon, and her family seems to be falling apart under the pressure. It seems like the only person she can count on is Chuin-mei, a Chinese revolutionary who Ruth becomes more and more involved with. That involvement can mean serious trouble for Ruth, Chuin-mei, and even Ruth's family when the police learn of the friendship between the two girls. Will Ruth and her family be able to escape China before something terrible happens? Sequel to *The Bomber's Moon.*

1.28 Westall, Robert. **Fathom Five.** Alfred A. Knopf/Borzoi Sprinters, 1990. 255 pp. ISBN 0-679-80131-6. Fiction.

Sixteen-year-old Chas McGill worries about his tall, thin body, but his brain is active as he enlists his friends to help catch a spy who is giving away secrets to the enemy. Trying to pacify his mother, who worries about what the neighbors might think, is the least of Chas's problems. Identifying a radio transmitter he has found on the beach leads him and his friends into both sabotage and murder. Sequel to *The Machine Gunners.*

1.29 Westall, Robert. **The Machine Gunners.** Alfred A. Knopf/Borzoi Sprinters, 1990. 186 pp. ISBN 0-679-80130-8. Fiction.

Chas McGill, a teenager growing up in Garmouth, England, during World War II, collects war souvenirs. Nightly blackouts and German air raids are a fact of life, and one morning Chas finds a downed German plane in the nearby woods. The pilot is dead, and Chas makes plans to detach the plane's machine gun, hide it from adults, and use it against the Nazis, should they invade. To do so, he enlists the help of his friends, Cem, Audrey, Clogger, and Nicky. Together they fight to keep their secret as suspense builds to an unexpected climax.

1.30 White, Ellen Emerson. **Long Live the Queen.** Scholastic Hardcovers, 1989. 343 pp. ISBN 0-590-40850-X. Fiction.

High school senior Meg thought she had problems: boyfriends, what to wear to the prom, how to ditch the secret service, and how to relate to the President of the United States, who just happens to be her mother. Things get unimaginably worse, though, when she is violently kidnapped from her high school. She begins a devastating fight to keep body and soul together as she deals with an alternately charming and abusive captor. Survival becomes a daily battle, and Meg is forced into a terrible sacrifice to save herself. But when she makes it home, battered, starved, and emotionally numbed, she realizes the hardest fight is still ahead of her. With humor and love on her side, Meg tries to recapture control over her life in a world that will never be the same for her again.

2 Animals

2.1 Brooks, Bruce. **On the Wing: The Life of Birds: From Feathers to Flight.** Charles Scribner's Sons, 1989. 192 pp. ISBN 0-684-19119-9. Nonfiction.

What is "the first step in being a bird"? Birds have feathers, and that is what distinguishes them from all other living creatures. This book looks at birds in great detail, from feathers to flight to food to "family life." In the many color photographs, you will examine their bills, feet, and wings and see them building nests, hunting, hatching, and singing. And in the last chapter you will learn about the relationship between birds and human beings.

2.2 Edwards, Hugh. **Crocodile Attack.** Avon Books, 1990. 238 pp. ISBN 0-380-71189-3. Nonfiction.

Following years of research and interviews with survivors and observers, Hugh Edwards tells you about crocodiles, including complete details of the better-known attacks on humans. You'll learn about the crocodile's living habits, its methods of attack, and safety hints to use in croc territory. A sense of awe and admiration for the reptile underlies the lore and legends surrounding these elusive creatures. The book blends tragedy and folklore as it teaches you about crocs.

2.3 Freethy, Ron. **Secrets of Bird Life: A Guide to Bird Biology.** Cassell/Blandford, 1990. 232 pp. ISBN 0-7137-2154-5. Nonfiction.

How do birds fly? Why do they migrate? How do they sing? Why do they sing? These commonly asked questions, and many more, are answered in this comprehensive introduction to ornithology. Line drawings, tables, and black-and-white and color photos clarify the text, which assumes no specialized biological knowledge on your part: the scientific terms are all explained in the text.

2.4 Gabhart, Ann. **For Sheila.** Avon/Flare Books, 1991. 149 pp. ISBN 0-380-75920-9. Fiction.

Life seems to be going well for Sydney. She has both a job she loves at a veterinarian's boarding kennel and the leading part in a play. But she still misses her sister, who has died, and her father, who has left home to marry one of his students. Then a little white dog shows up suddenly and mysteriously, but only when Sydney is alone. No one else sees the dog, but Sydney grows to understand why it has come.

2.5 Johnson, Rebecca L. **The Secret Language: Pheromones in the Animal World.** Lerner, 1989. 64 pp. ISBN 0-8225-1586-5. Nonfiction.

Many animals produce chemicals called pheromones that enable them to communicate with others of their species by sending chemical messages. This book explores the sending and receiving of such "secret language" messages, with special emphasis on the honeybee. An understanding of pheromones opens the way to practical applications that include attracting helpful insects and fighting insect pests.

2.6 Kilworth, Garry. **The Foxes of Firstdark.** Doubleday, 1989. 371 pp. ISBN 0-385-26427-5. Fiction.

O-ha the fox lives in a time of great change. Although the woods where she was born have been safe for generations, humans begin encroaching upon the area animals dwell in. When O-ha's first mate is killed by farm boys, she is pregnant and struggles for survival until she is taken in by a kindly badger. But when her cubs are murdered, she loses interest in life. When a new fox, Camio, escapes from a zoo and comes to her part of the woods, O-ha regains her will to live and the ability to love. Together they produce a dynasty of unusual foxes who adapt to the times and survive the changes that inevitably come to the woods.

2.7 Liotta, P. H. **Learning to Fly: A Season with the Peregrine Falcon.** Algonquin Books of Chapel Hill, 1989. 201 pp. ISBN 0-945575-15-7. Nonfiction.

P. H. Liotta was a graduate student and Air Force officer when offered the opportunity to spend seven weeks in continuous care and observation of five peregrine falcons at a peregrine recovery program in New York. The young birds spent their first two to three weeks with adult falcons, crucial for imprinting, and then were transferred to the release site. There the birds were kept in a 4-x-4-foot plywood box with a vinyl mesh front until their sixth week, when the mesh was removed and the birds were free to explore. In the absence of parents, the young fledglings had to teach themselves to survive, which for a falcon means speeding through the air at 200 mph to snap a prey's neck with the slap of a talon and the bite of a razor-sharp beak. Liotta describes the birds' stay in the box, their release, and their learning to fly and feed. But more than that, this is a personal memoir, in diary format, of Liotta's comparison between falcon and airplane and between falcon and pilot, both of whom must come to terms with their gifts of power and speed and with their physical limitations. It is also an exploration of Liotta's own inner feelings and views of life.

2.8 Mattison, Chris. **A–Z of Snake Keeping.** Photographs by the author. Sterling, 1991. 143 pp. ISBN 0-8069-8246-2. Nonfiction.

Colorful photos and simple instructions bring snake keeping into focus for those interested in a hobby that is rapidly growing in popularity. Making this a successful hobby involves selecting a suitable species, maintaining hygiene, using proper cages, and knowing feeding habits and normal behavior patterns. Enhance your knowledge as a backyard herpetologist who no longer finds snake keeping such an inexplicable hobby.

2.9 McHargue, Georgess. **The Horseman's Word.** Dell/Laurel-Leaf Books, 1988. 259 pp. ISBN 0-440-20126-8. Fiction.

Champion rider Leigh Powers goes to Kinloch Farms in Scotland to help her Aunt Connie and Uncle Will with their pony-trekking business. There she meets handsome Rob Tinto, hears Scottish folklore, and joins the Common Riding. The big challenge, however, comes when Rob helps Leigh disguise herself as a boy and participate in the for-men-only secret ceremony of the Horseman's Word. Will they be caught?

2.10 Morris, Desmond. **Catlore.** Jonathan Cape, 1987. 114 pp. ISBN 0-224-02520-1. Nonfiction.

Cat fanciers will enjoy learning more about the most popular pet in the United States. Designed as a sequel to *Catwatching, Catlore* answers the questions about cats and cat behavior posed by readers of the first volume, such as how sensitive is a cat's hearing, how does a cat purr, and why does a cat prefer to die alone. Cat haters or cat-phobic individuals might be interested to learn that cats really do seek them out in a room of people. Why? Because they are probably the only people who are not moving around to catch the cat's attention, not waving their hands, not talking in a shrill voice, and, above all, not staring at them—all mildly threatening behaviors to cats. Black-and-white line drawings.

2.11 Paulsen, Gary. **Woodsong.** Illustrated by Ruth Wright Paulsen. Bradbury Press, 1990. 132 pp. ISBN 0-02-770221-9. Nonfiction.

Gary Paulsen tells of his life in northern Minnesota, which is full of adventures with wolves, deer, and sled dogs. His tale of his race across Alaska is as adventurous as are his tales of wild animals, and he gives you an account of each day's life on that race, the Iditarod.

2.12 Peacock, Doug. **Grizzly Years.** Henry Holt, 1990. 288 pp. ISBN 0-8050-0448-3. Nonfiction.

Doug Peacock almost brings the grizzly bear into the living room with you as he tells of the adventures in the American wilderness. Humans and animals live in fear and distrust of one another; Peacock, unarmed and alone, recounts how that suspicion was broken down in the mountains of Wyoming and Montana.

2.13 Perry, Nicolette. **Symbiosis: Nature in Partnership.** Cassell/Blandford, 1990. 218 pp. ISBN 0-7137-2155-3. Nonfiction.

"Symbiosis" means living together; it is the term used to describe a relationship between two different species for the benefit of both. The text, color photographs, and line drawings help you understand such symbiotic relationships as a carp that cleans a hippo's mouth, a goby fish that protects a blind shrimp, and a mackerel living in a Portuguese man-of-war's poisonous tentacles. Hundreds of examples are given, ranging from algae, fungi, and pollination to coral reefs, hippos, and humans.

2.14 Phelps, Tony. **Poisonous Snakes.** Cassell/Blandford, 1989. 272 pp. ISBN 0-7137-2114-6. Nonfiction.

The newly updated *Poisonous Snakes* classifies over 200 venomous snakes by type and includes valuable reference sections on venom, keeping poisonous snakes in captivity, antivenin, and snakebites. This book, an informative study guide of one of nature's most mysterious and feared species, contains over a hundred full-color and black-and-white photographs.

2.15 Pringle, Laurence. **The Animal Rights Controversy.** Harcourt Brace Jovanovich, 1989. 103 pp. ISBN 0-15-203559-1. Nonfiction.

The author explores many questions central to the growing controversy about the human use of animals. He discusses the historical and philosophical backgrounds of the animal rights movement and offers an extensive bibliography.

2.16 Sedgwick, John. **The Peaceable Kingdom: A Year in the Life of America's Oldest Zoo.** William Morrow, 1988. 413 pp. ISBN 0-688-06367-5. Nonfiction.

John Sedgwick spent the year 1985–86 working at the Philadelphia Zoo. Opened July 1, 1874, the zoo claims to be the oldest zoo in the country. It measures forty-two acres in size, less than the average of fifty-five acres for the country's 175 zoos and dwarfed by the 265-acre Bronx Zoo. Sedgwick describes his tenure at the Philadelphia Zoo in a chronological manner, commenting on zoo births, the acquisition of animals from other zoos, crowd control for the more than one million annual visitors, and finances, and he provides portraits of some of the 1,700 individual animals (representing 550 species) and of the keepers and administrative staff of the zoo. Black-and-white photographs.

2.17 Tang, Xiyang. **Living Treasures: An Odyssey through China's Extraordinary Nature Reserves.** Bantam Books. Copublished by New World Press, 1987. 174 pp. ISBN 0-553-05236-5. Nonfiction.

Through this book you will visit a few of the 316 nature reserves which cover 42 million acres in China. The author tells of his experiences in finding and photographing natural ecosystems, rare animals and plants, and valuable geological features. In the Huaping Forest grows the Cathay silver fir, discovered in the 1950s; in Sichuan Province there is a special panda research center; and in Wudalianchi Nature Reserve there is a natural museum of live volcanoes. At the back of the book are pictures of the animals and plants under government protection.

3 Art and Architecture

3.1 Arenas, José Fernández. **The Key to Renaissance Art.** Lerner, 1990. 80 pp. ISBN 0-8225-2057-5. Nonfiction.

Looking for a brief overview of Renaissance art? The concise explanations and colorful illustrations of Professor Arenas's book reveal the fifteenth- and sixteenth-century artists' challenge: to assimilate in their works the renewed interest in classical and pagan ideals with the medieval period's Christian philosophy. This book shows how Michelangelo's, Filippo Brunelleschi's, Leonardo da Vinci's, and others' successful blending of these two conflicting ideas produced an art form for the period that celebrated the classical world, nature, and the human body. From the Key to Art series.

3.2 Greenberg, Jan, and Sandra Jordan. **The Painter's Eye: Learning to Look at Contemporary American Art.** Delacorte Press, 1991. 96 pp. ISBN 0-385-30319-X. Nonfiction.

This introduction to contemporary American art includes ways of seeing, experiencing, and appreciating twentieth-century art. The color plates of works by such modern notables as Willem de Kooning, Jackson Pollock, Mark Rothko, Roy Lichtenstein, Wayne Thiebaud, and Andy Warhol are presented with suggestions of how you can examine and appreciate them as well as works of their contemporaries. A bibliography, glossary, and biography section all contribute to this educational resource on modern American painting and artists.

3.3 Hamilton, John. **Sketching with a Pencil: For Those Who Are Just Beginning.** Cassell/Blandford, 1991. 48 pp. ISBN 0-7137-2284-3. Nonfiction.

This book for beginners presents the basics of drawing. Selection of materials to use, choices of easy subjects, and information about perspective and composition are first steps. Tips on drawing landscapes and still lifes are illustrated in simple sketches and finished drawings. You will also learn about shading, depth, distance, and reflection.

3.4 Mackay, Donald A. **The Building of Manhattan.** Illustrated by the author. Harper and Row, 1987. 150 pp. ISBN 0-06-015788-7. Nonfiction.

Did you know that when the topmost piece of steel is finished on a new skyscraper, an American flag and a small fir tree are set on top of it? That's one of the many facts you'll learn in this book. Donald Mackay describes the structures built throughout Manhattan's history—from the Native American longhouses to the skyscrapers. His line drawings show you in great detail the people, the machinery, the problems, and the construction involved in building both below and above the ground on the island of Manhattan.

3.5 Reyero, Carlos. **The Key to Art from Romanticism to Impressionism.** Lerner, 1990. 74 pp. ISBN 0-8225-2058-3. Nonfiction.

The nineteenth-century art world found itself split into five different styles following the Industrial Revolution. Throughout the century, Romanticism, Eclecticism, Realism, Impressionism, and Symbolism appeared in all art forms—town planning, architecture, sculpture, painting, drawing, image reproduction, and decorative art. This book explains the development of these styles by reference to the works of Paul Delaroche, Antoine-Louis Barye, Gustave Courbet, Claude Monet, and Dante Gabriel Rossetti. Photos are provided of each artist's works. From the Key to Art series.

4 Biography and Autobiography

4.1 Abdul-Jabbar, Kareem, with Mignon McCarthy. **Kareem.** Random House, 1990. 230 pp. ISBN 0-394-55927-4. Nonfiction.

This diary is a detailed account of Abdul-Jabbar's last season with the Los Angeles Lakers—the 1988–89 season, when the Lakers were going for their third consecutive world championship. As Abdul-Jabbar talks about his last year in the game he spent three decades playing, he also dwells on his boyhood in New York and the inspirational, eccentric, and comic people he has met, from his high school coach to Magic Johnson and even Jack Nicholson. This book is his farewell to basketball and the people he played the game with for so long.

4.2 Ashabranner, Brent. **The Times of My Life.** Cobblehill Books, 1990. 114 pp. ISBN 0-525-65047-4. Nonfiction.

Author Ashabranner has lived in times and places that most of us can only read about. He talks about the Depression, two wars, the Kennedy years, and civil rights; he lived in Africa and India, where he started and directed Peace Corps programs; he was a senior government official in Washington, D.C.; and he has also found the time to be a writer! His memories are a touching, personal, and sometimes funny look at places and events we learn about in a drier way at school.

4.3 Barnes, Jeremy. **Samuel Goldwyn: Movie Mogul.** Silver Burdett Press, 1989. 144 pp. ISBN 0-382-09586-3. Nonfiction.

This is the story of Sam Goldfish, later Goldwyn, a Polish Jewish immigrant who later became one of the United States's premier movie moguls, producing such movies as *Wuthering Heights* and *Porgy and Bess.* This book follows Sam's life from his arrival in the States in 1895, to his early involvement in the movies around 1911, to the height of his career. The book shows you a driven, sometimes difficult, but unusually successful personality. From the American Dream series.

4.4 Bentley, Judith. **Fidel Castro of Cuba.** Julian Messner, 1991. 124 pp. ISBN 0-671-70198-3. Nonfiction.

Fidel Castro was born to a wealthy Cuban farmer in a province that had a reputation for being rebellious. Could this have set the tone for the political life Castro was to lead in his rise to prominence as a world figure? The author makes the case that this well-educated guerilla who led Cuba in a revolution is solely responsible for Cuba becoming a socialist state. This biography not only details Castro's rise to power, his obsession with the revolution and the faulty Bay of Pigs invasion, but also criticizes socialism, listing problems like the failing economy and low morale under the Castro regime. What hope exists for Cuba beyond Castro, the aging revolutionary? From the In Focus Biography series.

4.5 Bonanno, Massimo. **The Rolling Stones Chronicle: The First Thirty Years.** Henry Holt/Owl Books, 1990. 221 pp. ISBN 0-8050-1301-6. Nonfiction.

These accounts of all the Rolling Stones's performances and related activities are recorded in chronological order, from 1960–1989. Photographs, quotes, newspaper articles, and eyewitness reports answer your questions about the famous rock group. Each member's career is briefly outlined in both words and pictures.

4.6 Bowman, John. **Andrew Carnegie: Steel Tycoon.** Silver Burdett Press, 1989. 128 pp. ISBN 0-382-09582-0. Nonfiction.

Imagine your family deciding to move far away from your home because your town had become a poor and even dangerous place to live. This is what happened to a thirteen-year-old named Andrew Carnegie when his family moved from Scotland to the United States. This is the story of Andrew, who earned $1.20 a week at his first job and who later was unable to give all of his money away because he had so much. This book tells of his wealth as a steel tycoon and his willingness to donate his money to good works. From the American Dream series.

4.7 Brandelius, Jerilyn Lee. **Grateful Dead Family Album.** Warner Books, 1989. 256 pp. ISBN 0-446-51521-3. Nonfiction.

The author has been associated with the Dead for twenty years now, and here she has compiled a textual and photographic retrospective of the band that is a way of life to thousands of its fans. She follows the band from the early years in the 1960s, through the Acid Test days, the pilgrimage to the pyramids, and the recent "Alone and Together" tour with Bob Dylan. There are hundreds of never-before-seen photographs, with cameo appearances by The Who and Janis Joplin, among others, as well as anecdotes, testimonials, memories, and poems by the band and its countless fans.

4.8 Brooks, Polly Schoyer. **Beyond the Myth: The Story of Joan of Arc.** J. B. Lippincott, 1990. 176 pp. ISBN 0-397-32423-5. Nonfiction.

In 1428 France was torn by religious strife, plague, and warfare. The last king believed he was made of glass, and no saner ruler appeared to be in the offing. In stepped a peasant girl named Joan, whose inner voices and visions helped her inspire a nation. Joan, with her faith and determination, led her country to victory at Orléans and made the coronation of a new king possible. She was ultimately burned as a witch, for reasons discussed in this book. Now the most popular French saint, Joan's story is retold here without glorifying her or belittling her achievements and impact.

4.9 Brown, Gene. **Duke Ellington.** Silver Burdett Press, 1990. 128 pp. ISBN 0-382-09906-0. Nonfiction.

This concise, comprehensive biography of the famous American musician Duke Ellington includes a chronology of the main events of his life and a list of his major compositions in both jazz and other types of popular music. From the Genius! The Artist and the Process series.

4.10 Catalano, Grace. **New Kids on the Block.** Bantam/Starfire Books, 1989. 128 pp. ISBN 0-553-28587-4. Nonfiction.

Five young men describe their climb from the streets of Boston to the top of the pop charts. Interviews and sixteen pages of photos highlight this introduction to the group that began as the Nynuk and ended as New Kids. From their love lives to their anti-drug stance, Donnie, Jordan, Jon, Joe, and Danny open up.

4.11 Catalano, Grace. **Richard Grieco: Hot 'n' Cool.** Bantam/Starfire Books, 1990. 99 pp. ISBN 0-553-28804-0. Nonfiction.

Richard Grieco is one of the most "in demand" talents of Hollywood today. From his beginnings as a male model to his first audition for "One Life to Live" to his role in "21 Jump Street" and then stardom as "Booker," Grieco has skyrocketed to success. This biography features photos, a chapter of facts, Grieco's opinions on various topics, and his interests, which include body conditioning, writing poetry, riding motorcycles, and doing charity work.

4.12 Chestnut, J. L., Jr., and Julia Cass. **Black in Selma: The Uncommon Life of J. L. Chestnut, Jr.** Farrar, Straus and Giroux, 1990. 432 pp. ISBN 0-374-11404-8. Nonfiction.

J. L. Chestnut grew up in the segregated South in a time of violence and dissension. As a lawyer who fought on the grass-roots level along with

Martin Luther King, Jr. and Jesse Jackson, Chestnut led a life which "both parallels and exemplifies the growth of the civil rights movement since the early sixties." Journalist Julia Cass presents his story and, at the same time, the story of the nation's struggle to overcome its legacy of inequality and hatred.

4.13 Cleary, Beverly. **A Girl from Yamhill: A Memoir.** William Morrow, 1988. 279 pp. ISBN 0-688-07800-1. Nonfiction.

Children's author Beverly Cleary tells her life story, beginning with the background of her mother's and father's families and continuing through her first eighteen years. She speaks of her earliest years with love and concern for all of her family and for doing what is expected of a good little girl. Although growing a bit more independent in her high school years, she saw how much her mother dominated her life; it was only with her dad's help that she was able to move to California and go to college, where she could develop the interest in books and writing she showed from the time she started school.

4.14 Coffey, Ellen Greenman. **John D. Rockefeller: Empire Builder.** Silver Burdett Press, 1989. 112 pp. ISBN 0-382-09583-9. Nonfiction.

From the first time he saved $50 and loaned it to a local farmer for 7% annual interest, John D. Rockefeller learned an important lesson he would never forget—to let money work for him. This book tells the story of one of America's greatest industrialists and philanthropists. Career-minded at sixteen, he later made his money in financing and in an oil refinery, naming his Cleveland business Standard Oil. Later he made investments in good works, establishing the Rockefeller Foundation in 1913. Part of the American Dream series.

4.15 Coman, Carolyn. **Body and Soul: Ten American Women.** Photographs by Judy Dater. Hill and Company, 1988. 134 pp. ISBN 0-940595-13-3. Nonfiction.

There is no single theme connecting all the women in this book. One is a nun who is a hermit; another is Geraldine Fitzgerald, a famous actress; and another is a Mormon who would not allow her children to attend public school. Carolyn Coman has put these life stories in the women's own words. She attempts to "make an unbelievable-sounding life understandable" and to "dig inside a quiet story and find adventure."

4.16 Conway, Jill Ker. **The Road from Coorain.** Alfred A. Knopf, 1989. 238 pp. ISBN 0-394-57456-7. Nonfiction.

Jill Ker Conway, the first woman president of Smith College, tells you her story. She spent the early years of her childhood on Coorain, her family's sheep ranch in Australia. Amidst the isolation, drought, and dust storms, she learned to love and appreciate the beauty of the land. After her father died, she lived in Sydney with her embittered, neurotic mother, which was not easy for her. She recalls her father's words, "Do something, Jill. Don't just put in time on this earth." What she did led her to become president of Smith College.

4.17 Dash, Joan. **The Triumph of Discovery: Women Scientists Who Won the Nobel Prize.** Julian Messner, 1991. 148 pp. ISBN 0-671-69332-8. Nonfiction.

This book takes a look at the lives and careers of four extraordinary women who won the greatest of all international honors, the Nobel Prize. The four women profiled are Maria Goeppert-Mayer, who won the prize in physics; and Barbara McClintock, Rosalyn Yalow, and Rita Levi-Montalcini all of whom won it in medicine. Their work in different fields of science is outlined, along with facts about their personal lives.

4.18 Donofrio, Beverly. **Riding in Cars with Boys: Confessions of a Bad Girl Who Makes Good.** William Morrow, 1990. 204 pp. ISBN 0-688-08337-4. Nonfiction.

Although she "makes good," the author of this book was the girl every "nice boy"'s parents had nightmares about. Riding in a car with boys was the least of her problems, as she drank and smoked and had a baby in high school. She kept the baby, got a college education, and has been published in *The Village Voice, Cosmopolitan,* and *New York* magazine. This is the humorous and bold story of an independent and quirky "bad girl" who had a lot of potential.

4.19 Dunphy, Don. **Don Dunphy at Ringside.** Henry Holt, 1988. 276 pp. ISBN 0-8050-0530-7. Nonfiction.

Don Dunphy, the well-known sports reporter, tells how he grew up as a poor child in Manhattan, later becoming an accomplished broadcaster, famous for his work in boxing. He tells of very special sports events from his own point of view, that of the athletes, and those of other sports reporters, newspapers, and networks he has been associated with. This book is a personal record of Don Dunphy's forty years of experience in the world of sports reporting.

4.20 Dunphy, Eamon. **Unforgettable Fire: The Story of U2.** Viking, 1987. 320 pp. ISBN 0-670-82104-7. Nonfiction.

The Irish rock band U2 (named after the American spy planes of the 1960s) got its start in Dublin in 1976, when Larry Mullen posted a note on the notice board of his multidenominational high school about forming a musical group. Adam Clayton, Paul Hewson (later called Bono), and Dave Evans (later called The Edge) agreed to join Mullen. When the group performed at a school talent show not long after, the response was enthusiastic, with people whistling for more, and U2 was on its way to becoming one of the hottest bands of the 1980s. Author Eamon Dunphy traces the band's rise to the top and the development of its music, examining the beliefs and convictions that lie behind the group's music and that help account for U2's popularity. He provides portraits of the band members and examines just how they achieved their phenomenal success. Black-and-white photographs (including childhood pictures), index.

4.21 Frazier, Nancy. **William Randolph Hearst: Press Baron.** Silver Burdett Press, 1989. 128 pp. ISBN 0-382-09585-5. Nonfiction.

This is the story of William Randolph Hearst, the well-known publisher of newspapers and magazines, including *The Ladies Home Journal, Harper's Bazaar,* and *The San Francisco Examiner.* Hearst, a press baron who developed the sensationalistic style of "yellow journalism," lived a life of intrigue, politics, and scandal. Read about the man who was accused of publicly assassinating the characters of political figures, who tried to push the United States into a war with Mexico, and who built a castle for a movie star. From the American Dream series.

4.22 Freedman, Russell. **Franklin Delano Roosevelt.** Clarion Books, 1990. 200 pp. ISBN 0-89919-379-X. Nonfiction.

Franklin Roosevelt is well known for his leadership during the Great Depression and World War II, despite his bout with polio. This book traces his life from 1882 through his youth, political career, and presidency to his death in 1945. It portrays him as a caring and determined individual whose wealthy upbringing did not deter him from acting on behalf of all citizens, regardless of wealth, and whose affliction did not weaken his ability to lead. Includes many black-and-white photographs.

4.23 Freedman, Samuel G. **Small Victories: The Real World of a Teacher, Her Students, and Their High School.** Harper and Row, 1990. 431 pp. ISBN 0-06-016254-6. Nonfiction.

The school where Jessica Siegel taught was in the worst ten percent of high schools in New York state. Located in Manhattan and attended by recent immigrants, the school was rife with problems from apathy and absenteeism to drugs and violence. But there were a host of caring, compassionate, and committed people involved in the education of these kids. During the 1987–88 school year, the author followed Jessica Siegel around and discovered through her, her students, truant officers, and other teachers what kind of people it takes to make a difference in even the bleakest situations.

4.24 Furlong, Monica. **Thérèse of Lisieux.** Pantheon, 1987. 144 pp. ISBN 0-394-53706-8. Nonfiction.

The popular Saint Thérèse of Lisieux, who lived to be only twenty-four, was born Marie-Françoise-Thérèse Martin in Alençon, France, in 1873. Thérèse's fervently religious family placed great emphasis on obedience and going to heaven, and by age nine Thérèse was determined to become a Carmelite nun. She asked her bishop for permission to enter the convent at age fifteen, some eighteen months too young, and actually begged the pope for his permission during a family audience. Thérèse was victorious and entered the convent a few months later. The religious life was rewarding but difficult for her, and she died an agonizing death from tuberculosis just nine years later. During those years she wrote her spiritual autobiography, which became an international best-seller. Author Monica Furlong describes Thérèse's childhood, her personality, and her decision to become a nun, and also takes a look at the role of women in the Catholic church. Black-and-white photographs.

4.25 Gelb, Arthur, A. M. Rosenthal, and Marvin Siegel, editors. ***The New York Times*** **Great Lives of the Twentieth Century.** Times Books, 1988. 697 pp. ISBN 0-8129-1625-5. Nonfiction.

The first in the *Times* biographies series, this book includes biographies of creative people of the arts and of the intellect, as well as historically prominent people from the early 1960s to the present, such as Louis Armstrong and Earl Warren; Picasso and Jackie Robinson; Coco Chanel and Mao Zedong; and many others. In addition to a biographical essay on each person, each section emphasizes his or her historical uniqueness by including interviews, like the one with John Lennon conducted just a few weeks before his death; news stories; reviews; and essays, like Vincent Canby's on Groucho Marx, and Ruth Gordon's on Helen Keller. A complete table of contents and index make this reference book easy to use.

4.26 Glassman, Bruce. **Arthur Miller.** Silver Burdett Press, 1990. 128 pp. ISBN 0-382-09904-4. Nonfiction.

One of America's leading playwrights, Arthur Miller is best known for his masterpiece, *The Death of a Salesman.* This biography, illustrated with color and black-and-white photographs, shows how Miller's Jewish upbringing and his exposure to Marxism affect the social and political aspect of his life and writings. From the Genius! The Artist and the Process series.

4.27 Glassman, Bruce. **J. Paul Getty: Oil Billionaire.** Silver Burdett Press, 1989. 112 pp. ISBN 0-382-09584-7. Nonfiction.

What would it be like to own close to one billion dollars? This story of J. Paul Getty gives you some idea. Getty was one of the most successful business and oil tycoons in the world. This book tells you his story: how he made his first investment at age eleven, how he became a shrewd oil entrepreneur, how he was linked to Hitler through his visits to Germany, and how his money provided him with more trouble, sometimes, than it was worth. From the American Dream series.

4.28 Glassman, Bruce. **Mikhail Baryshnikov.** Silver Burdett Press, 1990. 128 pp. ISBN 0-382-09907-9. Nonfiction.

A small boy's dream of dancing became reality for Mikhail Baryshnikov, renowned Russian ballet principal. He learned that while success and fame in his Communist Russia brought respect and admiration, they did not offer opportunities for self-expression and wealth. After learning of the successful experience of a close colleague who defected to the United States, "Misha" considered making the same move. The risk was great: performers were watched very closely by the KGB, and there were no guarantees that his career would flourish in the United States. This book deals with the events of Baryshnikov's life, leading up to his courageous defection and through the disappointments and successes of his career in the United States.

4.29 Goodall, Jane. **Through a Window: My Thirty Years with the Chimpanzees of Gombe.** Houghton Mifflin Company, 1990. 268 pp. ISBN 0-395-50081-8. Nonfiction.

Jane Goodall was a secretarial school graduate when she was sent to Tanzania by the legendary Louis Leakey to study chimpanzees. Now a world-famous scholar, she writes about her thirty years in the community at Gombe, a community of chimpanzees. She writes of war and love; murder and birth; rejoicing and sadness. She describes the rise to power of a dictator, and the defeat of old leaders. She allows us insight into lives surprisingly like our own and gives us food for thought in considering our place as a species on this planet.

4.30 Gordon, Jacquie. **Give Me One Wish.** W. W. Norton, 1988. 350 pp. ISBN 0-393-02518-7. Nonfiction.

Jacquie Gordon's daughter, Christine, was born in 1961 with a fatal disease—cystic fibrosis. At that time, the average life expectancy for her was five years, but she lived twenty-one courageous years. Her mother tells Chris's story and her own. She tells of Chris's love of music, dancing, people, life, and her love of laughter: toward the end, when she was in and out of the hospital and had to return after only a few days at home, Chris could say to the nurse, "I just missed the great food here."

4.31 Gray, James Marion. **George Washington Carver.** Silver Burdett Press, 1991. 144 pp. ISBN 0-382-09964-8. Nonfiction.

Uncle Moses and Aunt Sue, German farmers in southwest Missouri, were the only parents George Washington Carver ever knew. Upon the tragic death of his mother, who was a slave, the Carvers assumed responsibility for baby George and his brother, Jim. They helped mold George's character and promoted his interest in rocks and plants. Even as a small boy, George conducted simple experiments in his work on the farm. Recognizing George's talents and his need for more education, the Carvers sent him to a boarding school. His educational life was full of hope and despair as he struggled from one school to another, encountering financial and racial barriers. A college art teacher opened the door to George when she recognized his fine art talents. His keen interest in agriculture and plant hybrids, however, caused that same teacher to encourage George to enroll at Iowa State University, a step that began a lifelong career in agricultural experimentation. Respect, fame, and admiration came to this most widely recognized African American. From the Pioneers in Change series.

4.32 Greene, Marilyn, and Gary Provost. **Finder: The True Story of a Private Investigator.** Crown Publishers, 1988. 225 pp. ISBN 0-517-56490-4. Nonfiction.

Marilyn Greene began her career as a volunteer in search and rescue work. She trained her German shepherd to be an air/scent dog—a dog that can detect the scent of a human being from a half mile or more away. Eventually she became a private investigator specializing in missing persons. Ironically, her own son ran away from home, and she learned what it meant to be the parent of a missing person as well as an investigator.

4.33 Gutman, Bill. **Bo Jackson: A Biography.** Archway Paperbacks, 1991. 130 pp. ISBN 0-671-73363-X. Nonfiction.

Bo Jackson is the superstar athlete who plays two professional sports—football and baseball. This biography explores his adventures, hardships, and training regimen. The book, however, does not include the latest chapter in Bo's career: After suffering a serious hip injury while playing football for the Los Angeles Raiders, Jackson was released by the Kansas City Royals baseball team, signed but later waived by the Chicago White Sox, and now faces almost certain retirement from sports after undergoing hip-replacement surgery.

4.34 Hailey, Kendall. **The Day I Became an Autodidact and the Advice, Adventures, and Acrimonies That Befell Me Thereafter.** Delacorte Press, 1988. 278 pp. ISBN 0-385-29636-3. Nonfiction.

What is an autodidact? Kendall Hailey becomes one when she finishes high school early and decides not to go to college; that is, she becomes a self-taught person. Encouraged by her eccentric family, she reads, writes, travels, acts, and paints. At nineteen she concludes, "Thank God I graduated early. And thank heavens I did not go to college. What a terrible waste of life it would have been."

4.35 Hodges, Margaret. **Making a Difference: The Story of an American Family.** Charles Scribner's Sons, 1989. 196 pp. ISBN 0-684-18979-8. Nonfiction.

Mary and Sidney Sherwood's youngest child, Sidney, Jr., was only a month old in 1901, when his father died. Sidney and his four sisters, Gretchen, Helen, Jean, and Penelope, grew up in a farmhouse in Cornwall, New York. Living on very little money, Mary taught them to value education, the world around them, and other people. Gretchen became a writer and translator; Helen, an occupational therapist; Jean, an environmental activist; Penelope, an orthopedic surgeon; and Sidney, an expert in international economics. The Sherwood family truly has made a difference.

4.36 Hook, Jason. **American Indian Warrior Chiefs: Tecumseh, Crazy Horse, Chief Joseph, Geronimo.** Plates by Richard Hook. Firebird Books, 1991. 192 pp. ISBN 1-85314-103-8. Nonfiction.

Tecumseh was an uncommon genius according to General William Harrison, one of his fiercest adversaries. His attempts to unite all eastern Indian nations were imperative to saving these Native American cultures. Maps, illustrations, and photographs enhance the accounts of Tecumseh as well as those of Crazy Horse, who is credited with winning the greatest Indian victory in history. The military genius of Chief Joseph becomes apparent in the account of the Nez Percé in the struggle to keep their ancient homeland. Finally, the courage of Geronimo, who led twenty men against 5,000 U.S. soldiers to save his homeland of the Southwest, exemplifies the Native American heroes in their struggle to combat broken treaties of the white newcomers.

4.37 Jackson, Michael. **Moonwalk.** Doubleday, 1988. 287 pp. ISBN 0-385-24712-5. Nonfiction.

Superstar Michael Jackson shares his life story with his fans, relating how he rose from obscurity to stardom. Born in 1958, he was the seventh of nine children born to a crane operator in a steel mill and a department store clerk. He grew up in a tiny three-room house in Gary, Indiana, and his childhood memories are only of practicing and performing. Jackie, Tito, Jermaine, Marlon, and Michael began performing when Michael was only five. By the time he was nine, the brothers, then known as the Jackson 5, began to take off, moving from amateur talent shows and seedy clubs to television appearances, recordings, and tours. Michael cut his first solo record, *Got to Be There,* in 1971, the same year as "The Jackson Five" Saturday morning cartoon show began. Michael describes his continuing career as a performer, including producing *Thriller,* the best-selling record album of all time. Black-and-white and color photographs.

4.38 Kisor, Henry. **What's That Pig Outdoors? A Memoir of Deafness.** Hill and Wang, 1990. 270 pp. ISBN 0-8090-9689-7. Nonfiction.

"What's that big loud noise?" looks exactly like "What's that pig outdoors?" Or so claims Henry Kisor as he tells you about one of the humorous times he misread his son's lips. Kisor writes with tongue in cheek about his life, his deafness, the problems he had in dating, playing sports, and going to classes. He is now a successful journalist and writer, and the story of his success is filled with laughter and a sense of the determination that took him to the top in a highly competitive field.

4.39 Lanker, Brian. **I Dream a World: Portraits of Black Women Who Changed America.** Photographs by Brian Lanker. Stewart, Tabori and Chang, 1989. 167 pp. ISBN 1-55670-092-X. Nonfiction.

Lanker, a photojournalist, interviewed seventy-five black American women who have shown courage and intelligence in making a difference in the United States. Lanker's purpose is to celebrate the human spirit, as each woman relates stories or incidents of racism, sexism, or other circumstances which affected her life. Accompanying each woman's short sketch is a one-page photograph. Many of the women's names are readily recognized—Althea Gibson, Toni Morrison, Barbara Jordan, Alice Walker, Sarah Vaughn, Wilma Rudolph, Lena Horne—yet all the women, known or unknown, have one thing in common: all have poignant stories and hopes to share about America's past and future.

4.40 Larsen, Rebecca. **Paul Robeson: Hero before His Time.** Franklin Watts, 1989. 158 pp. ISBN 0-531-10779-5. Nonfiction.

Born in 1890, Paul Robeson did it all—All-American football player, Phi Beta Kappa member, graduate of the Columbia University School of Law, actor, singer, and political activist. What distinguished him from others with the same achievements was that Paul Robeson was black. He protested racism in the United States, noting that the Soviet Union treated their people better than the U.S. did. Observations like this led politicians during the McCarthy era to target Robeson as a Communist, ruining his career by calling him anti-American. Despite all the obstacles, Robeson pushed on, fighting discrimination, racism, and hatred, while foreshadowing the goals of the civil rights movement of the 1960s—that all people should be treated as equals.

4.41 Lord, Bette Bao. **Legacies: A Chinese Mosaic.** Alfred A. Knopf, 1990. 245 pp. ISBN 0-394-58325-6. Nonfiction.

Best-selling author Bette Bao Lord describes her life and experiences in this book, which explores her sense of a split identity as both Chinese woman and Western woman. Her marriage to the former ambassador to China, Winston Lord, made her part of the Western world, but her roots are Chinese, and Chinese history is what created her. She demonstrates her unyielding tie to China through her memories and the stories of her friends and relatives, among them dissidents, Communists, intellectuals, politicians, and citizens, all part and parcel of Chinese history.

4.42 Luo, Zi-ping. **A Generation Lost: China under the Cultural Revolution.** Henry Holt, 1990. 342 pp. ISBN 0-8050-0957-4. Nonfiction.

Zi-ping Luo was six at the beginning of China's first Cultural Revolution in 1957. The following year her father, who had supported the Chinese revolution nearly all of his life, was branded a Rightist by the Anti-Rightist Movement and was exiled to an isolated province for two years. The anti-intellectual climate continued, and in 1966 all schools beyond the elementary level were closed so that students could continue to carry out the revolution. Writing in the format of letters to a mathematics professor, Luo describes her family's struggle to avoid persecution and imprisonment while trying to educate its children. She describes copying textbooks by hand secretly, stashing controversial writings under mattresses and in other hiding places, and always being on guard. But Luo's family was able to maintain their contacts with some of China's best-known intellectuals, who taught Luo physics, chemistry, and Western languages and literature. When Chinese universities reopened in the mid-1970s, Luo was able to start her college program in a graduate chemistry program before coming to the United States.

4.43 Lyttle, Richard B. **Pablo Picasso: The Man and the Image.** Atheneum, 1989. 246 pp. ISBN 0-689-31393-4. Nonfiction.

When he died in 1973 at the age of ninety-three, Pablo Picasso left behind an amazing wealth of art, from drawings to stage settings to ceramic designs. What motivated this man to his constant creativity and originality? This book explores the life of Pablo Picasso, from his youth in Spain to France, where the streets of Paris were filled with art and artists. This book explores Picasso's relationships with women and other artists, examining how everyone he met and everything he did influenced Picasso's unique brand of art. Includes black-and-white photographs, black-and-white reproductions of some of Picasso's works, bibliography, and index.

4.44 Makeba, Miriam, with James Hall. **Makeba: My Story.** New American Library, 1988. 249 pp. ISBN 0-453-00561-6. Nonfiction.

Singer Miriam Makeba was born in South Africa during the 1930s. Music brought her some relief from the oppression and discrimination to which blacks were subjected by the ruling whites, but conditions were made worse when apartheid became the official policy in 1947. Makeba joined one of the biggest musical groups in South Africa when she was twenty-two. This was the start of her meteoric rise to fame, and soon she was performing in Europe and America. Her success led to the revocation of her passport by the South African government while she was on her first trip abroad, but once exiled, Makeba was free to speak out against the injustices in South Africa. She writes of the addresses she delivered at the United Nations, the political and entertainment celebrities that she has known, her marriages to jazz star Hugh Masekela and black activist Stokely Carmichael, and the ultimately tragic life of her troubled daughter, Bongi. Black-and-white photographs.

4.45 Mills, Judie. **John F. Kennedy.** Franklin Watts, 1988. 370 pp. ISBN 0-531-10520-2. Nonfiction.

John Fitzgerald Kennedy was the great-grandson of a poor Irish immigrant and the son of a multimillionaire. This book traces his family and his life from great-grandfather Patrick Kennedy's immigration to John's assassination. His parents, Joseph and Rose Fitzgerald Kennedy, had a great deal of influence on his life and career. In fact, it was his father's dream that John become president. In one of his speeches, John Kennedy used the verse from St. Luke that his mother often repeated to her children: "For of those to whom much is given, much is required."

4.46 Moates, Marianne M. **A Bridge of Childhood: Truman Capote's Southern Years.** Henry Holt, 1989. 256 pp. ISBN 0-8050-0971-X. Nonfiction.

Truman Capote based many of his fictional characters on relatives and friends in the town of Monroeville, Alabama, where he spent many of his early years, from 1928 to 1934. He and his cousin and their friend, Nelle Harper Lee, were nearly inseparable, but Capote never felt that he truly belonged. Stories he told then and things that happened in later visits are recorded as they were told to Marianne Moates, by Capote's cousin, Jennings Faulklater. This book gives insight into a period of Capote's life about which little has been written.

4.47 Monette, Paul. **Borrowed Time: An AIDS Memoir.** Harcourt Brace Jovanovich, 1988. 342 pp. ISBN 0-15-113598-3. Nonfiction.

Author, poet, and playwright Paul Monette begins his AIDS memoir by describing his intellectually challenging and personally fulfilling relationship with male companion Roger Horwitz. Then, in March of 1985, some ten years after they met, Horwitz developed a number of symptoms that were diagnosed as pneumocystis, a precursor of AIDS. Monette describes Horwitz's battle with the relentless disease that "comes like a slowly dawning horror," bringing Horwitz pain, blindness, and, finally, death. This is a story of devotion, sacrifice, and love, and also a story of anger—at the disease, at modern medicine's lack of effective weapons for fighting the ailment, and at the reaction of some friends and associates to Horwitz's diagnosis of AIDS.

4.48 Murphy, Wendy Buehr. **Frank Lloyd Wright.** Silver Burdett Press, 1990. 128 pp. ISBN 0-382-09905-2. Nonfiction.

Frank Lloyd Wright was one of America's most influential architects. This biography traces his life from his birth in 1867 to his death in 1959.

His strong-willed mother lavished attention on him but his father, unhappy with his marriage, left the family, leading Wright to do poorly in school. Nonetheless, he succeeded in becoming one of America's most innovative architects. Includes many color and black-and-white illustrations. From the Genius! series.

4.49 Ngor, Haing, with Roger Warner. **A Cambodian Odyssey.** Macmillan, 1987. 478 pp. ISBN 0-446-38990-0. Nonfiction.

Haing Ngor tells a harrowing tale of life in Cambodia during the brutal Pol Pot regime in which up to two million Cambodians died. Ngor was an obstetrician and surgeon in Phnom Penh when the city fell to the Khmer Rouge communists in 1975. To avoid persecution for being a physician, Ngor insisted that he had been a taxi driver, but three times he was jailed and tortured on the suspicion of being a doctor. Miraculously, each time he survived. Ngor watched execution squads carry off most of his relatives, and he stood by helplessly when his wife, Chang My Huoy, died in childbirth. When the Vietnamese invaded Cambodia in late 1978, Ngor made the grueling trek to Thailand and, eventually, to freedom in America. In an unusual turn to his life, Ngor brought attention to the plight of the Cambodian people by costarring in the film *The Killing Fields,* a role for which he received an Academy Award for Best Supporting Actor in 1985. Black-and-white photographs.

4.50 Parks, Gordon. **Voices in the Mirror: An Autobiography.** Doubleday, 1990. 342 pp. ISBN 0-385-26698-7. Nonfiction.

Gordon Parks puts his life into words as he records his early family days in Fort Scott, Kansas; his unhappy time in the city of St. Paul, Minnesota; and his trials on his own to his triumphs in becoming a famous photographer, writer, and film director. The rage at the racism he saw and experienced served him well in his attempt to create art and truth at the same time. He became creative in helping readers discover what was happening in the United States and the world over. This is a look at a man through his own eyes, a man who did not graduate from high school but who has received more than fifty honorary doctorates and awards.

4.51 Patterson, Charles. **Hafiz Al-Asad of Syria.** Julian Messner, 1991. 126 pp. ISBN 0-671-69468-5. Nonfiction.

Hafiz Al-Asad has been president of Syria since 1970 and was an important military leader before that. This powerful biography details Asad's life and rise to power and prominence in Middle Eastern politics. Includes a time line of Syria's history from around 2100 B.C. to 1990 and a complete glossary.

4.52 Ramusi, Molapatene Collins, and Ruth S. Turner. **Soweto, My Love.** Henry Holt, 1989. 257 pp. ISBN 0-8050-0263-4. Nonfiction.

The life of Molapatene Collins Ramusi is the story of growing up black under South African apartheid. Through great personal strife and sacrifice, he gained his independence, but lost his son to the violence of guerrilla activities. As a lawyer, Ramusi continues the fight today for a free South Africa.

4.53 Shuker, Nancy. **Elizabeth Arden: Cosmetics Entrepreneur**. Silver Burdett Press, 1989. 112 pp. ISBN 0-382-09587-1. Nonfiction.

Elizabeth Arden, or Florence Nightingale Graham as she was born, was one of the first women to create cosmetics; she built a cosmetics empire that is still alive today. She, with the help of two sisters and a $6,000 loan from her brother, opened a salon that bloomed into a mega-empire. This is the story of her dedication to her work, her involvement in the women's suffrage movement, and her interest in horse racing. Includes photos of early beauty treatments. Part of the American Dream series.

4.54 Shuker, Nancy. **Maya Angelou.** Silver Burdett Press, 1990. 128 pp. ISBN 0-382-09908-7. Nonfiction.

Maya Angelou was born with three strikes against her. She was poor, black, and female, making her rise to fame a difficult one. This biography provides insights into the obstacles she faced and how she rose above them to become a famous poet, musician, and actor. Included is a chronology of important dates in history and in her personal life as well. From the Genius! The Artist and the Process series.

4.55 Steltzer, Ulli. **The New Americans.** Introduction by Peter Martin. NewSage Press, 1988. 175 pp. ISBN 0-939165-07-4. Nonfiction.

In recent years, millions of immigrants have settled in the United States, looking for new lives. This book is an exploration into the lives of the New Americans. What traditions from their former countries do they bring with them? What new working conditions do they find in the United States? What are the reactions of other Americans to these immigrants? The experiences of these New Americans are unique ones, offering insight into the opportunities and pitfalls immigrants discover when they arrive on America's shores. Black-and-white photographs.

4.56 Sutherland, Christine. **Monica.** Farrar, Straus and Giroux, 1990. 231 pp. ISBN 0-374-21215-5. Nonfiction.

Monica Wichfeld led a glamorous life that seemed totally unsuited to producing this heroine of the Danish Resistance. She grew up in Ireland, lost a brother in 1918 to the Germans which began a lifelong hatred of Germans on her part, and eventually married a Dutch aristocrat. Her family lived in Paris and Italy before returning to their estate in Holland, by which time World War II and the Nazi occupation had begun. She joined the resistance movement and harbored refugees, rowed explosives across the lake at night, and devoted herself to destroying the Nazis. When she was caught by her enemies, her composure at the trial and her strength of character made her an example to the other prisoners. When she was deported to Germany and killed, she became a national folk heroine.

4.57 Vanilla Ice. **Ice by Ice.** Avon Books, 1991. 164 pp. ISBN 0-380-76594-2. Nonfiction.

For the first time, Vanilla Ice tells about his life as a youngster, teenager, and celebrity. He says he is not proud of the difficult times he made for his mother and that his life as a gang member is not an appropriate role model for teenagers, but he believes in telling the truth. His mother and later his stepfather, too, moved to what they hoped would be better environments for him, but school was just a place for him to skip class and make fun of teachers and the system. His interest in motorcross led him to win more than 400 trophies and to a possible career. Then he tried out for a talent contest, only on a friend's dare, and his self-taught abilities in rapping, beat-boxing, and dancing led him to a three-year climb to fame and success. Also included are bios of important persons in his life.

4.58 Willeford, Charles. **I Was Looking for a Street.** The Countryman Press, 1988. 143 pp. ISBN 0-88150-112-3. Nonfiction.

In this memoir, Charles Willeford describes his youth in Los Angeles and on the road before and during the Great Depression. His parents are dead, and he lives with his grandmother until she loses her job in 1933, when Charles is fourteen. He knows his uncle cannot support him as well as his grandmother can, so he runs away and becomes a bum. At that time, "there were thousands of boys my age riding freight trains to nowhere. But no one can tell me I didn't have a happy childhood."

4.59 Wolff, Tobias. **This Boy's Life: A Memoir.** The Atlantic Monthly Press, 1989. 288 pp. ISBN 0-87113-248-6. Nonfiction.

Forging checks and stealing cars, having a mother who travels constantly, dealing with an evil stepfather . . . not an average childhood! Award-winning author Tobias Wolff describes his escapades as a youth in the 1950s, coping as best he could with the constant upheavals in his life. Progressing through his travels as a child to his out-of-control, underachieving college days and ending after his time in the armed forces, Wolff unravels how he began to reevaluate his wild life and started moving in a new direction.

4.60 Worth, Richard. **Robert Mugabe of Zimbabwe.** Julian Messner, 1990. 103 pp. ISBN 0-671-68987-8. Nonfiction.

Robert Mugabe led the fight for black political power in the emerging African nation of Zimbabwe. He went on to become Zimbabwe's first prime minister. This biography offers current coverage of Mugabe's life and is organized for use in preparing reports and research papers. It includes photographs, a time line, and a glossary.

4.61 Zyskind, Sara. **Struggle.** Lerner, 1989. 284 pp. ISBN 0-8225-0772-2. Nonfiction.

This is the true story of a teenage boy who managed against great odds to stay alive through the Holocaust, surviving the ghettos and death camps of Poland. This is a dramatic, intensely human story of survival as well as an important historical document.

5 Careers and Jobs

5.1 Birnbach, Lisa. **Going to Work.** Villard Books, 1988. 416 pp. ISBN 0-394-75874-9. Nonfiction.

Lisa Birnbach, who gave us *The Official Preppy Handbook,* went to work to interview a thousand people at positions ranging from executive officers to entry level clerks. She compiles her findings about Americans and their jobs in large and small companies. Easy to find by location, businesses are listed under eleven major cities. This book offers something for both the young person preparing to enter the work force and for the executive planning to change jobs.

5.2 Brown, Margaret Fogel. **Careers in Occupational Therapy.** Rosen, 1989. 140 pp. ISBN 0-8239-0981-6. Nonfiction.

For those interested in occupational therapy, this title from the Careers in Depth series thoroughly covers everything a novice would want to know about the field: definition and tools, career options and descriptions, job settings, educational and personal requirements, trends, and professional organizations. In addition, the appendixes list scholarships and loans for studying occupational therapy, accredited institutions offering certification and degree programs, and information about military occupational therapy education programs.

5.3 Brown, Rita Mae. **Starting from Scratch: A Different Kind of Writers' Manual.** Bantam Books, 1988. 254 pp. ISBN 0-553-05246-2. Nonfiction.

If you want to be a writer of fiction, this book gives you a very personal view of what it takes. The author discusses her own beginnings as a writer, tools of the trade, language, construction, and exercises you can do to explore your creativity. She describes the various types of writing, including novels, magazine writing, short stories, plays, screenplays, and teleplays. The last two chapters contain a four-year program for the education of writers, and an extensive reading list.

5.4 Carter, Sharon. **Careers in Aviation.** Rosen, 1990. 127 pp. ISBN 0-8239-0965-4. Nonfiction.

Not all occupations in aviation involve flying. This book shows you a wide range of aviation careers, including those of flight attendant, airport manager, aircraft mechanic, air traffic controller, and pilot. You'll learn about other areas of aviation, like flying in air shows, aerial patrol, law enforcement, commercial airlines, news media, helicopter ambulance service, and corporate aviation. An experienced pilot, the author reveals not only the advantages but also the disadvantages of the field and recommends ways of entering it. From the Careers in Depth series.

5.5 Cohen, Paul, and Shari Cohen. **Careers in Law Enforcement and Security.** Rosen, 1990. 128 pp. ISBN 0-8239-1026-1. Nonfiction.

What is the life of a CIA agent really like? This book explores the lives and careers of special agents, parole and probation officers, sheriffs, security guards, detectives, and private investigators. The personal interviews with law enforcement officials and their families enhance the book's usefulness as a tool in career decision making. From the Careers in Depth series.

5.6 Collins, Robert F.. **America at Its Best: Opportunities in the National Guard.** Rosen, 1989. 139 pp. ISBN 0-8239-1024-5. Nonfiction.

Robert F. Collins is a retired colonel who tells you all about life in the National Guard. Today's National Guard traces its history to the militia and Minutemen of the Revolutionary War and, like those forces, believes that a force of citizen-soldiers is desirable. The National Guard serves two facets of government: it is available to states for emergencies like natural disasters and riots and it is also an important part of our national defense. This book tells you how to join the National Guard, how much you'll be paid, what kind of basic training you'll go through, and what kinds of jobs you'll do. Part of the Military Opportunity series.

5.7 Collins, Robert F.. **Basic Training: What to Expect and How to Prepare.** Rosen, 1988. 149 pp. ISBN 0-8239-0833-X. Nonfiction.

Have you ever thought of joining the military? This book tells you about all of the branches of the United States military, presenting their basic philosophies and information on how to enlist. Each branch has different recruit requirements, basic training locations, terminology, and purposes. The book also includes lists of items to bring to basic training, pay scales, educational offerings, and training schedules. Part of the Military Opportunity series.

5.8 Duncan, Jane Caryl. **Careers in Veterinary Medicine.** Rosen, 1988. 129 pp. ISBN 0-8239-0804-6. Nonfiction.

Interested in veterinary medicine? Veterinarian Jane Caryl Duncan tells you about many career possibilities. She reveals the rewards and demands of working in private practice, government and public health, the military, education, zoos, and private industry. Appendixes provide a directory of veterinary schools offering accredited programs in animal technology. From the Careers in Depth series.

5.9 Edwards, E. W. **Exploring Careers Using Foreign Languages.** Rosen, 1990. 135 pp. ISBN 0-8239-0968-9. Nonfiction.

Knowledge of a foreign language is an asset to any career. E. W. Edwards tells you how you can use the foreign languages you learn to prepare for careers in business, government, communication, education, and other professions. Sample résumés and a directory of international organizations appear in the appendixes. From the Careers in Depth series.

5.10 Figler, Howard. **The Complete Job-Search Handbook: All the Skills You Need to Get Any Job and Have a Good Time Doing It.** Henry Holt/Owl Books, 1988. 366 pp. ISBN 0-8050-0537-4. Nonfiction.

This practical guide to developing confidence and becoming successful in finding the right job includes tips on how to dress, what to say, and how to prepare for an interview. You'll find it helpful when you look for your first job and even later if you decide to change careers or return to the work force after being out of it for a while. Both beginners and "veterans" can find answers to often-asked questions about jobs and careers.

5.11 Fiske, Edward B. **How to Get into the Right College: Secrets of College Admissions Officers.** Illustrated by Nishan Akgulian. Times Books, 1988. 193 pp. ISBN 0-8129-1732-4. Nonfiction.

This book separates fact from the many myths about how to get into the best university. Based on the results of a national survey of professional college admissions officers, this guide carefully outlines the steps you need to take in order to be admitted to the better universities. It offers information on the importance of test scores, what to do when you're a junior and when you're a senior, how to write successful admissions essays (samples included), what to include in application packets, how to get good recommendations, and much more. It identifies the best college bargains and tells you the colleges with the best debate teams, unusual sports teams (from polo to rodeo), and the most comprehensive study-abroad programs.

5.12 Gilbert, Sara. **Lend a Hand: The How, Where, and Why of Volunteering.** Morrow Junior Books, 1988. 160 pp. ISBN 0-688-07247-X. Nonfiction.

Why volunteer? You can try out different kinds of work if you don't know what you want to do with your life. If you do know what you want to do, you can get valuable experience. You can connect with people and make friends. You can make a difference instead of just complaining about the state of the world. This book provides you with information about volunteering, why you should do it, how to pick an organization to work with, and a comprehensive list of organizations, national and international, that welcome young volunteers. Just do it!

5.13 Greenfield, Howard. **Books: From Writer to Reader.** Crown, 1989. 197 pp. ISBN 0-517-56840-3. Nonfiction.

Everything you could ever want to know about writing, editing, and publishing is gathered in this one book! From the time the writer finishes a manuscript, decisions have to be made. Is an agent a good idea? Which publishers should the manuscript be sent to? This book will guide you through every step of the writing and publishing processes, from getting the words down on paper to reaching the right audience for your work.

5.14 Haddock, Patricia. **Careers in Banking and Finance.** Rosen, 1990. 106 pp. ISBN 0-8239-0962-X. Nonfiction.

Patricia Haddock describes the many careers you can pursue in banking and finance, from those requiring a high school diploma to those requiring a college degree. Her concluding chapter tells you how to write résumés and covers other job-hunting topics. A glossary and a list of helpful publications are included. From the Careers in Depth series.

5.15 Johnson, Barbara L. **Careers in Beauty Culture.** Rosen, 1989. 101 pp. ISBN 0-8239-1002-4. Nonfiction.

This book provides a wealth of information and advice for aspiring cosmetologists, including personal and educational requirements, advantages and drawbacks of beauty professions, job responsibilities, résumé writing and interview techniques, and self-employment. A glossary of beauty terms and a list of recommended books and magazines are included. From the Careers in Depth series.

5.16 Klass, Perri. **A Not Entirely Benign Procedure: Four Years as a Medical Student.** New American Library/Signet, 1988. 286 pp. ISBN 0-451-15358-8. Nonfiction.

Perri Klass writes an autobiography which takes you through four years of medical school. She shares the drama, the failures, the learning, the humor, the anger, and the insider secrets of hospital life. She chose pediatrics for her specialty largely because she became pregnant and then cared for her son during her internship. If you are thinking about becoming a doctor, read this revealing account of the profession for insight and inspiration.

5.17 Koester, Pat. **Careers in Fashion Retailing.** Rosen, 1990. 146 pp. ISBN 0-8239-1007-5. Nonfiction.

This book gives you plenty of practical information on working in the fashion retail industry. It tells you about career paths, educational preparation, and job responsibilities in sales, management, specialty careers, and entrepreneurship. Suggestions on how to prepare for a career are enhanced by the directory of schools included in the appendix. From the Careers in Depth series.

5.18 Kurtzman, Harvey. **My Life as a Cartoonist.** Minstrel Books/Byron Preiss, 1988. 105 pp. ISBN 0-671-63453-4. Nonfiction.

Harvey Kurtzman, the editor who "discovered" Alfred E. Neuman for *Mad* magazine, takes you behind the scenes in the world of cartooning. He explains how comic books are created, how artists successfully tell a story through pictures, and how he personally followed his dream of drawing comic characters for a living. He even includes a step-by-step explanation of how to translate the idea for a joke into a finished cartoon, and he offers advice to aspiring artists about tools of the trade, pacing, and panel construction.

5.19 Lee, Richard S., and Mary Price Lee. **Careers for Women in Politics.** Rosen, 1989. 120 pp. ISBN 0-8239-0966-2. Nonfiction.

This book reveals the realities and career prospects for women seeking political careers. It describes the personal qualities needed, method of entry, financial resources for political study, and tips for running for office. A directory of women's political organizations is included in the appendix. From the Careers in Depth series.

5.20 Lo, Steven C. **The Incorporation of Eric Chung.** Algonquin Books of Chapel Hill, 1989. 199 pp. ISBN 0-945575-18-1. Fiction.

It's 1979 and Henry Kissinger is about to open the door for business between China and the U.S. Eric Chung, a Chinese student heading for college at Texas Tech, finds himself caught up in the corporate struggle without really trying. Swept up in events, he quickly becomes one of the wheelers and dealers in Texas's big business. How did all these whirlwind adventures happen to him? And will the bottom fall out in the end? This book offers a new look at the immigrant experience with an amusing twist.

5.21 Matheson, Eve. **The Modeling Handbook: The Complete Guide to Breaking into Local, Regional, and International Modeling.** Henry Holt/Owl Books, 1989. 225 pp. ISBN 0-8050-1126-9. Nonfiction.

Based on her research, interviews, and the experiences of her own teenage daughter, Eve Matheson tells you the requirements of modeling for both males and females, as well as problems models face and the solutions for them. Every topic of interest to beginning models is discussed: modeling specialties, competitions, conventions, terms, and successful modeling agencies in the United States and abroad.

5.22 Michelson, Maureen R., editor. **Women and Work: Photographs and Personal Writings.** Photographs edited by Michael R. Dressler and Maureen R. Michelson. NewSage Press, 1988. 179 pp. ISBN 939165-01-5. Nonfiction.

From judges to cashiers to zoo keepers, women hold jobs in every field, but they rarely have the opportunity to talk about their work. In this collection, eighty-five women discuss what being a part of the work force means to them in the context of the rest of their lives. They address many of the social issues of the 1980s as they describe the new place of women in American society. Is it harder for women to find career work? Are they paid as well as men? Are they satisfied with their work? Black-and-white photographs.

5.23 Nelson, Cordner. **Careers in Pro Sports.** Rosen, 1990. 143 pp. ISBN 0-8239-1027-X. Nonfiction.

A career in professional sports can offer wealth, fame, and fun, but also disillusionment, heartbreak, and failure. The author discusses both sides of a career in sports, along with tips on career planning, training for competition, and breaking into the profession. Professional associations and sports publications appear in the appendix. From the Careers in Depth series.

5.24 Pekhanen, John. **M.D. Doctors Talk about Themselves.** Delacorte Press, 1988. 294 pp. ISBN 0-440-50028-1. Nonfiction.

More than seventy physicians express their personal views of the medical profession in this book. John Pekhanen's cross section represents doctors from different geographical regions, with different specialties, and of different economic standings, ages, races, and points of view. Taken together, their comments give the reader a glimpse into the private world of doctors, an emotional world where doctors display their feelings of doubt, guilt, fear, anxiety, grief, and anger. They focus on such general topics as their medical training and residency, their colleagues, effects of governmental regulations, malpractice suits, impaired physicians, and the future of medicine.

5.25 Rhodes, Richard. **Farm: A Year in the Life of an American Farmer.** Illustrated by Bill Greer. Simon and Schuster, 1989. 336 pp. ISBN 0-671-63647-2. Nonfiction.

Rhodes writes about one Missouri farmer, his family, and their life on an American farm in the 1980s. Living with the family, Rhodes experiences the hard work, both physical and mental, in planning, planting, harvesting, and marketing plants and animals. The family is a portrait of the daily living on many Midwestern farms. In addition to dealing with the elements of nature, the family uses all of its resources to confront problems with the economy and with the changing times.

5.26 Roberson, Virginia Lee. **Careers in the Graphic Arts.** Rosen, 1988. 131 pp. ISBN 0-8239-0803-8. Nonfiction.

If you think you'd like to become an illustrator, a layout artist, a designer, or a pasteup artist, this book tells you the training, education, and skills you'll need. The author not only gives advice, but provides technical instruction on design and layout, typesetting and typography, using a camera, and pasteup. Added features include résumé writing, interview techniques, and portfolio tips. From the Careers in Depth series.

5.27 Schneider, Dorothy, and Carl J. Schneider. **Sound Off! American Military Women Speak Out.** E. P. Dutton, 1988. 259 pp. ISBN 0-525-24589-8. Nonfiction.

Though 11 percent of the United States Armed Forces is made up of women, there are still numerous problems and obstacles facing today's female veterans. Sexual harassment and combat eligibility are just a few of the difficulties women talk about in these interviews. Is it more difficult for women to get promoted in the military? Should women take part in combat? Do women in the military feel comfortable raising a family while serving their country? These and other tough questions are raised, and some of the answers may surprise you.

5.28 Schwartz, Perry. **Making Movies.** Lerner, 1989. 88 pp. ISBN 0-8225-1635-7. Nonfiction.

How are movies made and distributed? What careers are in films? Perry Schwartz explains film making from its inception, an idea, to a typical day on the set, concluding with film distribution and advertising. Included are photographs, a glossary, and a list of movie industry organizations.

5.29 Sigel, Lois Savitch. **New Careers in Hospitals.** Rosen, 1988. 113 pp. ISBN 0-8239-0802-X. Nonfiction.

Because of new regulations, hospitals now emphasize planning, image promotion, quality of care, and safety management as their primary functions. This book tells you about new careers that meet these priorities—careers in health education, infection control, marketing, patient advocacy, planning, public relations, quality assurance, risk management, and safety engineering. A glossary of medical terms is included. From the Careers in Depth series.

5.30 Smith, Lucinda Irwin. **Women Who Write: From the Past and the Present to the Future.** Julian Messner, 1989. 165 pp. ISBN 0-671-65668-6. Nonfiction.

The writer's life is seen through biographical sketches of seven authors from the past (from Jane Austen to Agatha Christie) and through interviews with a dozen contemporary women who write. Novelists, screenwriters, poets, playwrights, and journalists talk about the problems, rewards, practical and creative realities of writing, and their own different lifestyles. The book ends with practical guidelines for beginners. If you aspire to writing, this should be on your reading list.

5.31 Spencer, Jean W. **Exploring Careers in Word Processing and Desktop Publishing.** Rosen, 1990. 153 pp. ISBN 0-8239-0994-8. Nonfiction.

This book explains what word processing is and why it's so important. It suggests careers in word processing and desktop publishing and offers tips for success, information on specialty services, and a glimpse of the office place of the future.

5.32 Taub, Eric. **Gaffers, Grips, and Best Boys.** St. Martin's Press, 1987. 200 pp. ISBN 0-312-01150-4. Nonfiction.

The end credits of a film detail more than just who starred in and directed a movie; all of the production team is included in that list of names. But just what is a gaffer? What exactly do all those job titles mean? In this book, the author explains what each person on a film crew does, and through interviews with some of the leading technicians in

Hollywood, gives you insight into just how important all of these skilled professionals are. A complete glossary is included, in which a gaffer is defined: "This is the individual charged with the shaping of a location to fit the director's needs and the director of photography's needs. A gaffer typically scouts locations, determines lighting requirements, and helps all technical aspects of a production to run smoothly."

5.33 White, Carl. **Citizen-Soldier: Opportunities in the Reserves.** Rosen, 1990. 134 pp. ISBN 0-8230-1023-7. Nonfiction.

The reserves are combat-ready units that train and carry out military missions one weekend a month and two weeks a year. Carl White examines military life in each branch's reserve force, describing the effects of mobilization and military obligations of reservists' families and employers. Annual earnings for officers and enlisted reservists are shown in the appendixes. From the Careers in Depth series.

5.34 Young, Jeffrey S. **Steve Jobs: The Journey Is the Reward.** Scott, Foresman and Company, 1988. 440 pp. ISBN 0-673-18864-7. Nonfiction.

At the young age of twenty-one, Steve Jobs founded Apple Computer in order to produce an economical personal computer. Just four years later, Jobs's net worth was over $100 million. Author Jeffrey S. Young, one of the founders of the magazine *Macworld,* has known and worked with Steve Jobs for several years, so he is able to give a personal portrait of Jobs's life and career. Young describes Jobs's childhood in Mountain View, California, near Silicon Valley, his early fascination with electronics, his high school years as a bright, nonconformist "wirehead," and his brief stay at Reed College in Portland, Oregon, as well as his employment at Atari. Then, in 1976, Jobs and business partner Stephen Wozniak began Apple Computer, and it is Jobs's career at Apple that is the focus of this book, from the central role he played in developing the Macintosh and his computer empire to his bitter departure from Apple and the founding of his new company, NeXT.

6 Classics

6.1 Alcott, Louisa May. **Little Men.** Troll Associates/Watermill Press, 1988. 345 pp. ISBN 0-8167-1471-1. Fiction.

Nat arrives at Plumfield School with a letter recommending him for enrollment. He is pleasantly surprised to find himself welcomed by the Bhaers and all the children who live there. The Plumfield School is a rather liberal one, and each child is loved individually for his or her own personality. Of course, where there are children, there are also problems. Nat is accustomed to rejection and cruelty. Everyone at the school is so kind that he doesn't want to let them down. He hopes to become the fine man that Mr. and Mrs. Bhaer expect of "their" boys.

6.2 Alcott, Louisa May. **An Old-Fashioned Girl.** Troll Associates/Watermill Press, 1988. 348 pp. ISBN 0-8167-1462-2. Fiction.

Polly is an old-fashioned country girl. Her friend, Fanny Shaw, invites her to spend a month with the wealthy Shaw family in the city. Polly is introduced to the modern and sophisticated life of city young people, and they, in turn, find that her cheerful and honest nature affects them, too. After her visit, Polly returns home to the country. Six years later, she is a young lady who returns to the city as a working woman. She remains friends with Fanny, but she finds she doesn't fit in at the fine parties or with Fanny's wealthy friends.

6.3 Alcott, Louisa May. **Under the Lilacs.** Troll Associates/Watermill Press, 1988. 280 pp. ISBN 0-8167-1472-X. Fiction.

Ben Brown and his father have traveled with a circus for Ben's whole life. His father leaves, promising to send for Ben as soon as possible. But Ben is mistreated and runs away with his trick dog, Sancho. He meets Mrs. Moss and her two daughters, who offer him a home and introduce him to new friends and a new way of life. He is happy, except that he wishes he could find his father. Then the troubling news arrives that Ben's father is dead!

6.4 Dickens, Charles. **Hard Times.** Troll Associates/Watermill Press, 1988. 313 pp. ISBN 0-8167-1463-0. Fiction.

Charles Dickens describes life in an English industrial city during the Victorian era. It is a hard life, one without dreams. Raised in this setting, Louisa Gradgrind is incapable of recognizing or accepting the love of the man who cares deeply for her. Moving into the city, Sissy Jupe, a member of a circus family, is snatched from her "undesirable" environment and placed in one where imagination is trampled on. Without dreams and imagination, Louisa, Sissy, and other characters find little purpose for living.

6.5 Porter, Eleanor H. **Pollyanna.** Troll Associates/Watermill Press, 1989. 220 pp. ISBN 0-8167-1468-1. Fiction.

Maybe you've heard someone called a "Pollyanna" for being too cheerful and too naive to recognize trouble, but the real Pollyanna was anything but dim-witted. An orphan who comes to live with her stern and joyless aunt, she has been triumphing over adversity with the "Just Be Glad" game ever since her missionary father taught it to her when she was a small child. As she teaches it to everyone she meets, she brings happiness and warmth to a great many lives, eventually transforming an entire town.

6.6 Stevenson, Robert Louis. **Dr. Jekyll and Mr. Hyde.** New American Library/Signet Classics, 1987. 124 pp. ISBN 0-451-521-38-2. Fiction.

Have you ever felt torn between right and wrong, good and evil? Dr. Henry Jekyll has, and he finds it no laughing matter. Dr. Jekyll is a scientist who has created a horrible drug that transforms him into the hideous Hyde, an evil alter ego. As Hyde is turned loose on society with increasing frequency, Jekyll finds himself absorbed by the murderous Hyde personality. He is unable to control him, and London suffers repeatedly for Hyde's crimes. Will Jekyll be able to control Hyde before it's too late?

6.7 Twain, Mark. **Adventures of Huckleberry Finn.** Troll Associates/Watermill Press, 1988. 365 pp. ISBN 0-8167-1464-9. Fiction.

Huckleberry Finn, a homeless orphan of sorts, has a hard time living the civilized life with his guardian, the Widow Douglas. His misadventures in the story begin when he fakes his own death to escape his abusive father. He finds himself aiding Jim, a runaway slave, and together they begin an incredible journey down the Mississippi River—a journey that includes feuding families, con men posing as royalty, and stolen money. Find out how Huck saves his and Jim's skins while having the adventure of their lives.

7 Dating and Sexual Awareness

7.1 Bunting, Eve. **Will You Be My POSSLQ?** Harcourt Brace Jovanovich, 1987. 181 pp. ISBN 0-15-297399-0. Fiction.

What is a POSSLQ? Jamie McLaughlin is surprised when Kyle Pendleton explains it as "Persons of the opposite sex sharing living quarters." He assures Jamie that it will be a platonic arrangement, but beginning her first year at UCLA has caused enough changes in her life, and Jamie isn't sure that living together is a good idea. However, she is attracted to Kyle and accepts his offer. As their relationship moves onto a more personal level, Jamie is torn and confused by fear that the cancer she had when she was fifteen will recur, by family problems, and by her feelings for Kyle.

7.2 Calvert, Patricia. **Stranger, You and I.** Avon/Flare Books, 1988. 149 pp. ISBN 0-380-70600-8. Fiction.

Hughie McBride is a seventeen-year-old junior at Vandalia High School in a small town in Minnesota. He is the middle child, with older twin sisters and a nine-year-old brother, Beanie, with whom he shares an attic bedroom. Zee, also a junior, has been his best friend and buddy since the fourth grade. Hughie dreams of finding himself—leaving town, seeing the world, and becoming rich and famous. But there are problems at home, and Zee has a secret problem that she soon confides to him.

7.3 Carson, Michael. **Brothers in Arms.** Pantheon Books, 1988. 220 pp. ISBN 0-394-57213-0. Fiction.

Benson is a "fourteen-year-old boy who loves sweets, classical music, Jesus, and other boys. . . ." Unable to cope in regular school, Benson joins a seminary, but alas, it too is a pit of temptation, populated by "lecherous brothers and neurotic novices." Eventually, finding himself expelled from the seminary due to Brother Michael, who saw him as an easy target, Benson returns to his old school. This time, though, he finds a friend in the star pupil of the senior class, a boy who makes everything Benson finds difficult to cope with seem easy and natural.

7.4 Caseley, Judith. **Kisses.** Alfred A. Knopf, 1990. 186 pp. ISBN 0-679-90166-3. Fiction.

Hannah Gold is fifteen and already feels like a failure with boys. She is smart, a good violin player, and brunette—not what the high school Romeos are looking for at all! She does start to date, however, and between misadventures in the snow with cars and guys with colds spraying her when they sneeze, she starts to work out what is and isn't important about romance, self-confidence, and dating.

7.5 Chabon, Michael. **The Mysteries of Pittsburgh.** William Morrow, 1988. 297 pp. ISBN 0-688-07632-7. Fiction.

After four years of college in Pittsburgh, Art Bechstein needs the summer to review his past and to make decisions about his future. He makes new friendships with Arthur, a witty, debonair man whose homosexuality both attracts and repels him; Phlox, a bewitching woman of contrived appearance, currently imitating Joan Crawford; and Cleveland, an alcoholic biker who uses his troubled childhood as an excuse for the dangerous lifestyle he stumbles into. As Art tries to sort out his fondness for both Phlox and Arthur, his memories of the mysterious death of his mother, and his shame and repulsion for his gangster father, he finds that the two worlds he desperately tried to keep separate are on a collision course.

7.6 Clements, Bruce. **Tom Loves Anna Loves Tom.** Farrar, Straus and Giroux, 1990. 167 pp. ISBN 0-374-37673-5. Fiction.

Realizing their time together is limited, Tom Post and Anna Milton put together memories as they get to know each other. Anna comes to trust Tom enough to share her secret with him. When her Aunt Barbara becomes critically ill, Tom and his family are there for Anna. These two sixteen-year-olds form a deep friendship based on trust and understanding.

7.7 Cohen, Susan, and Daniel Cohen. **When Someone You Know Is Gay.** M. Evans, 1989. 170 pp. ISBN 0-87131-567-X. Nonfiction.

What would you do if your best friend came up to you and said, "I've got something to tell you. I'm gay." This book tries to help you answer that question. You will find statistics about homosexuality, its history, and family reactions to it. Included are excerpts from interviews with eleven gay and lesbian teenagers. At the back of the book are lists of helpful addresses, phone numbers, books, films, and videos.

7.8 Conford, Ellen. **Genie with the Light Blue Hair.** Bantam/Starfire Books, 1989. 150 pp. ISBN 0-553-05806-1. Fiction.

Utterly sensible, practical, down-to-earth Jeannie Warren can't imagine why her aunt and uncle bought that weird-looking antique lamp for her fifteenth birthday. In fact, if a storm hadn't caused a power failure that very night, she probably never would have bothered to light the candle inside; and then she wouldn't have met Arthur. A wispy, blue genie who looks and talks like Groucho Marx, Arthur appears to offer her not one, not three, but unlimited wishes. Not even a rational girl like Jeannie can turn down an offer like that. So she starts wishing (she makes a list first), but no matter how careful she is about what she asks for, things never seem to turn out right—like when she wishes her handsome English teacher loved her and the next thing she knows she's his daughter. Jeannie is sure there must be a way to figure this wishing thing out, so she keeps trying, and she learns a little more with each wish, especially that it doesn't always take magic to make dreams come true.

7.9 Fiedler, Jean, and Hal Fiedler. **Be Smart about Sex: Facts for Young People.** Illustrated by Hal Fiedler. Enslow Publishers, 1990. 128 pp. ISBN 0-89490-168-0. Nonfiction.

Why do boys and girls feel differently about love and sex? What is "safe sex"? Why does my body do things I don't want it to? Divided into chapters and organized in a question-and-answer format, this comprehensive, illustrated book about sex and sexuality is an easy-to-read, informative source on the concerns teens may have about their sexuality and about being sexually active. It also describes contraceptive options and sexually transmitted diseases, and it provides a bibliography.

7.10 Gabhart, Ann. **Only in Sunshine.** Avon/Flare Books, 1988. 152 pp. ISBN 0-380-75395-2. Fiction.

Wendi Collins and Rod Westmore are two high school juniors who find that opposites can attract—with a little help. Wendi's need to change—to open her wings and fly—reveals a charming and courageous young woman.

7.11 Hautzig, Deborah. **Hey, Dollface.** Alfred A. Knopf, 1989. 151 pp. ISBN 0-394-82046-0. Fiction.

Val Hoffman, fifteen years old and new to the Garfield School for Girls, feels completely out of place until she meets Chloe Fox, who's much more intriguing than the other students. The two girls become very close, sharing special secrets and much of their free time. Val eventually feels confused about the intensity of her feelings for Chloe. Could this be more than friendship? How does Chloe feel? Mature situations.

7.12 Hermes, Patricia. **Be Still My Heart.** G. P. Putnam's Sons, 1989. 144 pp. ISBN 0-399-21917-X. Fiction.

Allison is fifteen years old and very unsure of herself. She can't imagine that anyone would find her attractive or interesting. And how much help can her friend Leslie be to her when David, the only boy Allison likes, is attracted to Leslie? Can a friendship survive jealousy?

7.13 Johnson, Eric W. **Love and Sex in Plain Language.** Illustrated by Russ Hoover and Gary Tong. Bantam Books, 1988. 207 pp. ISBN 0-553-27473-2. Nonfiction.

This is a mature treatment of reproduction and sex, which includes information on the recent AIDS epidemic. The author is direct in his discussion of such topics as anatomy, sexual intercourse, heredity, homosexuality, sexually transmitted diseases, contraception, and sexual values. This book encourages thought based on up-to-date information. Mature situations and language.

7.14 Koertge, Ron. **The Arizona Kid.** Avon/Flare Books, 1989. 215 pp. ISBN 0-380-70776-4. Fiction.

Billy, with his Izod shirts and sunblock, heads west to Arizona to spend the summer with his Uncle Wes and to work at a racetrack. Things are certainly different there than in Missouri. The sun is hotter, the girls are cuter, and Uncle Wes is gay. In the next three months Billy learns about himself and growing up. He finds his direction, experiences his first romance, defends the helpless, saves the day, and comes to understand his uncle. Mature language.

7.15 Koertge, Ron. **Where the Kissing Never Stops**. Dell/Laurel-Leaf Books, 1988. 217 pp. ISBN 0-440-20167-5. Fiction.

At seventeen, Walker has more problems than the average teen: his father dies, his girlfriend moves, and his mother takes a job as a stripper. Everything is terrible until he meets Rachel, the perfect girl for him. But what will she think of his mother? He can see the headlines: "Stripper's son dies at late show." Walker's sense of humor helps him deal with his problems and with his relationships.

7.16 Kuklin, Susan. **What Do I Do Now? Talking about Teenage Pregnancy.** G. P. Putnam's Sons, 1991. 179 pp. ISBN 0-399-21943-2. Nonfiction.

Based on actual accounts, this book contains first-person stories of problems faced by teenage parents and their families. The teenagers talk openly about their pasts as they try to work through the rest of their lives. While some decide to keep their babies, others choose abortion or adoption. Counseling becomes an important part of this experience, as various organizations step forward to assist these young mothers and fathers. The true stories of these teenagers illustrate the uncertainties, the pains, and the joys parenthood brings for the very young.

7.17 Landis, J. D. **Looks Aren't Everything.** Bantam/Starfire Books, 1990. 183 pp. ISBN 0-553-28860-1. Fiction.

Rosie Duprey dates every boy who asks her out—but only once. Her best friend Jeanie can't understand why Rosie goes with guys she barely knows, especially since Jeanie is never asked out at all. Rosie's mother comes to her daughter for advice when a newcomer to Plainview invites her to dinner. As her role with her mother and best friend changes, Rosie makes changes in her own social life. Interested in Jeanie's older brother, she tries a different approach with boys. These best friends remain loyal to each other and their beliefs as they work side by side, sharing secrets and experiences, and Jeanie's new friend Spud helps them examine superficial values.

7.18 Levy, Elizabeth. **Cold as Ice.** Avon/Flare Books, 1989. 167 pp. ISBN 0-380-70315-7. Fiction.

Kelly Ross lives in New York City and loves it. She has lots of friends, a big dog to protect her on the streets, and a great job at the Empire Dome Sports and Entertainment Complex. She not only sees New York's best live entertainment for free, but she often gets to meet some of the stars who perform there. This week's attraction is the best yet—an Olympic figure skating team. Ken Swanson, one of America's top contenders, is a dream on ice, a dream to look at—and he's definitely interested in Kelly. She refuses to listen to warnings about Ken's shady past or his reputation for being unstable until strange things begin happening to the team members. When things go from near-miss "accidents" to outright attacks to kidnapping, Kelly must decide whether to follow her heart and believe in Ken or listen to her head and get out of harm's way.

7.19 Levy, Marilyn. **Rumors and Whispers.** Fawcett/Juniper Books, 1990. 153 pp. ISBN 0-449-70327-4. Fiction.

Changing schools during your senior year is trouble enough, but moving from the Midwest to glamorous southern California makes shy Sarah miserable. Friendless, she finds comfort in her art teacher's approval. But Mr. Hill is suddenly ill and hospitalized and the frightening word "AIDS" is bandied about. Nothing in Sarah's quiet Ohio background has taught her how to handle this problem. And the rumors even disturb her newfound peace with David Light, a fellow student with whom she is falling in love.

7.20 Maguire, Jesse. **Crossing Over.** Ballantine/Ivy Books, 1990. 184 pp. ISBN 0-8041-0446-8. Fiction.

Allison Laurel meets with friends from "Nowhere High" in an abandoned railroad station. Her problems, like how to deal with Mark and how to get a part in the high school play, are not the only ones she must work her way through. Her friend Josh has problems at home and at school which cause him to run away. Why does Allison feel a need to help Josh when their problems are so different? And what does the station mean to them?

7.21 Matthews, Phoebe. **Switchstance.** Avon/Flare Books, 1989. 169 pp. ISBN 0-380-75729-X. Fiction.

Divorce has swept high school sophomore Elvy into a new town in the suburbs of Seattle, a new home with her grandmother, and a new school. What she needs is a new boyfriend. Will it be wild Harry, who is into vandalism, or dull Paul, who is into cars? Escapades with effigies, grade books, and library "trees" lead her through danger to a true friend.

7.22 Mazer, Norma Fox, and Harry Mazer. **Heartbeat.** Bantam/Starfire Books, 1990. 192 pp. ISBN 0-553-28779-6. Fiction.

What do you owe a guy who saves your life? You promise you'll be there for him whenever he needs you—or at least that's the vow Tod Ellerbee made to Amos Vaccaro. Amos is loveable, comic, shy; Tod is smart, good-looking and popular. What happens when both guys want the same girl? And *is* it possible for a girl to love two guys at once? Romantic comedy gets serious when disease complicates this already complex story.

7.23 Meyer, Carolyn. **Gillian's Choice.** Bantam/Starfire Books, 1991. ISBN 0-553-28835-0. Fiction.

The Hotline series centers around a telephone hotline where trained teenagers try to help other teens in their community deal with their problems. In *Gillian's Choice,* Angie Martinez, one of the hotline members, is constantly arguing with her boyfriend Marcos, who is pressuring her to have sex with him. Angie loves him but wants to delay sex until after marriage. Then Gillian, a quiet classmate, confides to Angie that she is pregnant. Gillian is afraid to tell her parents or the baby's father; she asks Angie to help her decide what to do. Angie is so confused by the choices she is facing in her own life that she understands how overwhelmed Gillian must feel. Can Angie find the strength to help herself and to help Gillian?

7.24 Rench, Janice E. **Teen Sexuality: Decisions and Choices.** Lerner, 1988. 72 pp. ISBN 0-8225-0041-8. Nonfiction.

During your adolescent years, you are confronted with decisions about your sexuality and emotions, your standards for relationships, and your ethical obligations to others as well as to yourself. How will you make these decisions which affect the rest of your life? Janice Rench creates realistic teen situations and follows each with questions and answers, providing the information you need to make responsible decisions. The book is indexed and includes a bibliography.

7.25 Rench, Janice E. **Understanding Sexual Identity: A Book for Gay Teens and Their Friends.** Lerner, 1990. 56 pp. ISBN 0-8225-0044-2. Nonfiction.

Janice Rench gives basic information about gays and lesbians and attempts to dispel the myths surrounding the issue of homosexuality. Using a question-and-answer format, she offers support and guidance to gay teens and helps heterosexual teens to understand and accept their gay friends. There is an explanation of how the HIV virus is spread and instructions are given on how to use a condom. From the Coping with Modern Issues series.

7.26 Rue, Nancy N. **Stop in the Name of Love.** Rosen, 1988. 281 pp. ISBN 0-8239-0794-5. Fiction.

Kyle and Holly seem like the perfect teenage couple. But they find themselves in a vicious cycle of abuse and injury, followed by affection, apologies, and gifts. By reading one person's version of the story, and then flipping the book over for the other version, you get both sides of this love story and see the traps that lead to dating violence, as well as how the characters mature and come to understand their actions. From the Flipside Fiction series.

7.27 St. Pierre, Stephanie. **A Brush With Love.** Bantam Books, 1989. 166 pp. ISBN 0-553-28154-2. Fiction.

What a break! Melissa's father has hired two of her school's most popular senior hunks to paint the house. With all her friends away, Melissa had been expecting the last month of summer to be boring, but now things are definitely looking up. She is enchanted by fun-loving Matt Warner with his devil-may-care charm and dazzling smile. But

Kirk Gardener—serious, athletic, smart, and gorgeous—is also appealing. Basking in the glow of attention from both boys, Melissa is perfectly happy, but the boys are not. She's going to have to make up her mind. From the Sweet Dreams series.

7.28 Schultz, Marion. **Tracy Harmon: Love Specialist.** Fawcett/Juniper Books, 1989. 131 pp. ISBN 0-449-70325-8. Fiction.

Tracy used to be overweight; now her good looks have earned her the title "Miss Popularity." But although she writes advice to lovers in the school newspaper, Tracy has two big worries: how can she convince heartthrob Brent she's not just a pretty face, and how can she prevent her best friend from ruining her life with an older man?

7.29 Shuker-Haines, Frances. **Everything You Need to Know about Date Rape.** Rosen, 1990. 61 pp. ISBN 0-8239-1075-X. Nonfiction.

This book from the Need to Know Library series presents the sensitive issue of date rape for both males and females. It defines date rape and suggests ways in which both sexes can avoid it. The book also tells you what to do if you have been raped. A "Where to Get Help" section explains how to contact rape crisis centers.

7.30 Silverstein, Herma. **Teenage and Pregnant: What You Can Do.** Julian Messner, 1988. 154 pp. ISBN 0-671-65221-4. Nonfiction.

Herma Silverstein combines straight talk with emotional support as she gives pregnant teenagers the facts they need to know about pregnancy tests, abortion, prenatal care, childbirth, adoption processes, legal rights, social services, contraception, and protection from sexually transmitted diseases. She also includes information on getting counseling, lists of helpful organizations, and hotline numbers.

7.31 Wallach, Susan Jo. **Acting on Impulse.** Bantam Books, 1990. 167 pp. ISBN 0-533-28463-0. Fiction.

After successfully spearheading a campaign to raise money for a class trip to England, red-haired vivacious Savannah Wheeler is thrilled that at last the class is on its way. Even better, both her best friend Thea and Greg Edwards, the most popular boy in school, are going along. By the time the group arrives in Stratford-on-Avon to see a real Shakespearean play, Greg and Savannah have gone from friendship to romance. Though a bit troubled at Greg's tendency to criticize and try to change her, Savannah is convinced she loves him enough to become the girl he wants her to be. Then she meets Philip Wescott, a young Englisher who likes her just the way she is.

7.32 Wersba, Barbara. **Just Be Gorgeous.** Dell/Laurel-Leaf Books, 1991. 156 pp. ISBN 0-440-20810-6. Fiction.

Things aren't going well for Heidi Rosenbloom. Her best friend has moved away, her mother's one aim in life is to make Heidi beautiful, and her father has moved out after having an affair with a younger woman. Heidi wants a life of her own but cannot summon enough courage for that until she meets Jeffrey Collins. She finally has a friend who listens, shares secrets and interests, and needs her. His homelessness and gay lifestyle add to his mystique, and Heidi makes him a vital part of her life, much to her mother's horror. Jeffrey helps her to believe in herself and to step out on her own, while Heidi continues to hope that Jeffrey will change his ways and return her love. The story continues in *Wonderful Me.*

7.33 Wersba, Barbara. **Wonderful Me.** Dell/Laurel-Leaf Books, 1989. 156 pp. ISBN 0-440-20883-1. Fiction.

When you've spent sixteen years of your life thinking that you're weird and unattractive, it comes as a shock to discover that someone is sending you love letters. That's what's happening to Heidi—the girl who wants to walk dogs for a living instead of going to college. Is she really wonderful? Sequel to *Just Be Gorgeous.*

7.34 White, Edmund. **The Beautiful Room Is Empty.** Ballantine, 1988. 199 pp. ISBN 0-345-35151-7. Fiction.

Throughout his rapidly changing life during the 1950s and 1960s, the nameless narrator of this book manages to keep his sense of humor about who he is and where he's going. He drifts in and out of social castes, joining and abandoning causes while trying to figure out where he really fits in. His search for self-discovery and self-acceptance will lead him to New York City, where he will find that hidden piece of himself which will give his life meaning and purpose.

7.35 Willey, Margaret. **Saving Lenny.** Bantam/Starfire Books, 1990. 151 pp. ISBN 0-553-05850-9. Fiction.

When Lenny Stevens moves to town, Jesse Davis is ecstatic. Lenny is handsome, a senior like Jesse, and she's ready for a diversion from school. The two fall in love and soon fabricate a lie to tell their parents so that they can live together. Kay, Jesse's best friend, is nervous about the arrangements, but in the face of their happiness and confidence, she keeps quiet. Then things start going wrong. Jesse finally tells Kay that Lenny suffers from chronic depression, and despite their love for each other, Jesse realizes that she may have bitten off more than she could chew when she decided to save Lenny.

8 Death and Dying

8.1 Deaver, Julie Reece. **Say Goodnight, Gracie.** Harper and Row/Charlotte Zolotow Books, 1988. 214 pp. ISBN 0-06-021419-8. Fiction.

Best friends forever, Morgan and Jimmy even share acting as their main interest. As high school seniors, they work to get parts in the theaters in Chicago and are excited about each other's successes and sad about "turn downs." When Jimmy is killed in a car wreck with a drunk driver, Morgan is devastated. Only with her aunt's special help is she able to face life without Jimmy, who always made her look on the brighter side of life.

8.2 Donnelly, Katherine Fair. **Recovering from the Loss of a Child.** Macmillan, 1982. 226 pp. ISBN 0-02-532150-1. Nonfiction.

Losing a child is a parent's nightmare, but each year the nightmare becomes reality for the parents of the 400,000 American children under the age of twenty-five who die from catastrophic illness, accident, suicide, or murder. Donnelly describes how numerous bereaved parents and siblings have learned to deal with this anger, guilt, and grief, in order that their poignant comments can offer guidance and hope to other families who have lost a child. She also provides detailed descriptions and addresses of organizations that help bereaved families. This is an emotionally difficult book to read, but it conveys a spirit of survival and of overcoming shattered dreams. Directory, bibliography, index.

8.3 Forman, James D. **The Big Bang.** Charles Scribner's Sons, 1989. 148 pp. ISBN 0-684-19004-4. Fiction.

Fourteen-year-old Chris Walker survives a horrifying accident, a race to beat a train, and is left to sort out the pieces. The "big bang" in his life changes everything: his relationship with his father, his feelings for his lost brother, and his own shadowy memories of the night he, his older brother, and seven friends piled into a van and tried to outrace a train. Some memories just won't go away, memories that hurt him and confuse him; other memories just won't come back. And the memory of that night in the van just might be the last "big bang" that Chris can take. . . .

8.4 Fosburgh, Liza. **The Wrong Way Home.** Bantam/Starfire Books, 1990. 180 pp. ISBN 0-553-05883-5. Fiction.

Fifteen-year-old Bent Roland faces problems which are usually reserved for adults. Her mother, afflicted with a disease of the nervous system, needs more nursing care than Bent and Ani, their housekeeper, can give. Bent's father, who left them eleven years earlier, insists that his ex-wife be placed in a nursing center and Bent come live with him, his new wife, and their family. Realizing that she must give in, Bent goes along with the plan only to discover that her father is unfaithful to his wife. A new family, a new home, and life without visits to her mother present challenges that Bent faces with maturity.

8.5 Hoffman, Alice. **At Risk.** G. P. Putnam's Sons, 1988. 219 pp. ISBN 0-399-13367-4. Fiction.

Amanda Farrell is eleven years old, and she has AIDS from a blood transfusion she received five years before. Parents of the community organize to try to prevent Amanda from going to school. Her younger brother's best friend is forbidden to play with him. Friends and neighbors shun the family. Throughout it all, the Farrells cope, endure, and prevail.

8.6 Irwin, Hadley. **So Long at the Fair.** Avon/Flare Books, 1990. 149 pp. ISBN 0-380-70858-2. Fiction.

Joel and Ashley have everything—money, looks, brains, popularity. They've been best friends since grade school. Now, as they are graduating from high school and Joel begins to realize he wants to spend the rest of his life with Ashley, the unthinkable happens: Ashley kills herself, leaving Joel desperately struggling to go on living without her.

8.7 Leder, Jane Mersky. **Dead Serious.** Avon/Flare Books, 1989. 141 pp. ISBN 0-380-70661-X. Nonfiction.

Teenage suicide has reached epidemic proportions: nearly a half-million teens attempt to kill themselves every year. Jane Leder presents accounts of actual suicides, explores reasons that trigger the decision to commit suicide, defines the warning signals, and offers suggestions for helping someone who is thinking about suicide. Leder's main message is that it is possible to prevent suicide.

8.8 McCuaig, Sandra. **Blindfold.** Holiday House, 1990. 167 pp. ISBN 0-8234-0811-6. Fiction.

"Young brothers jump to deaths: Loved same girl." That's what the headline said about Benji and Joel Goldsteins' suicides, and Sally O'Leary was the girl. To Sally it seems that everyone from Mrs.

Goldstein, who has actually attacked her and called her an evil witch, to her best friend to her own mother blames her, so it must be true. But what on earth did she do? Sally's confusion, guilt, and pent up anger soon lead to such explosive behavior that her distraught mother seeks the help of a psychiatrist. At first savagely resisting Dr. Jago's prying, Sally finally admits her need for help and lets herself remember her friendship with blind Joel and his attractive brother, Benji.

8.9 Morrell, David. **Fireflies.** E. P. Dutton, 1988. 216 pp. ISBN 0-525-24680-0. Nonfiction.

David Morrell chooses a fiction format to tell the true story of his fifteen-year-old son Matthew's six-month battle with a rare and deadly bone cancer. Fact meshes with fantasy in the clever blending of the actual story of Matthew's struggle, with a flashback of Matthew's death which David experiences on his own deathbed forty years in the future and in which he attempts to save Matthew. David finds solace shortly after his son's death in several mystical experiences in which Matthew appears to him in different forms. First, Matthew comes back as a brilliant, colorful firefly that soundlessly tells David it is now happy and at peace. Then, during a service at the mausoleum, Matthew returns as a mourning dove that lets David pick it up and that soundlessly conveys that it, too, is all right. These events give David some emotional stability and the strength to write this book about Matthew.

8.10 Naughton, Jim. **My Brother Stealing Second.** Harper and Row, 1989. 213 pp. ISBN 0-06-024374-0. Fiction.

One of Bobby's best memories is of his brother stealing second base; Billy was a great baseball player. In fact, he did everything well, and Bobby always tried to be like him. But ever since Billy was killed in an automobile accident, Bobby just goes through the motions of life at home and at high school. Then Bobby discovers something that he thinks will make a difference.

8.11 Ruskin, Cindy. **The Quilt: Stories from the NAMES Project.** Photographs by Matt Herron. Pocket Books, 1988. 160 pp. ISBN 0-671-66597-9. Nonfiction.

Thousands of Americans have contributed three-by-six foot panels to the quilt started by the NAMES Project, the National AIDS Memorial. Each panel is sewn in memory of someone who has died of AIDS. Color photographs of the panels accompany the stories of those for whom they were made. The quilt was displayed for the first time in front of the United States Capitol in 1987.

8.12 Schwandt, Stephen. **Holding Steady.** Henry Holt, 1988. 161 pp. ISBN 0-8050-0575-7. Fiction.

In a tragic twist of fate, an old Volkswagen affectionately nicknamed "D.C." for "Death Car" becomes just that for Brendon Turner's father. How does a seventeen-year-old cope with death, growing up, and proving himself all in one summer? He meets a young girl who is trying to accept her father's new hold on sobriety and to reestablish a relationship based on trust. But Brendon and his new friend cross the limits of common sense and nearly lose their lives. It is then that Brendon realizes his oneness with his father and can accept him and his death.

8.13 Schwemm, Diane. **Always.** Fawcett, 1990. 151 pp. ISBN 0-449-14607-3. Fiction.

Being a good softball team captain and student government leader, making a straight-A average her final semester, and getting accepted into the right college were what mattered most to Shelly Carlson. But when she learns her boyfriend has cancer, her priorities quickly change, and she spends more and more time with him. Even while fighting Hodgkin's disease, Jay helps Shelly face her life and move onward. Support also comes from her best friend, Kate, and Jay's and Shelly's parents. Shelly must decide if she wants to do what's expected to graduate. From the Portraits Collection series.

8.14 Shannon, George. **Unlived Affections.** Harper and Row/Charlotte Zolotow Books, 1989. 135 pp. ISBN 0-06-025305-3. Fiction.

With the death of his grandmother, Will Ramsey is alone in the world. He knows his parents died, but "Grom," a bitter and quiet woman, shrouded their lives and deaths in mystery. All she told him was that his mother had beautiful hair as a girl, and his father was better off dead. Now about to leave for college, Will is cleaning out his grandmother's house when he discovers a box of letters in his mother's old room. The letters are from his father to his mother, ending with her death. But Grom had told Will that his father had died before his mother did. As Will starts to read the letters, he feels like he finally has a family. But then, reading further, he uncovers more lies, until he finally learns the truth about his parents' and grandmother's lives.

8.15 Uyemoto, Holly. **Rebel without a Clue.** Crown, 1989. 194 pp. ISBN 0-517-57170-6. Fiction.

Eighteen-year-old Thomas Bainbridge is a movie star and the highest-paid male model in the country. He is also Christian Delon's best friend. Although Thomas lives in New York, he visits his home of Marine County, California, frequently. Christian still feels very close to his famous friend, but when Thomas returns the summer after Christian's senior year, things have changed: Thomas has contracted AIDS. The author of this book, herself only nineteen, describes Christian and Thomas' summer together as they learn to cope with mortality, family, love, and sexuality.

8.16 Zindel, Paul. **A Begonia for Miss Applebaum.** Bantam/Starfire Books, 1990. 180 pp. ISBN 0-553-28765-6. Fiction.

Best friends Henry and Zelda are saddened to find that their favorite and rather eccentric teacher Miss Applebaum won't be returning to school. She has terminal cancer. So Henry and Zelda begin visiting Miss Applebaum together after school. Miss Applebaum turns ordinary visits to the museum, Central Park, and even her own apartment into extraordinary lessons about life, friendship, and charity. Her charity towards others, especially her devotion to the homeless, awakens Henry and Zelda to the fate and lives of those around them. Miss Applebaum teaches a zest for life and compassion for others. But Miss Applebaum can't escape the inevitable. Will Henry and Zelda be able to carry out her last desperate wish?

9 Diaries, Essays, and Oral Histories

9.1 Cormier, Robert. Edited by Constance Senay Cormier. **I Have Words to Spend: Reflections of a Small-Town Editor.** Delacorte Press, 1991. 206 pp. ISBN 0-385-30289-4. Nonfiction.

These essays, originally written as newspaper columns, bring the variety of Robert Cormier's writings into one book. Included are essays about movies, books, poetry, life at home, past happenings around the country, and "Follies and Fancies." They span several years and, with their focus on small town America, they echo the changes in the American lifestyle.

9.2 Jens, Inge, compiler. **At the Heart of the White Rose: Letters and Diaries of Hans and Sophie Scholl.** Translated from German by J. Maxwell Brownjohn. Harper and Row, 1987. 331 pp. ISBN 0-06-015705-4. Nonfiction.

Brother and sister Hans and Sophie Scholl could not remain silent against Adolf Hitler. In May of 1942, while Germany was still winning the war and martial fervor was at its peak, Hans, Sophie, and a few other students at Munich University, known collectively as the White Rose, began distributing leaflets that demanded passive resistance to Germany's war effort and that spelled out the terrifying truth about Hitler's "final solution." Not motivated by political beliefs or by an aristocratic contempt for Nazi barbarians, the Scholls were driven by a strong humanism and by rigorous personal convictions, shaped by their childhood and youth in a deeply humane family. On February 18, 1943, the brother and sister were arrested, and four days later the People's Court sentenced them to death. Hans and Sophie were executed that same afternoon at age twenty-four and twenty-one, respectively. Left behind are their letters to family and friends, which demonstrate their courage, goodness, and love of life.

9.3 Landau, Elaine. **Teenagers Talk about School . . . and Open Their Hearts about their Closest Concerns.** Julian Messner, 1988. 107 pp. ISBN 0-671-64568-4. Nonfiction.

Elaine Landau interviewed twenty-three teenagers who told her their views about school life. They talk about peer pressure, ethnic problems, grade pressures, drugs, and dating. Chapter titles are taken from key quotes from the interviews, like "Kids Don't Have Any Rights," "To Them We're All Alike," and "He Tried to Make Me into a Miniature of Himself."

9.4 Martin, Douglas. **The Telling Line.** Delacorte Press, 1990. 320 pp. ISBN 0-385-30048-4. Nonfiction.

The author interviewed fifteen illustrators and used what he learned to write about them and their works. The artists included are Michael Foreman, Anthony Browne, Janet and Allan Ahlberg, Quentin Blake, Raymond Briggs, John Burningham, Helen Oxenbury, Jan Pienkowski, John Lawrence, Shirley Hughes, Brian Wildsmith, Nigel Lambourne, Victor Ambrus, Faith Jaques, and Charles Keeping. Includes many of the artists' illustrations.

9.5 Moore, David L. **Dark Sky, Dark Land: Stories of the Hmong Boy Scouts of Troop 100.** Tessera Publishing, 1989. 191 pp. ISBN 0-9623029-0-2. Nonfiction.

Thousands of refugees fled Southeast Asia during the Vietnam War era, many of them arriving in the United States with no idea what their futures might bring. David Moore records in this book the stories of some of those refugees, recounting their incredible adventures as they escaped war-torn Laos. Many of these young men left behind families in Laos; in the United States, their family became other members of the Hmong Scouts of Troop 100. The camaraderie of the Scouts helped many of the boys to overcome the fear, prejudice, and confusing experiences they encountered when arriving in the United States.

9.6 Schami, Rafik. **A Hand Full of Stars.** Translated from German by Rika Lesser. Dutton Children's Books, 1990. 195 pp. ISBN 0-525-44535-8. Fiction.

Living in a society where free speech is denied to its citizens, a teenage Syrian boy starts keeping a journal to record his impressions of his life. He describes some typical teenage concerns, like his love for his new girlfriend Nadia, but soon his journal becomes a way of expressing his frustrations with the politics of his country. Ultimately, he becomes passionate enough to help start an underground newspaper and becomes one of many young people making a difference in his world.

9.7 Vaughan, Edwin Campion. **Some Desperate Glory. The World War I Diary of a British Officer, 1917.** Henry Holt, 1988. 232 pp. ISBN 0-8050-0671-0. Nonfiction.

Life in the trenches of France during the First World War becomes very real in Edwin Campion Vaughan's eight-month journal, written in 1917 and published nearly seventy years later. This young British officer had to violate army regulations to keep a diary. Nonetheless, he kept an honest, feeling record of his experiences.

10 Drugs and Alcohol

10.1 Bunting, Eve. **A Sudden Silence.** Fawcett/Juniper Books, 1990. 105 pp. ISBN 0-449-70362-2. Fiction.

Jesse Harmon was with his brother, Bry, when a drunk driver ran Bry down. Jesse shouted a warning to Bry, who was deaf and couldn't hear it. Because he feels he might have done more, Jesse is battling not only grief, but also guilt over his brother's death. He and Bry's girlfriend, Chloe, are determined to find the hit-and-run driver who killed Bry. Their search brings adventure and a surprise.

10.2 Cole, Barbara S. **Alex the Great.** Rosen, 1989. 143 pp. ISBN 0-8239-0941-7. Fiction.

Druggie Alex Starky and tennis star Deonna Johnson are best friends, but their attitudes toward school and drugs are completely opposite. Stealing, skipping school, selling drugs—Alex does it all. Will Deonna remain loyal to their friendship or rat on Alex in order to help her? You'll get the story from each girl's point of view. From the Flipside Fiction series.

10.3 Cole, Lewis. **Never Too Young to Die: The Death of Len Bias.** Pantheon, 1989. 252 pp. ISBN 0-394-56440-5. Nonfiction.

In June of 1986, Len Bias had it all. The college basketball player had just been named as a first-round draft pick of the Boston Celtics and his future seemed certain. Then it was all over when he died of a cocaine overdose. This book explores the night Bias died, the circumstances of his death, the arrest and trial of Bias's friend and accused drug dealer Brian Tribble, and the hidden world of drugs, sports, and the inner city. Why did Len Bias have to die? Why didn't those closest to him know about his problem? And if they did, why didn't they do something? This story is a shocking example of just how much can be lost to drugs—money, fame, and even life itself.

10.4 Dorris, Michael. **The Broken Cord.** Harper and Row, 1989. 300 pp. ISBN 0-06-016071-3. Nonfiction.

Fetal Alcohol Syndrome (FAS) results when a woman consumes alcohol during her pregnancy; the child is born with both physical and behavioral problems. This book is the story of one father's twenty-year odyssey to solve his adopted son's overwhelming handicaps. Michael Dorris adopted Adam, a Sioux Indian baby, in 1971, though he knew little about the child's background. All Dorris knew was that Adam's mother had died of alcohol poisoning. His two-decade struggle to understand FAS and its effects on the family, the society, and the individual is a struggle he continues to this day.

10.5 Fosburgh, Liza. **Cruise Control.** Bantam/Starfire Books, 1988. 217 pp. ISBN 0-553-05491-0. Fiction.

Sixteen-year-old Gussie Smith is a teen with parent problems. His mother is an alcoholic and his father is a critical man who refuses to seek outside help for his wife. When the pressures build, Gussie escapes temporarily by cruising in his mother's car until he feels more in control. After he meets Flame, a teenage runaway who has her own parent problems, they decide to do some long distance cruising, and Gussie's ten-year-old brother goes with them. Heading south, they face serious decisions about their families and their futures.

10.6 Morrison, Martha A. **White Rabbit: A Doctor's Story of Her Addiction and Recovery.** Crown, 1989. 240 pp. ISBN 0-517-56816-0. Nonfiction.

Martha A. Morrison was twelve when she started stealing her mother's painkillers. During her teen years she combined alcohol with a vast variety of drugs—including marijuana, LSD, mescaline, speed, PCP, opium, and heroin—and her drug abuse continued through college, medical school, and her medical residency. Morrison acknowledges that she grew up in a warm, supportive, financially secure, and religious atmosphere in Fayetteville, Arkansas; yet she always felt insecure, leading to seventeen years of pain and addiction. Finally, Morrison reached the point of drug consumption in which the dozen drugs that she took no longer worked—they were barely able to help her reach "normal" feelings. She was having blackouts and was close to death. Confronted by two other physicians, Morrison finally recognized her addiction and began the long, slow road to recovery. Black-and-white photographs.

10.7 Ryan, Elizabeth A. **Straight Talk about Drugs and Alcohol.** Facts on File, 1989. 144 pp. ISBN 0-8160-1525-2. Nonfiction.

In today's society teenagers have many questions about drugs, and they want answers without being preached to. Exactly how do drugs and alcohol affect the body and mind? What constitutes an addiction? Why do some people become addicted while others don't? This book has honest answers and deliberately avoids lecturing on what's right or what's wrong. It also examines the relationship between teens and their families, and the appendix contains a state-by-state list of where to find help if you or someone you know has a problem with drugs or alcohol.

10.8 Terkel, Susan Neiburg. **Should Drugs Be Legalized?** Franklin Watts, 1990. 159 pp. ISBN 0-531-15182-4. Nonfiction.

According to 1988 statistics, 14.5 million Americans use drugs regularly. Would these figures increase if drugs were legalized? What about the number of addicts, which in 1988 numbered around two million people? These and other social, economic, and political reasons for and against drug legalization in the United States are discussed in this book. Drug abuse is a leading concern to the American public, and this timely book clarifies much of the history, current status, and possible future of drug use, distribution, and law enforcement patterns.

10.9 Wood, Marcia. **The Search for Jim McGwynn.** Atheneum, 1989. 150 pp. ISBN 0-689-31479-5. Fiction.

Fifteen-year-old Jamie Hill wanted to spend the summer hiking in the Ozarks. Instead, he has to work for eccentric old Mrs. McCarthy, owner of the smelliest dog Jamie has ever met. Jamie hates the thought of hanging around all summer, watching his father's drinking problem worsen and his mother alternately trying to deny anything is wrong and then trying to overcompensate for his father's illness. Luckily, Jamie meets Shelby Lee, who, besides becoming a good friend, introduces him to secret agent Jim McGwynn novels. When they discover that the author of the Jim McGwynn books lives in their town, Jamie and Shelby decide to find out who that author is. Although the summer doesn't turn out as Jamie had hoped, when it is all over, he realizes that staying at home has helped him to grow up in important ways.

11 Family Relationships

11.1 Allen, R. E. **Ozzy on the Outside.** Dell/Laurel-Leaf Books, 1991. 196 pp. ISBN 0-440-20767-3. Fiction.

Ozzy is determined to become a famous writer, but he lives in a small Colorado town where nothing exciting ever happens. He sets out to create big experiences he can write about, but his first attempt backfires. Then his mother dies suddenly, and the family ignores her last wishes. Ozzy decides to head for a new location—New Orleans. Will Ozzy find his story on a bus in the company of a pretty girl even before he reaches the new city?

11.2 Angell, Judie. **Don't Rent My Room!** Bantam/Starfire Books, 1990. 138 pp. ISBN 0-553-07023-1. Fiction.

Lucy Weber can't believe it when her parents announce they are moving to the country to run an inn on the New England coast. They no longer want the hustle and bustle of city life. As a fifteen year old, Lucy can see no good in leaving her friends, school, and lifestyle. She agrees to move with her parents for a summer in exchange for their promise that she may return to New York and live with her grandmother in the fall. Her summer is busy as she unwillingly works in the dining room of the inn and learns about eccentric Mr. Ainsley.

11.3 Angell, Judie. **Leave the Cooking to Me.** Bantam Books, 1991. 185 pp. ISBN 0-553-29055-X. Fiction.

Shirley Melton's mother is a single working parent, so fifteen-year-old Shirley cooks the family meals. When she throws a last-minute dinner party together to help a friend's mother, she never dreams it will lead to a catering business. She feels she must keep her new business a secret from her mother, which leads to all kinds of complications.

11.4 Ansa, Tina McElroy. **Baby of the Family.** Harcourt Brace Jovanovich, 1989. 265 pp. ISBN 0-15-110431-X. Fiction.

When Lena McPherson talks to babies in photographs, allows a slave's ghost to crash a family picnic, and communes with phantoms in her sleep, no one is surprised. The child of an affluent black family in

Georgia in the 1950s, she was born a "caul baby," meaning that the membrane that covered her in the womb didn't break when she was born. There was rejoicing in her family, and she became a local celebrity, as caul-babies are supposed to have special powers. But as Lena grows up, she finds that her adolescent companions prefer a little more normalcy in their friends, and she must make peace between her powers, her loving and proud family, and the less-than-understanding world at large.

11.5 Babcock, Richard. **Martha Calhoun.** Random House, 1988. 310 pp. ISBN 0-394-56542-8. Fiction.

Although only sixteen, Martha Calhoun is the responsible one in the family. Rom, her older brother, has always been the one to get in trouble, and now he is in prison. Bunny, their mother, is a waitress with a weakness for men and quite a reputation in their small town of Katydid, Illinois. While Bunny has plenty of love for her children, she is unable to give them the security and structure that they need in their lives. One day Martha's judgment lapses, and she is taken into custody on a morals charge involving a young boy. As the police, her social worker, a young minister, and the juvenile court judge investigate Martha, her family, and the reasons why they don't conform to the standards for the 1950s, Martha herself begins to examine her relationship with her mother and how they have failed one another.

11.6 Barry, Lynda. **The Good Times Are Killing Me.** Real Comet Press, 1988. 114 pp. ISBN 0-941104-22-2. Fiction.

Nationally syndicated cartoonist Lynda Barry writes her first novel while retaining her tragicomic style. Edna Arkins comes home from a family that is fighting to stay together. She lives in an ethnically diverse neighborhood that is teetering on the edge of racial violence. Besides the usual afflictions of growing up, such as hard-hearted music teachers, as well as loud and nosey neighbors, Edna deals with racial tension that destroys friendships and loyalties. Through it all, however, Edna relies on music to keep her sane. In fact, the end of the book is a section of paintings the author has done of various musicians and musical styles, with informational text included. These paintings have been exhibited at galleries across the country.

11.7 Bennett, James Gordon. **My Father's Geisha.** Delacorte Press, 1990. 165 pp. ISBN 0-385-30097-2. Fiction.

Teddy, a child of a military family, is "on his way to an ulcer before he's old enough to drive." He and his movie-crazy sister, Cora, are constantly tense in a household where their parents' usual modes of communication alternate between arguments and stony silence. Cora decides their parents will separate because she "has seen the movie." Teddy doesn't know what to think. He just wishes he could start over with a new life! Since that doesn't happen, he and Cora survive their childhood in the 1960s, relying heavily upon their senses of humor.

11.8 Boissard, Janine. **Cecile.** Translated from French by Mary Feeney. Little, Brown, 1988. 312 pp. ISBN 0-316-10103-6. Fiction.

Eighteen-year-old Cecile Moreau is the youngest of four daughters. She's the blunt, impulsive one—always tramping through other people's gardens with her boots on, as her father puts it. Cecile lives with her parents in the village of Mareuil, just outside Paris. Anxious to stop being a spectator to life and to start her own life in motion, Cecile recklessly begins a relationship with Tanguy, a troubled actor who alternately attracts and repels her by his scornful, cynical views. Her feelings shift from love to disgust to the need to somehow heal his wounds. Cecile's struggle to find love leaves her with wounds of her own to heal, and in confronting her own emotions and sense of betrayal, she is able to recognize the power of love. Fourth in a series about the Moreau family. Originally published in French under the titles *Cecile la poison* and *Cecile et son amour.*

11.9 Bridgers, Sue Ellen. **All Together Now.** Bantam/Starfire Books, 1990. 184 pp. ISBN 0-553-24530-9. Fiction.

How long can twelve-year-old Casey keep a secret from someone as old as Dwayne? With her family scattered, Casey forms a close relationship with a very unusual person, a thirty-three-year-old man whose mind is like a child's. This one summer changes her whole life.

11.10 Brooks, Bruce. **No Kidding.** Harper and Row, 1989. 207 pp. ISBN 0-06-020723-X. Fiction.

It is midway through the twenty-first century; there are numerous changes in American society brought on by an epidemic of alcoholism. A young boy, Sam, rules his alcoholic mother's life and the lives of the couple who hope to become his brother Ollie's foster parents. Control is important to Sam, and he stretches the rules as far as he can in keeping the truth about his mother from Ollie. Little does he know about Ollie's real feelings and his secret nocturnal visits to a strange place in the heart of the city. Sam thinks he is the only one responsible for keeping his brother's life in order and comes to some startling conclusions about his own lost childhood and needs.

11.11 Buechner, Frederick. **The Wizard's Tide.** Harper and Row, 1990. 104 pp. ISBN 0-06-061160-X. Fiction.

"This is a story about Teddy Schroeder and his sister Bean, and some things that happened to them when they were children." The story is narrated by Teddy, years later, as he looks back on some of those questions that were left unanswered from his childhood during the Depression. Why was "Well, well, well" all his grandfather said when they got to Pittsburgh? Why did Mrs. Lundbeck want them to see the half-boy, half-crocodile? What happened that Christmas Eve when he and Bean fell asleep feeling that an unspoken family law had been broken? Looking back on those times, Teddy realizes that maybe he does have the answers after all.

11.12 Calvert, Patricia. **When Morning Comes.** Charles Scribner's Sons, 1989. 153 pp. ISBN 0-684-19105-9. Fiction.

When morning comes, Cat Kincaid will be gone. She has no intention of staying in her latest foster home, a bee farm which is a far stretch from the city streets she's used to. But her social worker, Mrs. Allen, has warned Cat that if this home—the most recent one in a long series of foster homes—doesn't work out, it will mean the detention center for Cat. Are people like Annie Bowen, her new foster caretaker, and Hooter Lewis, her newfound friend from school, enough to keep Cat from running away from her troubles again?

11.13 Caplan, Lincoln. **An Open Adoption.** Farrar, Straus and Giroux, 1990. 145 pp. ISBN 0-374-10558-8. Nonfiction.

Dan and Lee Stone decided to adopt after years of infertility. After a great deal of thought, they decided on an open adoption, in which they and the birth mother would meet, talk, and get to know each other. Peggy Bass, a twenty-year-old college student, was unmarried, seven months pregnant, and wanted to find parents for her baby. She chose the Stones from a group of letters written by prospective parents. This is the true story of the relationship the Stones and Peggy built up in the months prior to the baby's birth, and for a while afterwards. There is a great deal of controversy surrounding open adoptions, and this personal, vivid story helps expose both the benefits and the drawbacks of the two involved parties becoming friends.

11.14 Carter, Alden R. **Up Country.** G. P. Putnam's Sons, 1989. 256 pp. ISBN 0-399-21583-2. Fiction.

Sixteen-year-old Carl's plan for financing his college expenses involves breaking the law. He knows the risks he's taking, but he never dreams it will all be interrupted by his mother's drinking problem and his exile to the boonies of Wisconsin. Sent to live in the country with an aunt who is determined to get him on the right track, Carl struggles to cope with her and with his cousin who goes trapping in the wilderness. With the help of Signa, a farm girl who becomes his girlfriend, Carl begins to adjust to his new life, when suddenly his mother wants him to come back home. Does he dare go back and risk his past mistakes catching up with him?

11.15 Clarke, Judith. **The Heroic Life of Al Capsella.** Henry Holt, 1988. 152 pp. ISBN 0-8050-1310-5. Fiction.

Fourteen-year-old Australian Al Capsella is fed up with his family. His mother is a romance novel writer who, when the muse is not upon her, comes to his high school to wave at him through windows, harass his teachers, and make a spectacle of herself. She dresses in thrift store outfits, never cleans or does laundry, and is a source of endless embarrassment. His father, on the other hand, is a quiet guy, but he wears the same K-Mart sweater every day, and the lawn and garden look devastated through neglect. They just aren't what parents are supposed to be—but what can a guy do?

11.16 Cole, Brock. **Celine.** Farrar, Straus and Giroux, 1989. 216 pp. ISBN 0-374-31234-6. Fiction.

Celine concentrates on doing what her absent father told her to do—to show a little maturity while he's gone for two months. Then maybe she'll be able to spend the summer with her friend in Italy. She finds obstacles in her way, though: her young friend Jake; his artist father Paul, who seems interested in her personally; her very young stepmother, who goes to an unexpected conference with Professor Merkie; and her unfinished schoolwork—the paper on Holden Caulfield and her latest painting, entitled "Test Patterns."

11.17 Cooney, Caroline B. **The Face on the Milk Carton.** Bantam/Starfire Books, 1991. 184 pp. ISBN 0-553-28958-6. Fiction.

Jane Johnson is startled to recognize the face of the little missing girl on the milk carton as her own. She remembers the dress and collar in the picture and finally confronts her mother and father with some of what she's remembering. Her next-door neighbor, Reeve, helps Jane deal with some of the new discoveries she finds out about herself. There is a lot of sorting-out to do—decision making which will touch many lives, including those of her parents.

11.18 Cooney, Caroline B. **The Party's Over.** Scholastic, 1991. 187 pp. ISBN 0-590-42552-8. Fiction.

Hallie, or Helen Miranda, has it all—she is prom queen and captain of the cheerleaders and has the perfect boyfriend, Jaz. After her senior year, Jaz and her friends go away to college, while she chooses to remain at home in the small harbor town. But what will she do when she is no longer the center of attention, the one who's looked up to? Watch as Helen Miranda finds a new life.

11.19 Crew, Linda. **Children of the River.** Delacorte Press, 1989. 213 pp. ISBN 0-385-29690-8. Fiction.

Sundara, her aunt, her uncle, and two cousins escaped the Khmer Rouge army in Cambodia and have been living in Oregon for four years. Sundara does not know what has happened to her mother, father, brother, and sister. Her aunt feels responsible for bringing up Sundara in the Cambodian way. She can't go out on dates or even be seen talking to a male alone, and her marriage will eventually be arranged for her. But at high school she meets Jonathan, and Sundara must choose between her Cambodian upbringing and her life among Americans.

11.20 Cunningham, Laura. **Sleeping Arrangements.** Alfred A. Knopf, 1990. 195 pp. ISBN 0-394-56112-0. Fiction.

Orphaned at eight, Lily is taken in by her unmarried uncles, Gabe and Len. Len is an Abe Lincoln look-alike who turns up with his belongings in a manila envelope. Gabe is a Gershwin wanna-be who prides himself on living in a dream world. The establishment of their household is both touching and hilarious as Len cooks popcorn and steaks for breakfast, and Gabe warps the floors with his constant scrubbing. The heart of the book is how a family is created by three highly-unusual individuals.

11.21 Dana, Barbara. **Necessary Parties.** Bantam/Starfire Books, 1991. 310 pp. ISBN 0-553-26984-4. Fiction.

Chris Mills can't believe it when his parents tell him and his six-year-old sister that they are getting a divorce. Although Chris is unhappy about it himself, he swings into action when he sees how it is affecting Jenny, his little sister. He vows not to let it happen and ends up suing his parents. He enlists the help of a part-time lawyer who also works as a part-time mechanic. Chris's words and actions show him to be far beyond his fifteen years as he works to keep peace in the family.

11.22 Dann, Patty. **Mermaids.** New American Library/Signet, 1987. 191 pp. ISBN 0-451-15094-5. Fiction.

Charlotte tries to pray herself into sainthood but is weighed down by the normal everyday feelings of a fourteen-year-old. She and her younger sister are forced to move from town to town with their wanderlustful mother. Charlotte's sense of humor protects her from instability as all three try to bring order into their lives. Her friendship with Joe Peretti, a man twice her age, helps her mature.

11.23 Danziger, Paula. **Can You Sue Your Parents for Malpractice?** Dell/Laurel-Leaf Books, 1988. 141 pp. ISBN 0-440-91066-8. Fiction.

What happens when a ninth-grade girl learns she has legal rights? Lauren has found herself in a disgusting kind of slavery, with her parents, teachers, and society in general giving her orders. But her social studies law course opens her eyes: *Can* you sue your own parents?

11.24 Danziger, Paula. **The Cat Ate My Gymsuit.** Dell/Laurel-Leaf Books, 1988. 119 pp. ISBN 0-440-91612-7. Fiction.

Marcy is bright but bored. She hates school, her bullying father, and her own looks. When the only teacher who inspires her gets fired, Marcy is shaken out of her self-absorbing misery to fight for her teacher. But will she still be able to hang on to new friends, a new self-image, and a better relationship with her mother?

11.25 Danziger, Paula. **The Divorce Express.** Dell/Laurel-Leaf Books, 1988. 148 pp. ISBN 0-440-92062-0. Fiction.

Freshman Phoebe meets Rosie while riding the bus that takes her back and forth between her divorced parents. Her developing relationship with Rosie helps her weather the storm of Phoebe's mother marrying a man Phoebe hates and helps set the stage for a possible relationship between Phoebe's father and Rosie's mother. The story continues in *It's an Aardvark-Eat-Turtle World.*

11.26 Du Prau, Jeanne. **Adoption: The Facts, Feelings, and Issues of a Double Heritage.** Julian Messner, 1990. 129 pp. ISBN 0-671-69328-X. Nonfiction.

Many young people wonder if they were adopted, but most adopted children know very well that their parents are not their biological parents. While it was once extremely difficult to trace one's birth parents, modern laws have changed all this. Now adoptees can usually get access to records. But can a person handle all the emotional turmoil that might erupt as a result? And do birth parents have a right to silence and privacy?

11.27 Edgerton, Clyde. **The Floatplane Notebooks.** Algonquin Books of Chapel Hill, 1988. 265 pp. ISBN 0-945575-00-9. Fiction.

Albert has been building a floatplane in his shop for many years, Vera allows chickens to lay eggs on her bed, and the relatives meet once a year to clean graves. These and other eccentricities of the Copelands of Listre, North Carolina, are related by various members of the family and also by the wisteria vine which has witnessed the comings and goings of the Copelands since before the Civil War. Contains mature language and situations.

11.28 Faber, Adele, and Elaine Mazlish. **Siblings without Rivalry: How to Help Your Children Live Together So You Can Live Too.** Illustrated by Kimberly Ann Coe. Avon Books, 1988. 219 pp. ISBN 0-380-70527-3. Nonfiction.

The authors share much practical advice about dealing with sibling rivalry. Their use of exact dialogues, suggested techniques, and cartoon illustrations makes their advice easy to put into practice. All of their suggestions are based on experiences with their own children and those of other parents, which they learned of through interviews, questionnaires, and group counseling sessions. Directed toward parents, this book is also useful for mature teens.

11.29 Farish, Terry. **Why I'm Already Blue.** Greenwillow Books, 1989. 152 pp. ISBN 0-688-09096-6. Fiction.

Lucy's need to understand her father and mother's relationship keeps her life on hold. Gus, a disabled friend, helps Lucy to "accept the things she can not change" so that she can enjoy her family and her life more fully.

11.30 Fastman, Raisa. **A Portrait of American Mothers and Daughters.** Photographs by Raisa Fastman. NewSage Press, 1988. 127 pp. ISBN 0-939-165-04-X. Nonfiction.

Every woman is a daughter, and many more are mothers. This collection of portraits explores the unique bonds between mothers and daughters, examining what makes them the same, what makes them different, and what passes between them. Many of these women have contributed short essays to this book, describing their feelings about their parent or child. Their insightful comments have a universal appeal, revealing the often-neglected world of relationships between mothers and daughters.

11.31 Ferris, Jean. **Across the Grain.** Farrar, Straus and Giroux, 1990. 216 pp. ISBN 90-55472. Fiction.

After their mother dies, Will has to keep his older sister, Paige, together, even if she doesn't want his "mothering," because no one else is there to do it. But life at the Snakebite Café brings about a change:

Will takes more interest in his own life because he has found others to care about his needs and desires.

11.32 Feuer, Elizabeth. **Paper Doll.** Farrar, Straus and Giroux, 1990. 186 pp. ISBN 0-374-35736-6. Fiction.

There are many things getting Leslie down. As if being a high school senior isn't enough, she's also trying to get into the toughest music school in the country, her father and mother are overprotective and suffocating, she's caught in the conflicts between her older brother and their parents, and she feels like a social reject because a childhood accident left her without legs. When she meets Jeff, a boy with a brash sense of humor and cerebral palsy, she doesn't know how to react to his obvious interest in her. Eventually, as their relationship evolves, she becomes more independent, and her family is forced to reevaluate their motives for keeping a stranglehold on her.

11.33 Filichia, Peter. **What's in a Name?** Avon/Flare Books, 1988. 218 pp. ISBN 0-380-75536-X. Fiction.

Seventeen-year-old Rose Sczylanska is shy and self-conscious about her family name. To her family's dismay, she temporarily takes a false name and registers to have it permanently changed. Romance blooms as her confidence rises, but will Rose's new boyfriend still like her if he finds out her real name? And how can she reconcile her injured family to her rejection of the name?

11.34 French, Michael. **Split Image.** Bantam/Starfire Books, 1990. 192 pp. ISBN 0-553-07021-5. Fiction.

At sixteen, Garrett moves in with his father and becomes greatly interested in his dad's job until he realizes that his father is working as a spy for the communist Pyongyang government of North Korea. Having just regained a father, will he now lose him again? And having helped his father, Garrett himself is guilty of treason. Caught in this web, what is the right thing for him to do?

11.35 Hall, Barbara. **Dixie Storms.** Harcourt Brace Jovanovich, 1990. 197 pp. ISBN 0-15-223825-5. Fiction.

At fourteen, Dutch Peyton's life on the family farm in Virginia is fairly stable. Although the family has had its tragedies, as when Dutch's mother died and when Dutch's nine-year-old nephew was abandoned, the pain seems to have worn off. But then one drought-plagued summer, the farm is dying, wild and crazy cousin Norma comes to visit, and Becky, the woman who deserted Dutch's nephew, comes back to get to know her now nine-year-old son. As painful memories are dredged up, Dutch finally begins to mature. As she herself becomes involved in a relationship, she becomes less judgmental of others and starts to realize that love is neither simple nor easy.

11.36 Hamilton, Morse. **Effie's House.** Greenwillow Books, 1990. 208 pp. ISBN 0-688-09307-8. Fiction.

Effie is fifteen and burdened with the secret of her pregnancy. But the problems she has communicating with her busy mother and several stepfathers are only part of the reason she runs away from home. Her only true friends seem to be her ugly green notebook, Father Jude, and her long-absent father, who everybody besides her believes was killed in Vietnam. More secrets unfold revealing the complexities of Effie's young life.

11.37 Harris, Mark. **Speed.** Donald I. Fine, 1990. 285 pp. ISBN 1-55611-180-0. Fiction.

Set half a century ago in Mount Vernon, New York, this is a novel of two brothers growing up. Speed is a perfect boy, handsome, intelligent and athletic, with one devastating disability. His brother, the narrator, isn't in Speed's league, but he has a lucky streak that helps him succeed. They grow up in the midst of a strange assortment of characters: their mother, with a lover who, they *think*, never came back from the Great War; their father, police chief, with a secret nuptial agreement with their mom; and Chamberlain Johnson, the girl who introduces a boy to "manhood." The book chronicles the adventures of two charismatic siblings as they bumble through the loves, lessons, and losses of growing up.

11.38 Hinton, S. E. **Taming the Star Runner.** Delacorte Press, 1988. 181 pp. ISBN 0-440-50058-3. Fiction.

After a short stay in juvenile hall for an assault on his stepfather, a sixteen-year-old city boy, Travis, is taken in by his uncle, a lawyer who owns a horse ranch in Oklahoma. Facing a pending divorce and custody fight over his own young son, Uncle Ken gives Travis as much time as he can, but Travis still feels lonely. Unable to make friends at school, he relies on the girls around the stable for companionship. His first bright news comes in a letter from an editor whose publishing company seems truly interested in the manuscript he secretly sent them before moving west. Casey, who runs a riding school at the ranch, also presents a challenge for Travis, who realizes they have a lot in common even though he still looks like a city hood.

11.39 Hoffman, Alice. **Seventh Heaven.** G. P. Putnam's Sons, 1990. 256 pp. ISBN 0-399-13535-9. Fiction.

It is the 1950s when Nora Silk moves into a very normal suburban community. Nora, however, is far from normal, and she soon has everyone intrigued. She is a strong, sexy, mysterious, single mother who is determined to bring up her two children alone. She also has a gift for making people see themselves and their lives in new ways. The sense of wonder she brings to the townspeople is one they realize they should never have been lacking in the first place.

11.40 Homes, A. M. **Jack.** Macmillan, 1989. 220 pp. ISBN 0-02-744831-2. Fiction.

Jack is fourteen when his father tells him that he is homosexual. His mother and father are divorced, but Jack had been completely unaware that his father was gay. Jack's best friend, Max, has a family Jack thinks is just about perfect—until he discovers otherwise. With humor and courage Jack struggles to make sense of his life.

11.41 Hopper, Nancy J. **Carrie's Games.** Avon/Flare Books, 1989. 121 pp. ISBN 0-380-70538-9. Fiction.

Seventeen-year-old Carrie is used to getting her own way—until her dad begins to date his secretary, Lise Anders. Carrie must prevent this relationship from developing, but her plan to win back his attention spells trouble. Will she successfully manipulate everyone to suit her own needs?

11.42 Howard, Clark. **Hard City.** Dutton, 1990. 513 pp. ISBN 0-525-24857-9. Fiction.

Twelve-year-old Richie is on his own on the streets of 1940s Chicago. The disappearance of his Tennessee bootlegger father, and the heroin addiction of his mother, have "orphaned" him, but he sets out without a cent to find his dad. As he grows up, he becomes a thief, a boxer, and a survivor in the indifferent city. He also discovers the mystery of his parents' past and, finally, creates his own standards and codes to live by.

11.43 Howe, Norma. **The Game of Life.** Crown, 1989. 181 pp. ISBN 0-517-57197-8. Fiction.

Sixteen-year-old Cairo Hays has her hands full playing the game of life—she has to stop her older sister from marrying a jerk, help her desperate Aunt Lucille lose weight, and sort out her own confused feelings about Rocky Nevin. On top of all this, she has to confront guilt left over from a childhood accident, while searching for truth. Is Cairo in control of the game of life, or is she just another pawn in the hands of fate?

11.44 Jensen, Kathryn. **Pocket Change.** Scholastic/Point, 1990. 182 pp. ISBN 0-590-43419-5. Fiction.

When Josie sees behavior changes in her dad, she suspects alcohol or drug abuse. As she searches through their house, she finds records of his hospitalization for mental instability following his service in Vietnam. Her stepmother, who is only a few years older than Josie, seems to be hiding some of her own anxieties and terror as she blames overwork for her husband's trouble. Josie is distraught when her dad forbids her to see her boyfriend, Brian. She knows they have to get professional help for her dad, but it is not until a hostage situation develops that real help comes to this dysfunctional family.

11.45 Kincaid, Jamaica. **Lucy.** Farrar, Straus and Giroux, 1990. 164 pp. ISBN 0-374-19434-3. Fiction.

During her teens, Lucy comes from the West Indies to North America to work as an *au pair* for a married couple. The couple, Lewis and Mariah, seem to have it all; they are intelligent, attractive, rich, and they have four children whom they love. But as Lucy gets to know the family she sees that they are not as happy as they pretend to be. When Lucy herself becomes involved in a relationship, she brings to both her own, as well as Lewis and Mariah's situation, a unique perspective through her vivid recollections of her native land.

11.46 King, Buzz. **Silicon Songs.** Delacorte Press, 1990. 164 pp. ISBN 0-385-30087-5. Fiction.

Seventeen-year-old Max lives on the streets. Those streets are better than the foster homes and unloving relatives he has had to deal with since the suicide of his mother five years earlier, and it's better than the subsequent withdrawal of his father. As if being on the streets weren't bad enough, Max's beloved uncle, Pete, is dying of brain cancer. Max escapes from his life through computers, working as a part-time programmer at a university. He discovers that someone is stealing computer time at the university and selling it to a South African company. Desperate for money, Max takes over the scam, despite his ethical qualms and his growing friendship with his uncle's nurse's daughter, Lindy. Will his life ever be in order?

11.47 Kirby, Susan E. **Shadow Boy.** Orchard Books, 1991. 153 pp. ISBN 0-531-08469-8. Fiction.

Artie suffers a head wound in an accident that leaves him brain damaged. The trials and pain of his father, mother, and sister as they adjust to a new Artie equal those of a boy who realizes that he once knew where his shoes were, how to set a table, how to take a walk by himself, and what to do when an elevator door closed. Told in the first person, this story brings you along on Artie's journey of slow, slow recovery in finding the "shadow boy" he once was. His family, torn by Artie's dependency and their love for him, learns new ways to cope and accept him for what he is and can do. Yet they can't let go of what they remember, nor can they trust Artie's friend in helping him regain some independence.

11.48 Klein, Norma. **No More Saturday Nights.** Fawcett/Juniper Books, 1988. 264 pp. ISBN 0-449-70304-5. Fiction.

When eighteen-year-old Tim decides to raise the baby that his teenage ex-girlfriend puts up for adoption, everyone thinks he is crazy. No one except Tim believes he can carry through with his plans to go to college and take care of the baby at the same time. He finds that parenting is both demanding and joyful—and that it helps him understand his relationship with his own father.

11.49 Latiolais, Michelle. **Even Now.** Farrar, Straus and Giroux, 1990. 211 pp. ISBN 0-374-14993-3. Fiction.

Lisa Sandham's parents had a bitter divorce six years ago, when Lisa was ten. Now Lisa finds it harder and harder to cope with her conflicting feelings about her beautiful, willful, demanding mother, whom she lives with, and her father and his new friend, Mary. Things become even more complicated when her mother's former lover, David, comes back into their lives. Feeling nothing but tension, loss, and guilt no matter which parent she is with, Lisa starts an independent process of self-discovery that is both frightening and exhilarating.

11.50 Lukas, Cynthia K. **Center Stage Summer.** Square One Publishers, 1988. 157 pp. ISBN 0-938961-02-0. Fiction.

Johanna Culp is delighted when Ms. Gant, Public Affairs manager at Byron, Inc., gets her a scholarship to study drama at the University of Arkansas. But then Johanna's rebellious older sister, Dana, with whom she's never gotten along, gets Johanna involved in a No Nukes movement against the proposed Arkansas Weller nuclear power plant, which Byron, Inc., makes electrical equipment for. Ms. Gant threatens to take back the scholarship if Johanna continues protesting the plant. Johanna must make up her mind about what matters most to her—her convictions or her scholarship.

11.51 MacKinnon, Bernie. **Song for a Shadow.** Houghton Mifflin, 1991. 311 pp. ISBN 0-395-55419-5. Fiction.

Eighteen-year-old Aaron Webb is the son of a famous rock star and an emotionally unstable mother. Aaron sells his guitar and ditches his new Mazda, the two reminders he has of his father. With no real plan in mind, he starts hitchhiking. He finds friends and a job in a small town in Maine, but he finally realizes that he cannot deny his heritage and talent forever.

11.52 Mahy, Margaret. **Memory.** Margaret K. McElderry Books, 1988. 278 pp. ISBN 0-689-50446-2. Fiction.

A chance meeting with a woman afflicted with Alzheimer's disease changes nineteen-year-old Jonny's life. He himself is searching for lost memories of his sister's death five years before. As he and Sophie West give support to each other, he discovers something new in himself. He learns to take on responsibility for Sophie's well-being and for his own mixed up life. Meeting up again with Bonny, his dead sister's best friend, helps him work towards self-discovery.

11.53 Malmgren, Dallin. **The Ninth Issue.** Dell/Laurel-Leaf Books, 1990. 181 pp. ISBN 0-440-20734-7. Fiction.

Moving to a much bigger school just before his senior year, Blue Hocker tries out for the football team. It is not a fair tryout, and Blue responds by hitting the team's star quarterback, so there is no football for Blue in his senior year. Instead he joins the school's newspaper staff. With the journalism teacher's encouragement, the students write articles which attract new readers around the school. The staff bands together to save the journalism teacher's job when he is accused of vandalizing a fellow teacher's car.

11.54 Marsden, John. **So Much to Tell You. . . .** Little, Brown/Joy Street Books, 1987. 117 pp. ISBN 0-316-54877-4. Fiction.

Marina is fourteen the year she attends boarding school in Australia. Her face has been disfigured in an attack, and she has refused to speak ever since. She has been in a mental hospital, and her mother thinks that the school will be good for her. Maybe she will learn to accept her disfigured face and start to speak again. Marina begins to write a journal for her English class and writes about her life at school and with her mother and father. Does she really hate her father for what he did to her?

11.55 Mazer, Harry. **Someone's Mother Is Missing.** Delacorte Press, 1990. 166 pp. ISBN 0-385-30161-8. Fiction.

Cousins Sam and Lisa are forced to share a home when Lisa's weak mother simply walks away from the family, unable to face poverty. Sam's own tactless mother simply complicates things; besides, Sam wants to help Lisa locate her mother. Can they each learn to understand their very different mothers—and manage a romance in spite of being cousins?

11.56 Mazer, Harry. **The War on Villa Street.** Dell/Laurel-Leaf Books, 1988. 182 pp. ISBN 0-440-99062-9. Fiction.

Run, Willis, run. Willis runs for exercise, of course, as everyone else does, and for the "high" aerobic exercise gives. But he begins to realize he is running away, not just running. A street gang of bullies, a drunken father, an involvement with a retarded boy—can Willis really run fast enough to leave his problems behind him? The idea of giving up has made him furious, and from his anger comes the strength to face his problems.

11.57 Mazer, Norma Fox. **Babyface.** Avon/Flare Books, 1991. 165 pp. ISBN 0-380-75720-6. Fiction.

Toni Chessmore had been lucky to have such loving parents and such a happy homelife. Following her father's heart attack, however, she goes to New York City to stay with her much older sister, and it is there that she begins to hear about her parents' "agreement." Problems continue for Toni upon her return home because she cannot talk with her parents about their "happy-family facade." And Toni's best friend is unavailable, so Toni is alone. When L. R. Faberman offers friendship, Toni ignores the fact that her best friend likes L. R. and begins to date him. Family life grows even more complicated before things get better.

11.58 Mazer, Norma Fox. **D, My Name Is Danita.** Scholastic Hardcovers, 1991. 163 pp. ISBN 0-590-43655-4. Fiction.

Danita, or Dani, and her family are really close and seem to be a perfect family. She and her younger sister bicker a bit but get along well. Dani's worst problem is the excessive attention her mother and father pay her because she weighed only a pound when she was born and has had a few health problems while growing up. Then one day a young boy walks into their lives and changes the family's relationships forever. Mysterious telephone calls and chance meetings with him in the mall and on the street begin to trouble Dani. Then she learns that the boy is her father's son. The family has to work through this new discovery together.

11.59 Mazer, Norma Fox. **Silver.** Avon/Flare Books, 1989. 202 pp. ISBN 0-380-75026-0. Fiction.

Sarabeth Silver is not eager to go to a new school, even if it has marvelous opportunities for kids. Her mother wants more for Sarabeth: she does not want her daughter to have to follow in her footsteps, cleaning house for rich folks. Fitting in goes well for Sarabeth until one of her new friends discloses a disturbing secret which becomes too much for Sarabeth to handle alone. But what can she do? Where can she go?

11.60 McCorkle, Jill. **Ferris Beach.** Algonquin Books of Chapel Hill, 1990. 343 pp. ISBN 0-945575-39-4. Fiction.

Kate lives in a small Southern town in the 1970s. She is at the stage in life where change, especially in her perceptions of the people and things around her, is a daily occurrence—especially when her father dies, she gets involved with her first boyfriend, and conflict with her mother becomes routine. Through these changes, Kate stubbornly refuses to allow the people she loves to reach out to her. Her ideas about people are too rigid: her mother is prim, sensible, and boring; her beautiful cousin Angela is uninhibited, free, and happy; and that's just how it is. Kate learns a painful but rewarding lesson about childhood stereotypes and the fact that once you grow up, black and white become harder and harder to define.

11.61 Meyer, Carolyn. **Killing the Kudu.** Margaret K. McElderry Books, 1990. 202 pp. ISBN 0-689-50508-6. Fiction.

Eighteen-year-old Alex is relieved to be getting away from his over-protective mother for the summer by going to visit his grandmother. Alex is a paraplegic—years ago his cousin Scott accidentally shot him. Now the two boys are meeting at their grandmother's for the first time since the tragedy. Initially they are uncomfortable with each other, but they grow closer through their shared attraction for Claire, the pretty girl from Northern Ireland who their grandmother hired to help out around the house. For all three of the young people, it is a summer of growing up, becoming independent, and coming to terms with the past.

11.62 Mickle, Shelley Fraser. **The Queen of October.** Algonquin Books of Chapel Hill, 1989. 301 pp. ISBN 0-945575-21-1. Fiction.

Sally calls it the year of the bust-up. Her parents are separating, and she is sent to Coldwater, Arkansas, to stay with her grandparents. She finds a very different life there: her grandfather, Dr. Maulden, makes homemade medicines and is being accused of mail fraud; her grand-mother writes letters to the editor about an outhouse spoiling the view from their backyard; and the parrot, Toulouse, reveals an extremely colorful vocabulary. The guilt and loneliness she feels ease as she encounters the life, love, and humor of the people of Coldwater.

11.63 Miklowitz, Gloria D. **Suddenly Super Rich.** Bantam Books, 1989. 150 pp. ISBN 0-553-05845-2. Fiction.

Fifteen-year-old Danielle Armandy is busy with homework, an after-school job, tutoring a ten-year-old boy who can't read, and dating when suddenly her mother wins a $5.3 million lottery. This sends the family into turmoil. Through each member's experiences, the value of wealth and the meaning of social status are explored. Danielle and her family come to the understanding that family love and trust are what mean the most and can't be bought.

11.64 Miller, Frances A. **Cutting Loose.** Fawcett/Juniper Books, 1991. 246 pp. ISBN 0-449-70384-3. Fiction.

Life in the past two years has been good for Matt McKendrick. He's been adopted by the police lieutenant who had tried to uncover the facts about his sister Kate's death. Matt himself had been the prime suspect and had taken abuse from young and old alike. But now he has just been named his high school's runner of the year, and a summer of fun lies ahead. A telephone call asking him to come back to work on the ranch opens old pain, but he feels drawn to the summer job. He takes his best friend Meg with him. Before the summer is over, he, Meg, and her brother Will must come to grips with their relationships with their family members, each other, and their futures.

11.65 Miller, Jim Wayne. **Newfound.** Orchard Books, 1989. 213 pp. ISBN 0-531-05845-X. Fiction.

Robert Wells grows up in Newfound Creek, Tennessee, surrounded by stories. He hears stories about bees, about ghosts down at the swinging bridge, and about dogs and squirrels and people. And he has his own stories. When his parents divorce, he goes with his mother, brother, and sister to live with his mother's parents, who are sharecroppers on his father's parents' farm. Robert comes of age absorbing the lore of Appalachia.

11.66 Myers, Walter Dean. **Scorpions.** Harper and Row, 1988. 216 pp. ISBN 0-06-024365-1. Fiction.

Jamal Hicks has enough problems helping his mother at home and with his work at school, but he finds it harder when his brother goes to prison for a holdup in which someone was killed. Mack, his brother's friend, gets out of jail and tells Jamal that his brother wants him to take over the leadership of the Scorpions, a Harlem gang. Problems continue for Jamal and his best friend Tito when they use a gun given them by Mack. Members of the Scorpions make it hard on Jamal, and he finds himself in a fight to the death when his friend Tito shows up with the gun. Their friendship binds them together, even as Tito has to leave the country for Puerto Rico.

11.67 Nixon, Joan Lowery. **Encore.** Bantam Books, 1990. 196 pp. ISBN 0-553-07024-X. Fiction.

Encore is the third book in the *Hollywood Daughters: A Family Trilogy* series, which reveals the lives of three generations who struggle for Hollywood fame. In *Encore,* teen star Erin Jenkins's TV sitcom is cancelled. Her parents disapprove of her career so Erin turns to her grandmother, Hollywood legend Anny Grant, who is struggling to regain her own superstar status. Can they both reestablish their Hollywood popularity?

11.68 Peck, Richard. **Those Summer Girls I Never Met.** Delacorte Press, 1988. 179 pp. ISBN 0-440-50054-0. Fiction.

Drew Wingate had big plans for his sixteenth summer, and those plans revolved around getting his driver's license and meeting some girls. Instead, he is on the cruise ship *Regal Voyager,* touring the Baltic Sea with his sister, Steph, who is two years younger and in a rebellious phase, and with his grandmother, an independent woman whom he has seen only once before in his life. But his grandmother is Connie Carlson, a famous singer of the 1940s. She amazes Drew with her vitality and the way her performance can charm a roomful of people and take them back to an earlier time in their lives. As Connie reveals some of the secrets of her own past to Drew and Steph, they find themselves growing and changing.

11.69 Pershall, Mary K. **You Take the High Road.** Dial Books, 1990. 245 pp. ISBN 0-8037-0700-2. Fiction.

Samantha, a young Australian high school student, is ecstatic when her mother announces she is pregnant. Sam has always dreamed of a little sister, and after her mother gets over the shock, the two of them name the baby Miranda and look forward to its birth. When the baby is born, Sam is present; it is the most magical moment of her life, despite the fact that Miranda turns out to be a Nicholas. After a year and a half, Nicky dies in an accident, and the family is shattered. Her parents' marriage starts falling apart, and Sam is sure she will never pull through this period of her life. But with the help of a dynamic, concerned, and handsome young writing teacher, her first boyfriend, and her best friend, Sam manages to pull through and even helps her mother deal with her own grief and guilt.

11.70 Pfeffer, Susan Beth. **Sybil at Sixteen.** Bantam/Starfire Books, 1990. 182 pp. ISBN 0-553-28614-5. Fiction.

In the Sebastian Sisters series, each sister tells of personal and family life as she turns sixteen. In this novel, Sybil, the youngest of the five sisters, is sixteen. Against all odds, she has learned to walk again after a devastating accident that left her disabled. But her newfound happiness and security are threatened when her father announces his plan to help the family financially by selling their home and moving again. Sybil is determined to find a way to keep the family together in the house left to them by their mother's Aunt Grace. But her efforts expose long-kept secrets and betrayals. How could she have foreseen the consequences of her efforts?

11.71 Phipson, Joan. **Bianca.** Margaret K. McElderry Books, 1988. 166 pp. ISBN 0-689-50448-9. Fiction.

Hubert and Emily Hamilton, along with their younger brother, Paul, are wandering the countryside when they see a frail, blond girl rowing across a misty lake. At the same time, a woman frantically searching for her daughter Bianca collapses and is taken to a doctor, Hubert and Emily's father. Bianca and her mother had suffered a traumatic emotional scene and the sensitive teenager had run away, suffered from exhaustion, malnutrition, and exposure, and lost her memory. Now the large, bustling, and loving Hamilton family attempts to restore both Bianca's memory and her relationship with her mother.

11.72 Pringle, Terry. **The Preacher's Boy.** Algonquin Books of Chapel Hill, 1988. 270 pp. ISBN 0-912697-77-6. Fiction.

Growing up in a small Texas town with a Baptist preacher for a father, Michael Page rebels at every opportunity. He wants to believe what his father believes, but he simply cannot. The town gossips keep Brother Page informed of Michael's activities. Lottie Swenson lives behind Michael's girlfriend Amy Hardin's house, where Michael spends his spare time; Lottie spends her spare time at the window with binoculars. Away at college, Michael begins to wonder if he will ever be able to tell his father the truth about himself. Mature language and situations.

11.73 Qualey, Marsha. **Everybody's Daughter.** Houghton Mifflin, 1991. 201 pp. ISBN 0-395-55870-0. Fiction.

Beamer Flynn spent her first ten years on the northern Minnesota commune that her parents helped create. Although the group disbanded, they remained in the area, and the friends consider Beamer's home their meeting place. After experiencing unusual relationships with two exceptional boys, Beamer is forced to examine her uncommon life and how it has shaped her personality.

11.74 Ross, Rhea Beth. **Hillbilly Choir.** Houghton Mifflin, 1991. 166 pp. ISBN 0-395-53356-2. Fiction.

At age fifteen, Laurie Hargrove returns to her grandmother's home in Arkansas. Her mother has failed as an actress in New York, but Laurie is happy to be back with her grandmother and old friends. She finds that life changes even in a small town, but none of her family or friends has the talent or means to escape the small town—except for Laurie.

11.75 Ryan, Mary C. **Who Says I Can't?** Avon/Flare Books, 1990. 159 pp. ISBN 0-380-70804-3. Fiction.

Garth Parker, the celebrated movie photographer, hints that Tessa is like her mother, Tatiana Talbert. Fifteen-year-old Tessa wishes this were true, that she were slim, beautiful, and self-confident. One day she decides to make her dream become a reality. Assuming the position of student director of the school talent show, Tessa hopes to prove herself a leader like her mother. For a while everything runs smoothly, but then her new personality backfires.

11.76 Rylant, Cynthia. **A Kindness.** Orchard Books, 1988. 117 pp. ISBN 0-531-05767-4. Fiction.

Chip's mother, Anne Becker, is going to have a baby, and Chip doesn't know who the father is. His own father had deserted them and moved to Australia when Chip was a baby, so Anne and Chip have been a family for the last fifteen years. Why is his mother going to have this baby? And why does she refuse to tell him the name of the father?

11.77 Sauer, James. **Hank.** Delacorte Press, 1990. 260 pp. ISBN 0-385-30034-4. Fiction.

Sixteen-year-old Richard is plagued by a younger brother with a highly developed sense of right and wrong. Hank, in Richard's words, "had this idea that everything had a way it was supposed to be. A right way that wasn't easy . . . but that was right just the same." As Richard chronicles Hank's efforts to march to the beat of his own drummer, Richard finds himself learning some valuable lessons about life and even about love.

11.78 Snyder, Zilpha Keatley. **The Birds of Summer.** Dell/Laurel-Leaf Books, 1983. 195 pp. ISBN 0-440-20154-3. Fiction.

Sixteen-year-old Summer has a heavy burden. She must finish high school, watch over her little sister, and try to rescue her aging flower-child mother from drug dealers. Her search for a father underlines her daily fears. How can a teenager handle life with no father and an irresponsible mother?

11.79 Staples, Suzanne Fisher. **Shabanu: Daughter of the Wind.** Alfred A. Knopf, 1989. 240 pp. ISBN 0-394-84815-2. Fiction.

Like all Pakistani girls of the Cholistan Desert, eleven-year-old Shabanu's and her older sister Phulan's husbands have been selected by their parents. But a few days before Phulan's wedding, a tragedy strikes. In order to protect Phulan's future, Shabanu has been pledged in marriage to the wealthy brother of a despised landlord. Shabanu is faced with a decision: should she dutifully submit to a marriage that will bring honor to her family but unhappiness to herself or rebel against her parents and bring shame upon them?

11.80 Steiner, Barbara. **Tessa.** Morrow Junior Books, 1988. 218 pp. ISBN 0-688-07232-1. Fiction.

The world that fourteen-year-old Tessa Mae has always known is shattered when her mother decides to divorce the father Tessa idolizes. Gone are the days she spent with her daddy, searching river bottoms for Indian relics to sell by mail order. Gone are the days of having her family all to herself—now a slick young apprentice has attached himself to her father. Gone are the days of lazy living in the country; instead, Tessa finds herself living in town with her mother. The only thing that hasn't changed is her friendship with Jec, but having a black boy for a best friend can be hard for a white girl in Arkansas in 1946. It will be a summer of growth that changes Tessa Mae's young life forever.

11.81 Sullivan, Faith. **The Cape Ann.** Crown, 1988. 342 pp. ISBN 0-517-56930-2. Fiction.

Lark's childhood is filled with adventures and dreams, but her biggest dream is the one she shares with her mother: House catalog #127, a Cape Ann with two baths and three bedrooms. Mama has worked hard and, even though the Great Depression makes her dream house seem out of reach, she has managed to save enough money for the down payment. The biggest problem they face is Papa, whose gambling debts might cost them their Cape Ann unless Mama takes matters into her own hands. Through it all, Lark begins to learn things about her parents that trouble her. How do you handle the realization that your Mama and your Papa don't belong together?

11.82 Tan, Amy. **The Joy Luck Club.** Ballantine/Ivy Books, 1989. 332 pp. ISBN 0-8041-0630-4. Fiction.

This book is based on the lives of four Chinese women and their American-born daughters. Using alternating narrators, the book, through reminiscences, stories, myths, and dialogue, creates the two interrelated worlds in which these immigrant parents and their American children live. The author poignantly presents the conflicts that are bound to arise between a mother who believes there is a Moon Lady who can grant any wish, who was engaged to be married at two and then married at twelve, and a Californian daughter who has a profession and lives with her boyfriend. Mostly though, the book is about love, no matter how hard or easy it is to give and to receive.

11.83 Thesman, Jean. **Erin.** Avon/Flare Books, 1990. 139 pp. ISBN 0-380-75875-X. Fiction.

Orphaned fifteen-year-old Erin Whitney is about to run out of places to stay. If she does not get along with Uncle Jock's family, the next place is a foster home. Since the age of ten, when her parents were killed in an automobile crash, she has been hurting inside. Erin's bizarre clothing and behavior regularly result in trouble for her. But who cares? Seemingly not Erin—or does she? Part of The Whitney Cousins series.

11.84 Thesman, Jean. **Heather.** Avon/Flare Books, 1990. 153 pp. ISBN 0-380-75869-5. Fiction.

Fifteen-year-old Heather Whitney begins a new life in the unfamiliar town of Fox Crossing. It is difficult getting to know her new, quiet stepfather Dr. Will Carver and unemotional stepsister Tracy. It is even more difficult dealing with Mrs. Brier, the grouchy housekeeper. Life in Fox Crossing is so different from life as she shared it with her cousin Amelia's family. How can she possibly adjust to all the changes? Part of the Whitney Cousins series.

11.85 Thesman, Jean. **The Rain Catchers.** Houghton Mifflin, 1991. 182 pp. ISBN 0-395-55333-4. Fiction.

Growing up in a house full of older women, Grayling is happy and loved, but she wants to ask her mother what happened the night before her mother left her behind. It is not until her fourteenth year that she has a chance to talk seriously with her mother, who is now a successful businessperson in San Francisco. Following a brush with danger in the guise of a strange man near the Wharf, Grayling is sent home to Seattle. A custody battle between her best friend Colleen's father and her grandmother brings yet more unease into Grayling's life. Grayling and Colleen's adventures growing up together are a story in themselves.

11.86 Thon, Melanie Rae. **Meteors in August.** Random House, 1990. 275 pp. ISBN 0-394-57664-0. Fiction.

Lizzie Macon was ten when her beautiful older sister, Nina, left town. Nina's pregnancy was a disgrace, but it was also a way to escape from Willis, Montana, a town where all the men spend their lives working at the mill, starting with a summer job at age sixteen and retiring at age sixty-five. Willis is a town of abuse, anger, and hatred between men and women, children and parents, whites and Indians, and have-nots and those who have a little. As Lizzie grows up in this atmosphere, she learns that to look at people as they are, without fear or shame, is a kind of healing.

11.87 Van Raven, Pieter. **Harpoon Island.** Charles Scribner's Sons, 1989. 150 pp. ISBN 0-684-19092-3. Fiction.

Frank Barnes moves to harsh, cold Harpoon Island hoping to find a place where his "slow" ten-year-old son, Brady, will fit in. Frank is hired as a school teacher, but the preacher who hired him, and who is apparently the island dictator, turns him away because of his son's handicap. Luckily, they are taken in by Amanda Coffin, and as Brady Barnes begins to open up and turn into a "normal" child, Frank wins respect as a teacher. But then World War I breaks out, and the Barnes' German roots are discovered!

11.88 Wolitzer, Meg. **This is Your Life.** Crown, 1988. 263 pp. ISBN 0-517-56929-9. Fiction.

Fame and family sometimes don't mix very well. Dottie Engels is a successful but overweight stand-up comic with two daughters, Opal and Erica. As they grow up, Opal and Erica find that they have almost nothing in common. Opal lands a great job in TV's hottest show, "Rush Hour," while Erica slips into the world of drugs and depression. Their futures seem to have nothing to do with each other, but, in fact, they have *everything* to do with each other. When their mother's fantastic future begins to crumble, Opal and Erica have to come together as a family to support a woman they've never really known. The hidden strength of all three women may be the only thing that can save their future and make them whole again.

12 Fantasy

12.1 Babbitt, Lucy Cullyford. **Children of the Maker.** Farrar, Straus and Giroux, 1988. 232 pp. ISBN 0-374-31245-1. Fiction.

Paragrin and Cam are the mortal rulers of the Melde Colony, servants of Jentessa, their Half-Divine Ruler. They have no idea that Jentessa has a sister, Magramid, who is Half-Divine Ruler of another colony and who is a fierce rival of Jentessa's. So when Paragrin goes on an exploration mission, leaving just Cam to rule the Melde, Magramid sees the opportunity to destroy the colony while the powers that rule are divided. She disguises herself as an old woman, sneaks into the Melde, and sets out to prove that the people of Jentessa's colony are not as "good" as their Half-Divine Ruler claims they are. But Magramid doesn't realize how truly good-hearted Cam is, and her reaction to this kindness threatens to destroy Cam and the colony completely.

12.2 Barker, Clive. **Weaveworld.** William Collins and Sons, 1987. 722 pp. ISBN 0-00-223254-5. Fiction.

As he attempts to capture his father's escaped racing pigeon, twenty-six-year-old Calhoun Mooney climbs a brick wall on an unfamiliar street in Liverpool. His attention shifts to an exquisite carpet being removed from a dying old woman's house, a carpet which contains a multitude of colors and patterns and which seems to come to life before his eyes. Little does Cal know that the forces of good—the Seerkind—have woven their existence and culture into the carpet, although he immediately senses that his life will never again be the same. Soon Cal and the old woman's granddaughter, Suzanna Parrish, are fighting the forces of evil—the Incantatrix Immacolata and the ghosts of her two dead sisters.

12.3 Bell, Clare. **Tomorrow's Sphinx.** Dell/Laurel-Leaf Books, 1988. 292 pp. ISBN 0-440-20124-1. Fiction.

The story is set in Africa thousands of years in the future when humans have long since migrated into space, leaving only the other animals to face the dying planet around them. In this world, the cheetahs have evolved into intelligent creatures. Despite the unique coloring that has made her an outcast among her kind, perhaps the most exceptional of all the cheetahs is Kichebo, a young, black female. The story is also set in Africa thousands of years in the past, when the Egyptian cult of the sun god is being pushed aside and the young Pharaoh Tutankhamen is master of the only remaining sacred black cheetah left alive. Only the boy king retains knowledge of the ancient lore which allows the minds of humans and cats to fuse, creating two new creatures, each with all the skills and senses of the other. The two black cats—one from the past, one from the future—form a link across time, bringing the two worlds together and opening the way to a third world, where the descendants of the ancient Egyptians live among the stars.

12.4 Bradley, Marion Zimmer, Julian May, and Andre Norton. **Black Trillium.** Doubleday, 1990. 410 pp. ISBN 0-385-26185-3. Fiction.

The King of Labornok has summoned an evil sorcerer to circumvent the defenses surrounding the beautiful land of Ruwenda. The three princesses of Ruwenda are sent on a quest by the Archmage Binah as invading forces swarm the land. They must each search for a talisman, and only when the three talismans are brought together will the princesses have a chance of regaining their kingdom. All depends on the strength and integrity of Haramis, heir to her father's throne and too easily tempted by power; Kadiya, impetuous huntress, who must learn to look before she leaps; and Angel, kind and timid, who must learn to control both her fears of and her love for the enemy!

12.5 Cherryh, C. J. **Rusalka.** Del Rey, 1989. 374 pp. ISBN 0-345-35953-4. Fiction.

Pyter Kochevikov and his friend, Sasha, seek refuge at the old Wizard Uulamet's out-of-the-way cottage. Russia is full of tales of ghosts at this time, most of which Pyter scoffed at, but now he believes. Ghosts seem to hate him, but then he meets the ghost of Uulamet's murdered daughter, a rusalka, one of the most feared ghosts of all! She desperately needs his energy to maintain even her ghostly presence, although it is a terrible drain on him. But Pyter is willing to risk everything for her because, strange as it seems, he and the ghost have fallen in love!

12.6 Duane, Diane. **High Wizardry.** Delacorte Press, 1990. 268 pp. ISBN 0-385-29983-4. Fiction.

Nita, at fourteen, has talked to animals, has traveled through space and time, has been a whale, and has journeyed to the moon. She, like her best friend Kit, is a wizard. But now, her younger sister, Dairine, has taken the wizard's oath without being asked and, worse, has been sent off on her Ordeal! She apparently opened a door to Mars in the

Women's Room of the Museum of Natural History, and was gone. Now Nita and Kit must follow her and bring her back, or else Dairine may have to go up against the Lone Power by herself, and the Lone Power is death!

12.7 Fletcher, Susan. **Dragon's Milk.** Atheneum, 1989. 242 pp. ISBN 0-689-31579-1. Fiction.

If Kaeldra can't get dragon's milk, her foster sister will die—and Kaeldra is the only one who stands a chance of succeeding! But all of the dragons have fled to the north, and there are obstacles to overcome—wrathful ancient dragons, dragonslayers, and hungry baby draclings. Despite the strange closeness Kaeldra feels for the mythical dragons, can she fight for what she needs while still embracing the unusual gift she harbors deep inside herself?

12.8 Gilluly, Sheila. **Greenbriar Queen.** New American Library/Signet, 1987. 330 pp. ISBN 0-451-15143-7. Fiction.

Once the fairest kingdom in the land, Ilyria has suffered twenty years of cruel oppression under the rule of the usurper King Dendron and the evil Warlock Rasullis, who had used sorcery to slay the true Greenbriar King and the rest of the royal family. Known as the Fallen because he is the only Ilyrian sorcerer ever to break the Wizard Rule and interfere in the affairs of humans, Rasullis has grown ever more reckless in his quest to increase his magic powers. When he begins to experiment with forces which could unlock the gate between Earth and the Underworld, the other wizards know the end of the world is at hand. They now must try to unmake Rasullis, but his power has grown so strong that they may have waited too long. Hope lies in a small band of mortals, the old king's First Watch: Kursh, the Dwarf; Peewit, the Littleman; Cedric, the Physician; Immris, the Yoriandir; and Tristan, the Man. Aging and horribly maimed in the war so long ago, the Watchmen are nonetheless recalled to duty and charged to find Ariadne, the only surviving child of the true Greenbriar line. For only through her can the powers of good be brought together and made strong enough to stand a chance in the coming final battle against the dark force of evil.

12.9 Golds, Cassandra. **Michael and the Secret War.** Atheneum, 1989. 183 pp. ISBN 0689-31507-4. Fiction.

Michael sees the letters SEI scratched in the sand on a rainy day and doesn't know what they mean. That same day, the mirror in his room cracks, and the Secret War is begun. Reality and fantasy begin to cross over one another, and Michael is unable to distinguish what's real from what's not. Visitors from other worlds begin to appear, refugees begin to arrive at Michael's home, and Michael finds himself caught up in a mysterious mission which he doesn't understand. Is it worth the sacrifices he must make to keep the princess, the saint, the Gray Man, and the others in his life? What if it costs him his life?

12.10 Hesse, Hermann (Foreword by Theodore Ziolkowski). **The Glass Bead Game: Magister Ludi.** Translated from German by Holt, Rinehart, and Winston. Henry Holt/Owl Books, 1990. 558 pp. ISBN 0-8050-1246-X. Fiction.

Hermann Hesse's last major work, **The Glass Bead Game,** is a novel which echoes the Faustus story. Far in a future, after most of the world has destroyed itself, intellectuals play an almost mystic mind game—especially Knecht the Rainmaker, who makes prayers he thinks to be unheard while the worlds crash around him.

12.11 Holt, Tom. **Who's Afraid of Beowulf?** St. Martin's Press, 1988. 206 pp. ISBN 0-312-02669-2. Fiction.

Ancient Vikings meet modern technology in this humorous tale of age-old powers awakened from their resting places. Hildy Frederiksen is an archaeologist who discovers a Viking longship sunk in a Scottish marsh. This discovery leads to the revival of Hrolf Earthstar, the Viking leader, and his twelve champion warriors. Earthstar, unimpressed with the changes that twelve hundred years have brought to the world, joins forces with Hildy to combat the sorcerer-king, another ancient being who is now a corporate shark planning to rule the world with computers. But it might be the old methods, not the new ones, that decide the battle between good and evil.

12.12 Huff, Tanya. **Child of the Grove.** Donald A. Wollheim/DAW Books, 1988. 288 pp. ISBN 0-88677-432-2. Fiction.

The Elder Races have withdrawn almost completely from the world of humans, and gone, too, are the dreaded wizards, or so the Elder Races think. Learning that a wizard survives with the sole intent of working sorcery for his own benefit, the Elders choose to intervene one more time. Crystal, the Child of the Grove, is the last chance for the mortals against the immortal wizards.

12.13 Jordan, Robert. **The Eye of the World.** Illustrated by Matthew C. Nielsen. Tom Doherty Associates/Tor Fantasy, 1990. 670 pp. ISBN 0-312-85009-3. Fiction.

A boy on the brink of adulthood, born within a special time period, is needed to fulfill an ancient and horrifying prophecy. Unfortunately for them, Rand and his two best friends seem to fit the bill. Caught up in a legendary adventure, complete with disgusting beasts, confusing prophecies, handsome warriors, and beautiful women with mysterious powers, Rand and his companions fight to save their world from oblivion and to grow up as best they can. Maps by John M. Ford.

12.14 Kay, Guy Gavriel. **Tigana.** Roc, 1990. 673 pp. ISBN 0-670-83333-9. Fiction.

The people of the land are so cursed by the dark sorcery of the tyrant King Brandin that they cannot even remember the name of their once-beautiful country, Tigana. But the seeds of revolution are planted as a closely guarded secret leader begins a crusade to free the land. Characters of every description participate in the quest to restore the heirs to their rightful throne. But through this intricate web of rebellion, seduction, betrayal, and vengeance, the ultimate challenge in regaining Tigana lies in deciphering the biggest enigma of all—love.

12.15 Lackey, Mercedes. **Arrow's Fall.** Interior maps by Larry Warner. Donald A. Wollheim/DAW Books, 1988. 319 pp. ISBN 0-88677-255-9. Fiction.

Legendary heroine Talia from Holderkin becomes important in saving the kingdom of horses, Valdemar, for Queen Selenay. A traitor in the Court deviously plots acts of evil against Talia and her mentor, Kris. Dirk, although in a lifebond with Talia, is unable to stop the arrows which puncture Talia and Kris in their pursuit of information about the evil army of traitors.

12.16 Lackey, Mercedes. **Arrow's Flight.** Donald A. Wollheim/DAW Books, 1987. 318 pp. ISBN 0-88677-222-2. Fiction.

Volume 2 of Mercedes Lackey's *Valdemar* trilogy centers on Talia, the Chosen of one of Valdemar's intelligent horses. Talia and her Companion Horse, Rolan, serve the Queen; Talia, as Herald. Talia has been gifted with empathy and mind-seeing—and people are suspicious and afraid of her. Does she manipulate people's emotions? Does she control the Queen herself? And what of Dirk, with whom she is falling in love? Talia's inner struggle to understand her own mind and heart is matched with real storms, raiders, mad women, and murderers as she goes on her first assignment as Herald.

12.17 Lackey, Mercedes. **Magic's Pawn.** DAW, 1989. 349 pp. ISBN 0-88677-352-0. Fiction.

Vanyel is born with the wild magical ability to work both Herald and Mage magic, but he wants nothing to do with it. Nor does he want to pursue the warrior arts; he would rather become a Bard and roam the world as a minstrel. But Vanyel's father does not approve of this goal—such magical talent left untrained can be very dangerous—so he sends Vanyel to be tutored by his aunt, Savil, and famous Herald-Mage in Valdemar. Even Savil, however, cannot foresee the dangers surrounding Vanyel as his wild magic is manipulated by evil forces to unleash horrible wyr-hunters on the land. Worse than that, Vanyel's magic becomes so powerful that it begins to slip from his control. If that happens, the whole land could be destroyed. Followed by *Magic's Promise* and *Magic's Price.*

12.18 Le Guin, Ursula K. **Tehanu: The Last Book of Earthsea.** Atheneum/Jean Karl Books, 1990. 226 pp. ISBN 0-689-31595-3. Fiction.

The child has been raped, beaten, and badly burned, but the aging widow Tenar is determined to raise her as her daughter. If only Ged the archmage could come to heal her. But what hope is there when Sparrowback, the archmage of Earthsea, has lost his powers? Witches and dragons, human love, and murder all climax to save the little girl.

12.19 Longyear, Barry B. **The God Box.** Signet, 1989. 235 pp. ISBN 0-451-15924-1. Fiction.

Korvas has been a rug merchant, a magician, a thief, a soldier, an assassin, a pauper, a priest, and a prince. Now he is the guardian of the god box, and he has inherited an obligation to fulfill the previous owner's final mission. The box which Olassar, the previous owner, left to him contains many puzzles and riddles, and one of these will lead Korvas to his role in destiny. When the prophecy of the Hero and the Destroyer is fulfilled, will the world be saved or destroyed? More important to Korvas, will *he* survive?

12.20 Mace, Elisabeth. **Under Siege.** Orchard Books, 1990. 214 pp. ISBN 0-531-05871-9. Fiction.

Sixteen-year-old Morris Nelson doesn't want to go with his mother to his eccentric Uncle Patrick's country home for the holidays. Once there, however, he becomes fascinated with his Uncle's three-dimensional computerized game board that features a medieval castle and its surrounding fields and forests where oppressed surfs live. When programmed, the landscape comes alive as the serfs besiege the castle. By chance, the lonely Morris finds he can interact with the tiny figures and becomes both friend and god to two of the serfs, Vail, a spirited girl, and Sam, a survivor. Will he be able to help them take the castle—and will his separated parents reconcile?

12.21 Mazer, Norma Fox. **Saturday, the Twelfth of October.** Dell/Laurel-Leaf Books, 1989. 247 pp. ISBN 0-440-99592-2. Fiction.

Zan's teacher said time circled back on itself, and Zan half believes it. When she is furious and humiliated, she fervently wishes herself in some other time and place—and her wish is granted. How will she learn the language of the "loonies" she finds herself among or go naked or eat bugs? Must she become one of them, or can she find a way to go home?

12.22 McKillip, Patricia A. **The Changeling Sea.** Del Rey, 1989. 139 pp. ISBN 0-345-36040-0. Fiction.

Fifteen-year-old Peri looks on the sea with hatred—it took her father's life and her mother's spirit so that the woman is now lost in her dreams. Yet Peri is drawn to the sea and goes to live in a driftwood house on the edge of the sea with an old woman who, before she vanishes, tells tales of a land beneath the sea. Peri remains, and there she meets Kir, prince of the island kingdom, and he, too, is drawn to the sea. Peri places a hex on the sea for what it has done to her, and Kir has a message to deliver to the sea as well. When the sea-dragon rises up from the deep, bound by a golden chain, Peri knows she must try to set the creature free, despite the consequences.

12.23 Moon, Elizabeth. **Surrender None: The Legacy of Gird.** Baen Books, 1990. 530 pp. ISBN 0-671-69878-8. Fiction.

Gird is a self-assertive peasant who becomes a legend. Through his courage, skill, and integrity, Gird becomes the leader of a ragtag band of rebels who liberate their country from oppression. He paves the way for others to become paladins, dedicated to the extermination of evil. This is his story—the story of how a single peasant boy changed a country, leaving behind a legacy which will never die.

12.24 Pratchett, Terry. **Truckers.** Delacorte Press, 1989. 246 pp. ISBN 0-385-29984-2. Fiction.

You wouldn't think the closing of a department store was any big deal. But when Torrit and Dorcas discover that *their* department store is closing, it sends a shock wave throughout their whole community. This community, you see, lives under the floorboards of the store, and most of its gnome inhabitants have never even seen the outside world. It falls upon Masklin, the last gnome to join the community from the outside, to engineer their move into a new home in the perilous world beyond the store.

12.25 Smith, Julie Dean. **Call of Madness.** Del Rey, 1990. 311 pp. ISBN 0-345-36327-2. Fiction.

Magic equals madness as far as the people of the land of Caithe are concerned. The power strikes unpredictably, leaving the populace at the mercy of wizards who neither understand nor can control their capabilities. The solution the people have found is to kill the wizards "for their own good." Brooding in a tavern, twenty-year-old Athaya Trelane ponders the unwelcome realization that she is manifesting magical powers. Her future, unless she can change it, seems grim: death at the hands of panic-stricken Caithians, or insanity!

12.26 Voigt, Cynthia. **On Fortune's Wheel.** Atheneum, 1990. 276 pp. ISBN 0-689-31636-4. Fiction.

Birle, fourteen years old and discontent, is about to marry. But then she goes out one night and spies a thief stealing a boat. In attempting to stop him, she is carried off with him. As it turns out, he's a noble, and she falls in love with him. Their adventures come to a halt when she is enslaved in an evil prince's citadel. Will she and her noble ever live happily ever after?

12.27 Wharton, William. **Franky Furbo.** Illustrated by the author. Henry Holt, 1989. 228 pp. ISBN 0-8050-1120-X. Fiction.

Life for a fox named Franky Furbo begins in combat during World War II when he rescues two soldiers—one German, the other American. Without realizing it, he is transformed from a fox into a human, the deceased American, and given a family. Together he and his new family experience a miraculous life and a future in helping foxes survive as a race.

12.28 Wilson, David Henry. **The Coachman Rat.** Carroll and Graf, 1989. 171 pp. ISBN 0-88184-508-6. Fiction.

Ever wonder what happened to the rat that Cinderella's fairy godmother turned into a coachman? Robert, that very rat, had always been fascinated by humans. The other rats warn him that humans' power to destroy makes them dangerous, but Robert won't listen. So when he actually gets the chance to become human permanently, he is overjoyed. Although the story borrows heavily from Cinderella, this is no fairy tale. Robert is forced to consider and deal with the serious issues of our human capacity for good and evil, rationality and irrationality, love and hate.

12.29 Wood, Robin, and Anne McCaffrey. **The People of Pern.** Illustrated by Robin Wood. Donning Company, 1988. 151 pp. ISBN 0-89865-634-4. Fiction.

Anne McCaffrey's mystical world of Pern is filled with amazing and mysterious characters, from masterharpers to weyrleaders. Now seventy-two of the most memorable people of Pern are collected together in this book, each with a distinctive portrait by Robin Wood. Each character is accompanied by a brief biographic sketch by McCaffrey, many of which include new insights into the popular characters she created years ago.

12.30 Woolley, Persia. **Queen of the Summer Stars.** Poseidon Press, 1990. 415 pp. ISBN 0-671-62201-3. Fiction.

This is the second book in a trilogy about Guinevere, King Arthur's queen. The book traces her life as a new, young, and spirited monarch. She is not beautiful—some think her boyish—but she is very energetic. In fact, she is not regal at all, but she is determined to create the most glorious court in the world. And she does. Here is another legend of Arthur's England, complete with the knights of the Round Table, the romance of Tristan and Isolde, and the introduction of Lancelot into all of their lives.

12.31 Wrede, Patricia C. **Dealing with Dragons.** Harcourt Brace Jovanovich/ Jane Yolen Books, 1990. 212 pp. ISBN 0-15-222900-0. Fiction.

Cimorene is bored to tears with being a princess. She has no interest in lessons on how loudly to scream when being carried off by a giant; she wants to learn economics, Latin, and fencing. When her parents decide to marry her to a handsome drip of a prince, she runs away and becomes a dragon's employee. Between sending away knights who've come to rescue her and making cherries jubilee for the dragon, she manages to get involved in dragon politics. She becomes instrumental in foiling the evil schemes of a bunch of oily wizards and a nasty dragon, who kill the king of dragons and want to set themselves up in his place. Book one of The Enchanted Forest Chronicles.

12.32 Wrede, Patricia C. **Snow White and Rose Red.** Tom Doherty Associates, 1989. 273 pp. ISBN 0-312-91380-8. Fiction.

Snow White and Rose Red live in Elizabethan England. They live in a time when scientific thought is pushing out faerie magic, and mortals are turning away from the old superstitions and beliefs. However, the two sisters live on the forest's edge which hides the border of the land of Faerie, and they frequently go back and forth to collect herbs for their mother. They soon notice strange things taking place near the border, and are swept up in a plot that involves the Queen of Faerie, her two half-mortal sons, and the spirit Madini, who wants to see all ties between the human and the faerie worlds cut off forever!

13 Friendship

13.1 Beatty, Patricia. **Sarah and Me and the Lady from the Sea.** Morrow Junior Books, 1989. 182 pp. ISBN 0-688-08045-6. Fiction.

Twelve-year-old Marcella Abbott has to get used to the idea of being poor when the Flood of 1894 ruins her father's business and forces the family to live like "natives." One of the first people she has to deal with is fun-loving Sarah Kimball, who rubs Marcella the wrong way right from the beginning. But a tragedy brings the two together, a shared mystery—that of the strange shipwrecked lady from the sea—leads them to become the best of friends. Their summer is filled with adventure—including an exciting episode with a beached whale!

13.2 Bennett, James. **I Can Hear the Mourning Dove.** Houghton Mifflin, 1990. 197 pp. ISBN 0-395-53623-5. Fiction.

When sixteen-year-old Gracie Braun's father dies, she goes into a severe depression and attempts suicide. Exceptionally gifted, Gracie is a sensitive young woman who struggles to heal herself with humor and insight into herself and the world around her. With the help of her psychiatrist and a rebellious delinquent, Luke Wolfe, Gracie finds the friendship and support she needs to help her come out of her dark world.

13.3 Betancourt, Jeanne. **Not Just Party Girls.** Bantam/Starfire Books, 1989. 165 pp. ISBN 0-553-05497-X. Fiction.

The Party Girls, sixteen-year-olds Anne, Kate, and Janet, make money by throwing theme parties for kids. When they are not working, they talk about clothes, boys, family problems, and plans for a trip to Europe. Then Anne gets involved in an internship as a missionary for migrant farm workers as part of a social studies project. She finds her values and lifestyle challenged and wants to leave the business she started with her friends. How will she resolve her dilemma?

13.4 Cannon, A. E. **The Shadow Brothers.** Delacorte Press, 1990. 179 pp. ISBN 0-385-29982-6. Fiction.

Marcus and Henry are best friends, partners in crime, and foster brothers. Whether it's driving around in a hearse to impress girls, running track, or making fun of their boss, they do everything together—until their junior year in high school, that is. Henry, a Navajo, starts expressing his feelings about being cut off from his roots. Suddenly his Native American heritage starts making a big difference in his life, and Marcus feels left out. Marcus is going through his own turmoil in feeling the pangs of his first love. As they get further and further apart, each worries that the bonds of brotherhood will not be strong enough to combat their feelings of fear, resentment, betrayal, and loneliness.

13.5 Covington, Dennis. **Lizard.** Delacorte Press, 1991. 198 pp. ISBN 0-385-30307-6. Fiction.

Bright but deformed Lucius Sims has been put in Leesville Louisiana State School for Retarded Boys. Nicknamed "Lizard" by a fellow inmate, he looks for ways to be himself but still fit in and survive the taunts and brutality of both inmates and staff. When his guardian tells him his father is dead, he seizes the opportunity to run away from the school with a visiting actor who poses as his father. The adventures with the alcoholic actor and his girlfriend open doors to the outside world. Lucius forms a relationship with a young black woman named Rain and her brother Sammy. Lies have become so common to Lucius that he welcomes love and learns what real caring can mean in a relationship.

13.6 Derby, Pat. **Goodbye Emily, Hello.** Farrar, Straus and Giroux, 1989. 153 pp. ISBN 0-374-32744-0. Fiction.

Robin and Emily are best friends—and Robin has no idea why. They have no common interests, no common goals, and have completely different personalities: Robin is shy and quiet while Emily is brassy and outgoing. All through grade school and junior high they stick together until Emily discovers boys and the popular crowd. The two girls begin to drift apart, leading Robin to discover talents she never knew she had as well as an independence she never thought she'd find. In high school she joins the Drama Club and makes her own friends. Then one day, after months of not seeing each other, Emily appears again—in trouble and in need of help that only Robin can provide.

13.7 Dines, Carol. **Best Friends Tell the Best Lies.** Delacorte Press, 1989. 213 pp. ISBN 0-385-29704-1. Fiction.

Fourteen-year-old Leah Lucas copes with disappointments from people important to her. Her best friend, Tamara, who has been lying about her mother being a murderer, runs away. Leah's mother is seriously considering marrying José, a Mexican whom Leah doesn't like. And her father, attempting to upset her mother's vacation plans with José, cancels Leah's Christmas vacation with him. Leah discovers that these disappointments are changing her.

13.8 Herlihy, Dirlie. **Ludie's Song.** Dial Books, 1988. 212 pp. ISBN 0-8037-0533-6. Fiction.

Growing up in Georgia in the 1950s, Marty wonders about Ludie, the washerwoman's daughter who was disfigured in a suspicious fire and is now unable to speak. Marty, although told at thirteen that she is getting too old to play with black children, does not accept racism as a fact of life. Looking beyond Ludie's race and appearance, Marty takes the time to see an artistic and intelligent girl she is proud to call friend. However, the friendship puts the girls and their families in danger as the racist community reacts to what it sees as a threat to white supremacy.

13.9 Hopper, Nancy J. **The Truth or Dare Trap.** Avon/Flare Books, 1988. 106 pp. ISBN 0-380-70269-X. Fiction.

How far should Megan go with Angie's practical jokes to belong to the popular crowd? At first everything is funny, surprising, and harmless. But sometimes a prank can go too far, and the need to belong can be too great. For Megan, when the dares become dangerous, it's time to reconsider friendships.

13.10 Kaye, Marilyn. **Attitude.** Fawcett, 1990. 153 pp. ISBN 0-449-14605-7. Fiction.

Lindsay Crawford's attitude changes during her first year at Benedict Academy, a private high school, as she makes some serious decisions. Does she love the wealthy, athletic, popular Parker Holland or debater and scholarship student David Jeffries? Should she remain loyal to her sorority sisters or take a stand against them over an issue she believes in? Will she accept Aunt Margaret as her family after the accidental death of her parents? The choices she makes will affect her chance for happiness.

13.11 Korman, Gordon. **Losing Joe's Place.** Scholastic, 1990. 233 pp. ISBN 0-590-42768-7. Fiction.

When sixteen-year-old Jason's older, body-builder brother Joe jets off to Europe for the summer, leaving his city apartment to Jason and two of his friends, he gives them only one piece of advice: not to lose his lease. He does not, however, warn Jason about his diabolical landlord, or his godzilla-like friend, who crashes on the floor every night. As Jason and his buddies bumble, feud, and party their way through the summer, they are constantly challenged in their efforts to keep Joe's lease. When the evil landlord decides to go condo, partly because of something Jason and his friends did, there is nothing for them to do but wait for a very big, very angry Joe to come home. They survived a summer alone in the city, but is there life after losing Joe's place? Easy reading.

13.12 Maguire, Jesse. **Just Friends.** Ballantine/Ivy Books, 1990. 185 pp. ISBN 0-8041-0445-X. Fiction.

Going to a new high school is never easy, but Marcy Jenner has unique problems. From one of the town's wealthier families, she also has the distinction of having been kicked out of her boarding school. She wants new friends but has difficulty being accepted, especially by Josh Hickham. She ruins her chances when he has to use his hard-earned money for a dinner she invited him to. Being accepted goes hand-in-hand with her discovering who she is.

13.13 Maguire, Jesse. **On the Edge.** Ballantine/Ivy Books, 1991. 180 pp. ISBN 0-8041-0447-6. Fiction.

Caroline, Darcy, Allison, T.J., and Jason are high school friends who unite in a secure and accepting group. All of them feel rejected by their parents, so the five of them turn to each other for love and support. Together, they deal with crises like running away from home, alcoholism, promiscuity, and pregnancy.

13.14 Major, Kevin. **Blood Red Ochre.** Delacorte Press, 1989. 147 pp. ISBN 0-385-29794-7. Fiction.

David's desire to find out more about his heritage leads him to Red Ochre Island and the Beothuk Indians. Nancy, a classmate and a friend, helps him to understand himself and respect the past. The author gives two pictures of young men—David and Dauvoodaset, a Beothuk Indian—which unfold in alternating chapters.

13.15 Manes, Stephen. **The Obnoxious Jerks.** Bantam/Starfire Books, 1988. 212 pp. ISBN 0-553-05488-0. Fiction.

Ullman Griswold Memorial High is known as "ugh" by a group of nonconformist students who call themselves The Obnoxious Jerks. Frank Weiss, the newest member, and his clubmates ridicule pedantic stupidity, bad cafeteria food, and the "untalent show." Other than detentions and official reprimands, the main problem the Jerks face is that a girl—Leslie Frieze—wants to join the club. Can a girl take part successfully in their outrageous pranks and clever banter? Easy reading.

13.16 Montgomery, L. M. **The Story Girl.** McClelland-Bantam/Seal Books, 1987. 258 pp. ISBN 0-7704-2285-3. Fiction.

When their father's job takes him to Rio de Janeiro, he sends Felix and Beverley to live with relatives in Carlisle. They like their new surroundings, especially their new cousins and playmates. The most unusual of these is the "story girl," who makes words live as she spins stories about every family happening and mystery on the island. She has a hard time accepting Peter, the hired boy, but the story girl helps weave her magic even into that.

13.17 Mulford, Philippa Greene. **The World Is My Eggshell.** Dell/Laurel-Leaf Books, 1989. 157 pp. ISBN 0-440-20243-4. Fiction.

After sixteen-year-old Abbey's father dies, her family moves from Upstate New York to Norwalk, Connecticut, and into a very different life. At first, her twin brother, Sheldon, seems to adjust to the changes much more easily than Abbey does. Soon, however, friendships with Mona Lisa and Packy give her new confidence. Abbey learns to stand up for herself in romance, sports, and school.

13.18 Savage, Deborah. **Flight of the Albatross.** Houghton Mifflin, 1989. 256 pp. ISBN 0-395-45711-4. Fiction.

Susan is soon bored and disappointed that she has come to visit her mother, a scientist involved in marine research in New Zealand. She finds an injured albatross and nurses it back to health, but it is when she meets Mako, a Maori boy, and Hattie, a mystical old woman, that Susan becomes involved in the conflicts of New Zealand cultures. Could it be that the albatross had the power to help Susan discover herself?

13.19 Stone, Bruce. **Been Clever Forever.** Harper and Row, 1988. 376 pp. ISBN 0-06-025918-3. Fiction.

Stephen Douglass is a genius—or, at least, everyone thinks so. And they expect acts of genius from him when all Stephen wants is to be left alone. His strange biology teacher, Mr. Truelove, seems to be the only person tuned in to what's really going on around Stephen, from Peggy (who wants Stephen to run for class president) to Stephen's divorced parents (who can't seem to grow up). But Truelove comes with many secrets of his own, secrets Stephen thinks he'll find out when he becomes involved in a plan to have Truelove fired while helping the teacher seek revenge. In the end, being clever may just be Stephen's greatest skill.

13.20 Sweeney, Joyce. **Face the Dragon.** Delacorte Press, 1990. 231 pp. ISBN 0-385-30164-2. Fiction.

Three friends enter a new accelerated program in high school. They are one-half of the program's population and are aware of the responsibility they have to make the experiment work. They want to learn, but they have the usual teenage worries. Eric, who has always been in his friend Paul's shadow, steps out on his own. Risking the loss of that long-standing friendship, Eric tries to date a girl who likes Paul. He is astonished when Paul has doubts about who he is and what he wants. But the time comes when Eric has to make a decision about remaining Paul's friend, even with what he knows.

13.21 Ure, Jean. **The Other Side of the Fence.** Delacorte Press, 1986. 164 pp. ISBN 0-385-29627-4. Fiction.

What do you do with your life when you're eighteen and have just been thrown out of your home by your father? For middle-class Richard, who finds himself alone in the world after being exiled from his family, life is suddenly purposeless and scary until he meets Bonny, a streetwise teen with fierce independence but little self-esteem. She, too, has no home and no plans; she, too, is alone in the world. Together, Richard and Bonny head out across England in search of their futures and themselves, learning from each other what the other side of the fence is really like. Their friendship deepens as they bring out the hidden best in each other, forging a bond that no force—ex-lovers, family, time, or distance—can break.

13.22 Van Raven, Pieter. **The Great Man's Secret.** Charles Scribner's Sons, 1989. 166 pp. ISBN 0-684-19041-9. Fiction.

Paul Bernard is the greatest writer alive. He has won every major award and refused the Nobel Prize for Literature. However, after suffering from an accident no one knows anything about, he lost his legs and has become a silent, withdrawn recluse, living on a farm with his daughter and brooding about the human condition. Jerry Huffaker, on the other hand, is an unknown, wanna-be high school newspaper writer who works up the nerve to ask the "great man" for an interview. The two become friends, and each helps the other to work out suppressed pain from events in their lives that neither has ever talked about much.

13.23 Van Raven, Pieter. **Pickle and Price.** Charles Scribner's Sons, 1990. 202 pp. ISBN 0-684-19162-8. Fiction.

John Pickle Sherburn, a slow-learning white boy living on a prison farm run by his parents, and Price, a young black man who has just finished serving a two-year term there, befriend each other and set off on a road trip to California. Each is dealing with issues that he cannot work out alone. Price was convicted of a crime he did not commit, while Pickle was abused by his father. In traveling together, searching for a life free from discrimination, each discovers the capabilities and dreams of the other. Price wants to go to college, while Pickle isn't as slow as he appears. Together, they develop a sense of self-worth.

13.24 Weyn, Suzanne. **The Makeover Campaign.** Avon/Flare Books, 1990. 153 pp. ISBN 0-380-75850-4. Fiction.

Marsha Kranton wasn't expecting to run for sophomore class president; her best friend Sara entered Marsha's name in order to defeat phony Doris Gaylord. In order to look like a serious candidate, Marsha cuts her hair and wears glasses. But when the campaign turns nasty due to Doris's dirty tricks, Marsha must decide whether or not to use the damaging information she knows about Doris. Must Marsha fight fire with fire, or can she win with dignity? Easy reading.

13.25 Williams-Garcia, Rita. **Blue Tights.** Bantam Books, 1989. 138 pp. ISBN 0-553-28293-X. Fiction.

More than anything else, fifteen-year-old Joyce Collins hungers for popularity. When she is excluded from her high school ballet show, she discovers that her dance talents lie not in ballet, but in African dance. She joins an African dance group and meets its young Muslim drummer, J'had, and through them, she begins to experience a feeling of belonging.

13.26 Wolff, Virginia Euwer. **Probably Still Nick Swansen.** Henry Holt, 1988. 144 pp. ISBN 0-8050-0701-6. Fiction.

Being in special education classes and battling to overcome the memory of his older sister's accidental drowning nine years earlier, sixteen-year-old Nick Swansen struggles with feelings of inferiority. Even so, he has the courage to ask Shana Kirby, the girl he likes, who had "gone up" from special ed to regular classes, to go to the prom with him. She accepts but doesn't show. Nick is crushed to the point of resenting his parents' love. Did Shana mean to hurt him? This story tells how Nick copes and learns to accept himself and others.

14 Health Issues

14.1 Arnold, Madelyn. **Bird-Eyes.** Seal Press, 1988. 201 pp. ISBN 0-931188-62-8. Fiction.

Sixteen-year-old Latisha is a patient at the Illinois Eastern Central State Hospital in 1963. Unlike the other women patients in her ward, she isn't really mentally ill; she's a runaway and a lesbian, and she is considered too "incorrigible" and threatening to be locked up with other teenage girls. Like all the patients, Latisha is given vast quantities of drugs to keep her calm, but she is spared the electric shock treatment that some receive. She learns to counteract the drugs by consuming vast quantities of coffee or by hiding the pills under her tongue and then spitting them out. Latisha becomes friends with Anna, an older deaf woman committed to the hospital due to depression following her husband's death, and it is Anna who gives Latisha the name Bird-Eyes. Their alliance against the oppression of the hospital is the catalyst for Latisha's eventual act of defiance.

14.2 Blake, Jeanne. **Risky Times: How to Be AIDS-Smart and Stay Healthy: A Guide for Teenagers.** Workman, 1990. 158 pp. ISBN 0-89480-656-4. Nonfiction.

This valuable resource book is filled with important information that every teen should know. It covers subjects such as safe sex, condoms, and how AIDS is transmitted. It also includes pictures, quotes, stories of people with AIDS, and tales of their friends, families, and lovers. These people discuss frankly how they got the disease and what they would change for themselves or recommend to others in order to prevent getting infected. The message is important: AIDS is not just a disease that homosexuals or promiscuous people get, and without being responsible and knowing what the disease is and how it is transmitted, there is no way to be safe.

14.3 Bombeck, Erma. **I Want to Grow Hair, I Want to Grow Up, I Want to Go to Boise: Children Surviving Cancer.** Harper and Row, 1989. 174 pp. ISBN 0-06-016170-1. Nonfiction.

The nurse left the cup for the urine sample. The girl secretly poured apple juice in it, and said casually, "It looks a little cloudy. I think I'll send it back through," as she drank it off in front of the horrified nurse. Another girl, confronting two kids who were staring at her, said, "Want to see what happens when you don't eat your vegetables?" and pulled off her wig. Both of these girls have cancer. Both also have a sense of humor. This is the point Erma Bombeck is making in this collection of anecdotes, interviews, and observations both by and about families and their children with cancer.

14.4 Brancato, Robin F. **Winning.** Alfred A. Knopf/Borzoi Sprinters, 1989. 211 pp. ISBN 0-394-80751-0. Fiction.

Gary Madden, the hero of the high school football team, has a freak accident which leaves him totally paralyzed. It will take the support of friends, family, and one remarkable teacher to put Gary back on the road to recovery. This book is an account of his adjustment and how he finally gets on with his life.

14.5 Busselle, Rebecca. **Bathing Ugly.** Orchard Books, 1988. 184 pp. ISBN 0-531-08401-9. Fiction.

Betsy Sherman, new to Camp Sunny Days, is truly embarrassed when Miss Mack, the camp director, announces that Betsy's mom wants her to lose weight this summer. She goes from shock to self-criticism to envy to determination. Even her best friend, Herm-the-Worm, and her swimming pal, Lolly Sharp, are unaware that she hoards candy and writes secret love letters. But summer ends better than either Betsy or her mom ever dreamed.

14.6 Callahan, John. **Don't Worry, He Won't Get Far on Foot: The Autobiography of a Dangerous Man.** William Morrow, 1989. 219 pp. ISBN 1-55710-010-1. Nonfiction.

After a terrible auto accident, John Callahan was paralyzed for life. But this didn't stop him from pursuing life. He overcame alcoholism, learned to function from a wheelchair, and turned his troubled life to cartooning and humor. His works have appeared in a variety of national magazines, and his life has turned around from the time when he was an angry young man, drinking, smoking, and hating his home life. Mature language and situations.

14.7 Callahan, Mary. **Fighting for Tony.** Fireside Books, 1987. 173 pp. ISBN 0-671-64456-4. Nonfiction.

Just after his second birthday, Tony Randazzo was diagnosed as autistic. He was aloof, unresponsive to most people and objects, and sometimes cried as many as twelve hours a day. Although her difficult son ended author Mary Callahan's marriage and career, as well as nearly destroying her sanity, she never gave up her desire to help Tony. Callahan, a registered nurse, discussed Tony's disabilities with numerous colleagues, enrolled him in several preschool programs, and read as much as she could find about autism. Tony made slow progress, learning alongside his younger sister, Renee, and his condition was "upgraded" from "autistic" to "retarded," but Callahan persevered in her fight. By the time Tony was five, his doctor admitted that his original diagnosis was wrong and that Tony's main problem was a difficulty in processing verbal commands and messages. Shortly thereafter, Callahan made a startling discovery that she felt pinpoints the cause of his autistic-like behavior—Tony seemed to have a cerebral allergy to milk. Black-and-white photographs, bibliography, references.

14.8 de Vinck, Christopher. **The Power of the Powerless.** Doubleday, 1988. 153 pp. ISBN 0-385-24138-0. Nonfiction.

Christopher de Vinck's brother, Oliver, was totally helpless—he was blind, mute, immobile, and mentally disabled. Oliver spent his thirty-two years of life in an upstairs bedroom, doing little more than eating, sleeping, and breathing. Despite his impairments, Oliver was one of the most powerful people that Chris had ever known. Unable to realize that he was different from others, Oliver was at peace with himself and instilled a sense of peace in others. His natural trust and gentleness produced loyalty, kindness, and, above all, love in his family. Chris tells Oliver's story and also introduces the reader to three other special people: Lauren, a baby who died shortly after birth due to an accident during the delivery; Anthony, a ten-year-old boy born with part of his brain protruding from an open skull; and Paul, a thirty-five-year-old man with Down's Syndrome.

14.9 Gardner, Sandra, with Gary B. Rosenberg. **Teenage Suicide.** Julian Messner, 1990. 116 pp. ISBN 0-671-70200-9. Nonfiction.

Teenagers give their reasons for trying to commit suicide. They tell of failures, loneliness, and the hopelessness of the future. Included are ways others can help, clues to note, and professionals to contact. Why would anyone want to end his or her life after such a short time? And what can be done to prevent more suicides? Read this book and find out.

14.10 Gilbert, Sara. **Get Help: Solving the Problems in Your Life.** Morrow Junior Books, 1989. 130 pp. ISBN 0-688-08010-3. Nonfiction.

If you've been troubled by some problem and needed help, this book might very well be the one you need. Eating disorders, addiction, legal and health problems, mental and sexual problems, education complications—whatever your problem, this directory should guide you to one or more of the 100-plus national groups ready to help and keep your privacy intact.

14.11 Hautzig, Deborah. **Second Star to the Right.** Alfred A. Knopf/Borzoi Books, 1989. 151 pp. ISBN 0-394-82028-2. Fiction.

Leslie Hiller is driven by something inside her to lose weight. She has everything going for her—a nice home, loving parents, and personal success. She does well in schoolwork, art, and music. Yet she cannot overcome the disease destroying her body and mind. Perfection and control are two forces pushing Leslie to anorexia nervosa.

14.12 Hyde, Margaret O., and Elizabeth H. Forsyth. **Medical Dilemmas.** G. P. Putnam's Sons, 1990. 112 pp. ISBN 0-399-21902-1. Nonfiction.

Many remarkable developments in modern technology have given doctors new ways of healing and prolonging life, but along with these advances come new and painful decisions. Choices have to be made by doctors, nurses, lawyers, and patients and their families as to who should receive organ transplants or how long expensive and painful treatment should be continued for brain-damaged babies. Who has the right to discontinue the use of life-support systems is another question not easily answered. The authors examine many of the issues involved. This book provides a thought-provoking look at some ethical questions and invites readers to make up their own minds.

14.13 Johnson, Julie Tallard. **Understanding Mental Illness: For Teens Who Care about Someone with Mental Illness.** Lerner, 1989. 72 pp. ISBN 0-8225-0042-6. Nonfiction.

Sara, Lisa, Johnnie, Erica, and Walter are caring teens. What did they do to help their family members with depression or schizophrenia? Teens' questions and fears are answered frankly and sincerely, and symptoms and suggestions are provided.

14.14 Kuklin, Susan. **Fighting Back: What Some People Are Doing about AIDS.** G. P. Putnam's Sons, 1989. 110 pp. ISBN 0-399-21621-9. Nonfiction.

Susan Kuklin has worked as a volunteer in a buddy program in New York City for persons with Acquired Immune Deficiency Syndrome (AIDS). Through interviews with other volunteers, doctors, and support personnel, as well as individuals with this terminal illness, she has presented personal stories of courage and dignity. People are fighting back, fighting for their lives and for the education and understanding of their families and communities about this disease. Fourteen stories are recounted. Glossary and photographs included.

14.15 Langone, John. **AIDS: The Facts.** Little, Brown, 1988. 239 pp. ISBN 0-316-51413-6. Nonfiction.

Research and facts about AIDS are explained in terms that all readers can understand. The author documents the background of the disease and its spread in America, as well as the historical perspective behind the theory that the virus transferred from monkeys to humans. One chapter outlines ways to prevent AIDS and another considers what to do when someone near to you has AIDS. The facts are those collected before the October 1988 foreword by Langone.

14.16 MacCracken, Mary. **Turnabout Children: Overcoming Dyslexia and Other Learning Disabilities.** New American Library/Signet, 1987. 252 pp. ISBN 0-451-15876-8. Nonfiction.

Therapist and teacher Mary MacCracken works miracles with learning-disabled children. Realizing that her earlier learning difficulties were caused by a learning disorder, she completed graduate school and set up a private practice working one-on-one with children suffering from different disorders. She concentrated on five students and their stories as she provided safe places for trust and learning to occur. "Children need safe places for courage and confidence to grow as they overcome feelings of failure and pain from society and family," says MacCracken.

14.17 Madaras, Lynda. **Lynda Madaras Talks to Teens about AIDS: An Essential Guide for Parents, Teachers, and Young People.** Drawings by Jackie Aher. Newmarket Press, 1988. 106 pp. ISBN 1-55704-009-5. Nonfiction.

Aimed at teens, parents, and teachers, this candid, informal guide explains in detail the facts about AIDS, the ways in which it is transmitted, and how it can be prevented. Specific information is easy to find, and at the back of the book is a list of AIDS hotlines, AIDS pamphlets, films and videos for teens, and information about AIDS antibody testing.

14.18 Miller, Caroline Adams. **My Name Is Caroline.** Doubleday, 1988. 278 pp. ISBN 0-385-24208-5. Nonfiction.

Caroline Adams Miller was fifteen when friends introduced her to bulimia: binging on huge amounts of food and then purging it from the body by means of vomiting, laxatives, and diuretics. She became addicted almost overnight—here was a way to keep in shape for her prep school swim team without constant dieting. And once Miller fell into the binge/purge habit, she lost all control. Food became an obsession and a way to deal with uncomfortable situations and problems. Her addiction continued during her four years of college at Harvard and during her first year of marriage. Finally Miller realized that she couldn't stop the bulimia on her own and joined a support group for people with eating disorders. Slowly, she conquered her problem following the group's step-by-step method. Included are a bulimia self-test, a test to help family and friends identify a suspected bulimic, a list of resources for those with eating disorders, and a list of national organizations that can help bulimics and other victims of eating disorders. Black-and-white photographs.

14.19 Wesson, Carolyn McClenahan. **Teen Troubles: How to Keep Them from Becoming Tragedies.** Walker and Co., 1988. 144 pp. ISBN 0-8027-1011-5. Nonfiction.

The ten long teenage years are a time of transition from childhood to adulthood, a transition that is rarely smooth and without problems. Author Carolyn McClenahan Wesson, a family therapist, explains that an eight-inch growth spurt, the presence of new hormones, and a one-third increase in the brain's size all contribute to making the teenage years a time of turmoil. But if these problems reach a crisis stage, then outside help is needed. Wesson helps teens recognize when troubles are too intense by, for example, identifying signs of depression, suicide, or drug addiction. She provides suggestions for coping with and overcoming teenage problems and includes advice for dealing with a seriously depressed friend. Bibliography, index.

15 Historical Fiction

15.1 Anderson, Margaret J. **The Druid's Gift.** Alfred A. Knopf/Borzoi Books, 1989. 211 pp. ISBN 0-394-91936-X. Fiction.

In this fantasy set on the remote Scottish island of Hirta, the sweep of history is shown through one character, a young girl who appears in four different time periods. She is Caitlin in the time of the Druids, Cathan in the time of the Vikings, Catie in the Middle Ages, and Catriona in the nineteenth century. Because she remembers snatches of both past and future, she is able to change the destiny of her people, reaching out with love and understanding rather than fear and hatred to each new group who invades the island. Sometimes it is difficult to follow Caitlin's switch between one alter-ego and another but this story has appeal, especially for those fascinated by time-travel fantasy, druidic lore, or the sea.

15.2 Appel, Allen. **Twice Upon a Time.** Carroll and Graf, 1988. 351 pp. ISBN 0-88184-384-9. Fiction.

Alex Balfour is a historian with the uncanny, but uncontrollable, ability to travel back in time. His girlfriend, Molly Glenn, a reporter for the *New York Times,* is sent to South Dakota to cover the attack on two white men by an Oglala Sioux claiming to be a direct descendant of the great chief Crazy Horse, who defeated General George Custer. Alex suddenly finds himself first in Philadelphia in 1876, where he spends time with Mark Twain, and next taken captive on a Mississippi riverboat, along with Twain, Indians Little Spring and High Cloud, and Abraham, a black who befriends Alex in Philadelphia. As Molly arrives at the Little Bighorn, site of Custer's Last Stand, so does Alex, but he is still back in 1876, just before the battle. Can he prevent the massacre? And can either he or Molly do anything about the racial intolerance that they have witnessed in two centuries?

15.3 Bond, Nancy. **Another Shore.** Margaret K. McElderry Books, 1988. 308 pp. ISBN 0-689-50463-2. Fiction.

On vacation in Nova Scotia, seventeen-year-old Lyn Paget and her mother visit the reconstructed eighteenth-century village of Louisbourg, a project of Parks Canada to recreate the living conditions of two hundred years ago. Everyone in Louisbourg dresses in costume and pretends to be part of that historical society. Then something impossible happens and Lyn finds herself transported back in time! Louisbourg is no longer a twentieth-century theme park; it's now a real village in 1744, and Lyn is trapped there! The villagers accept her as one of them, but soon enough Lyn finds that there are others who share her fate of time-travel. Can they get back to their own time? To complicate the situation even more, Lyn finds herself falling in love with Mathieu Martell, an eighteenth-century Frenchman who believes Lyn belongs in 1744. When the time comes, will she be able to leave him behind?

15.4 Cable, Mary. **The Blizzard of '88.** Atheneum, 1988. 197 pp. ISBN 0-689-11591-1. Nonfiction.

The blizzard of March 12, 1888 devastated the Eastern Seaboard, and these are the adventures and misadventures of many New Yorkers who experienced it. Telegraph lines were down, trains were stalled, businesses were closed, and people were stranded in hotels, in restaurants, or in the bitter cold. Thousands of people decided to meet annually to reminisce about that fateful day, and so they founded the Society of Blizzard Men and Blizzard Women.

15.5 Childress, Mark. **Tender.** Harmony Books, 1990. 566 pp. ISBN 0-517-57603-1. Fiction.

Leroy Kirby at twenty is a guitar-picking truck driver from a poor Mississippi family. Leroy at twenty-one is the most famous rock-and-roll star in the history of music. This novel describes it all—Leroy's childhood, with his father in prison and his overprotective mother; his transformation into a wild young man; the overnight success; the drugs, sex, and booze; and, ultimately, the fall from glory. *Tender* explores in detail what it would be like to be so successful at so young an age.

15.6 Collins, Alan. **Jacob's Ladder.** E. P. Dutton, 1989. 149 pp. ISBN 0-525-67272-9. Fiction.

Jacob and his younger brother, Solly, are orphaned and placed in a home for Jewish children in Australia during the Depression. They live with refugee children from Hitler's atrocities in Europe. With their past lives almost completely stripped away, Jacob doesn't know how he and Solly can remain a family. Outside influences like Uncle Siddy begin to separate the two boys and, despite Jacob's best efforts, Solly begins to drift away. Even as a day in court for Solly draws near, Jacob is certain that they can get back to the life they used to know.

15.7 Corcoran, Barbara. **The Sky Is Falling.** Avon/Camelot Books, 1990. 185 pp. ISBN 0-380-70837-X. Fiction.

Annah Perry is one of the lucky ones. Daughter of a bank vice president, she lives in a charming home and enjoys her select group of friends, her exclusive private school, and her carefully structured social life. But it is 1931, the Depression is in full swing, and Annah's life is about to turn upside down. The first hint comes on her fourteenth birthday when her uncle jumps to his death from his twenty-second story office window. Within weeks her father, too, has lost his job, and Annah learns that all of their investments have failed. The family scatters, each member trying to cope with disaster in his or her own way. Annah is sent to the family's primitive summer cottage in New Hampshire to stay with Aunt Edna, who is there trying to put her life back together after her husband's death. Already feeling rejected by those she loves, Annah finds she is treated as an outsider by the kids in her new school and scorned even more because she was once one of "those rich summer people." But Annah is made of strong stuff; she soon begins learning what's really important and what's not, the first steps on her path to a new life.

15.8 Fox, Paula. **The God of Nightmares.** North Point Press, 1990. 225 pp. ISBN 0-86547-432-X. Fiction.

In 1941, twenty-three-year-old Helen Bynum arrives in New Orleans, looking for her strange Aunt Lulu. Fresh from "the land of turnips and potatoes," where she helped her mother run a set of vacation cabins, Helen is eager to expand her horizons. Her expectations are fulfilled as she falls in love with Len and meets a variety of intriguing characters. Then the rumbles of war come over from Europe, disturbing her summer dream. Years later, after she has married Len and moved to New York City, her mother's death forces her to return to the home she left so long ago and to confront the past she and Len shared during that magical summer in New Orleans.

15.9 Green, Connie Jordan. **The War at Home.** Margaret K. McElderry Books, 1989. 136 pp. ISBN 0-689-50470-5. Fiction.

It is the middle of World War II, and Mattie's father has taken a new job in Oak Ridge, Tennessee. No one knows what Mr. McDowell does, and he is not allowed to talk about it. Mattie's cousin, Virgil, comes to stay with her family, and Mattie resents his presence and the attention he receives from her father. When the war ends in August 1945, everyone finally discovers what has been going on in Oak Ridge, and Mattie discovers something about herself and her family.

15.10 Gregory, Kristiana. **Jenny of the Tetons.** Harcourt Brace Jovanovich, 1989. 119 pp. ISBN 0-15-200480-7. Fiction.

When her family is killed by an Indian attack, young Carrie Hill finds herself living with the English trapper Beaver Dick Leigh and his family. Carrie soon learns, to her dismay, that Beaver Dick Leigh's wife, Jenny, is a Shoshone Indian, and Carrie hates all Indians for what happened to her family. At first she plans to run away from the Leighs; as the family travels through the Tetons, however, Carrie comes to respect Jenny and to appreciate the Shoshones' feelings of oneness with nature.

15.11 Harrison, Sue. **Mother Earth, Father Sky.** Doubleday, 1990. 313 pp. ISBN 0-385-41159-6. Fiction.

Set in the Ice Age, this book follows the young Native American woman Chagak, who witnesses the brutal murder of her family and is then forced to marry a man who participated in the killing. Drawing on her inner strength, Chagak begins a quest for revenge that takes her to people and places both magical and strange to her. Finally, her journey becomes more than one of revenge, as she must come to terms with the devastation that brutality has wreaked on her spirit, and part of her success lies in regaining her ability to love.

15.12 Houston, James. **Running West.** Crown, 1989. 318 pp. ISBN 0-517-57732-1. Fiction.

William Stewart is a Scottish clerk, banished from his homeland to Hudson Bay. Thanadelthur is a young Indian woman who was taken into the Hudson Bay Company's York Factory when her whole family was massacred. Set in the 1700s and based on historical facts and real people, this story revolves around their arduous trip back to Thana's homeland to collect furs and valuable metals for enterprising James Knight, the company governor. And, despite near starvation, violence, and deprivation on their journey, it is also the story of how they fall in love.

15.13 Lexalt, Robert. **The Basque Hotel.** University of Nevada Press, 1989. 124 pp. ISBN 0-87417-145-8. Fiction.

Pete's immigrant parents own the Basque Hotel in Carson City, Nevada, the smallest capital city in the United States in the 1930s. Pete's heroes are a motley crew of characters: Hallelujah Bob, who chases his demons with a shotgun when he drinks too much; Pansey Gifford, a handyman who always wears a suit with a flower in the lapel; and Mizoo, a cowboy with a ten-gallon hat. Pete faces the usual teenage problems of growing up and coming to terms with the world in this touching and funny book about a period long gone. A Basque Series book.

15.14 McKinley, Robin. **The Outlaws of Sherwood.** Greenwillow Books, 1988. 282 pp. ISBN 0-688-07178-3. Fiction.

Sherwood Forest comes to life again in this retelling of the Robin Hood legend based on new research. A new twist in the classic tale will give readers fresh insight into Robin, Marian, Little John, Will Scarlet, and all the others who fight injustice at the hands of ruthless tyrants like the evil Sheriff of Nottingham.

15.15 Morrison, Toni. **Beloved.** Borzoi Books, 1987. 275 pp. ISBN 0-394-53597-9. Fiction.

Sethe, an escaped slave, settles just outside Cincinnati shortly after the end of the Civil War. She cooks in a nearby restaurant and does sewing to raise money for her family—three children and her mother-in-law, Baby Suggs. Sethe has lost a husband and buried a child. Her two sons, Howard and Buglar, run away to escape the family's house, and Baby Suggs finds her escape through death, so the family is reduced to just Sethe and her daughter Denver—and the ominous ghostly presence that Sethe attributes to Beloved, the daughter who died at age two. Sethe tries to escape her past, but the raging Beloved is a constant reminder of Sethe's years of slavery and inhumane treatment by whites. This past is further called up with the arrival of Paul D, another former slave who worked with Sethe at Sweet Home before the war, and by the vivid stories they tell of their years in captivity some eighteen years earlier. As her past makes itself heard, Sethe must struggle to keep Beloved from gaining possession of her.

15.16 Namioka, Lensey. **Island of Ogres.** Harper and Row, 1989. 197 pp. ISBN 0-06-024373-2. Fiction.

"Have you come to our island, sir, because you have heard of our ogres?" Kajiro thinks the fisherman who says this must be joking. Kajiro, a sixteenth-century Japanese ronin (an unemployed samurai, trained for war), is sent to the island to spy on the commander of the garrison. But when Kajiro actually sees an ogre, can he believe his eyes? Is this why the farmers, the fishermen, and even the abbess of the convent are all afraid?

15.17 Newth, Mette. **The Abduction.** Farrar, Straus and Giroux, 1989. 247 pp. ISBN 0-374-3000-89. Fiction.

Osugo, an Inuit Eskimo from Greenland, and Christine, a Norwegian servant girl, tell their own stories of lives that intertwine in the seventeenth century. Osugo and Poq, who is to be her husband, are kidnapped by the crew of a Dutch ship sent from Norway. They are abused, kept in chains, and thought to be wild creatures. Osugo and Christine meet when the Inuits are imprisoned in Norway and Christine is forced to guard them. Have the Inuits met someone who considers them to be human, someone who might help them escape from slavery?

15.18 Paulsen, Gary. **The Night the White Deer Died.** Delacorte Press, 1990. 104 pp. ISBN 0-385-30154-5. Fiction.

It was meant to be. It was destiny revealed in the dream. Janet Carson, a fifteen-year-old Anglo in search of herself, and Billy Honcho, an old, tired Indian who has lost a special part of himself, meet to fulfill a haunting dream.

15.19 Pearson, Gayle. **The Coming Home Café.** Atheneum, 1988. 200 pp. ISBN 0-689-31338-1. Fiction.

When fifteen-year-old Elizabeth Turnquist realizes she will never find a job in Depression-ravaged Chicago, she decides to try to help her family by riding the rails, looking for work. She meets up with Eddie, another young vagabond, and Lenora, a young black woman, on the trains, and the three settle into an old, abandoned café in Jacksonville. The Coming Home Café really feels like home and Eddie and Lenora feel like family, as Elizabeth becomes a wage earner and comes to grips with the fact that she alone cannot save her family and that it may be time to start building a life of her own.

15.20 Perez, N. A. **Breaker.** Houghton Mifflin Company, 1988. 206 pp. ISBN 0-395-45537-5. Fiction.

At fourteen, Pat loses his father and is forced to go to work in the coal mines, in the breaker that looms above the small Pennsylvania village of Scatter Patch. A tall wooden structure, the breaker is filled with noise, coal dust, and boys his own age, boys already bent from the effort of being collier lads. Pat wants something more from life than this! Then the mine workers strike. Set in 1902, the actual time of this big strike, *Breaker* is the story of a boy who decides to change his fate and does it!

15.21 Pullman, Philip. **The Tiger in the Well.** Alfred A. Knopf/Borzoi Books, 1990. 407 pp. ISBN 0-679-90214-7. Fiction.

Sally Lockhart has a successful career and financial independence, unusual for a twenty-four-year-old woman in London in 1881. She also has an infant daughter who is her lover's child, conceived the evening of the deadly fire which took his life. Then a man by the name of Arthur

Parrish appears and claims to be her husband with legal documents to prove it. Faced with the possibility of losing everything, Sally is forced to search for answers herself before she loses her little Harriet. The plot thickens as Parrish is tied into a more sinister plot against immigrant Jews and an earlier time in Sally's life. Sequel to *Ruby in the Smoke* and *The Shadow in the North.*

15.22 Rinaldi, Ann. **Wolf by the Ears.** Scholastic Hardcovers, 1991. 252 pp. ISBN 0-590-43413-6. Fiction.

Harriet Hemmings is a slave at Monticello, home of Thomas Jefferson. She lives there with her mother Sally, who has been with the Jefferson family for many years, and her brothers. Freedom is granted to each one of Sally's children when they reach age twenty-one, but they struggle with the decision to go to an unknown world or to stay in the world that feels comfortable. They are unsure of their past, their parents, or their future in the "white" world.

15.23 Taylor, Mildred D. **The Road to Memphis.** Dial Books, 1990. 290 pp. ISBN 0-8037-0340-6. Fiction.

In 1941, Cassie, a high school senior, is confronting the confused overseas political situation and her imminent graduation. But in three short days, Cassie's priorities go through a radical shift. Suddenly she is confronted by brutal racism in her small Mississippi town when three white boys mercilessly tease one black boy and violence erupts. Cassie must deal with the results of this act as a friend and confidant to many of the people involved, and ultimately she must decide whether to help the black boy flee the state.

15.24 Westall, Robert. **Blitzcat.** Scholastic, 1989. 230 pp. ISBN 0-590-42771-7. Fiction.

A lost cat wanders through England during World War II. She meets several humans in her travels, and the series of stories about these people describes life during the blitz.

15.25 Wiley, Richard. **Soldiers in Hiding.** New American Library/Signet, 1987. 237 pp. ISBN 0-451-14954-8. Fiction.

A Japanese American, Teddy Maki, finds himself trapped into fighting his American homeland as a member of the Japanese army. His experiences in watching his friend die in a meaningless show of power by their Japanese commander affects his entire life. Drawn back to Tokyo by his love for his best friend's wife, Teddy, although a famous entertainer, walks through life in a vacuum. Eventually, he gains support for a strange act of revenge.

16 History and Geography

16.1 Armor, John, and Peter Wright. **Manzanar.** Photographs by Ansel Adams. Times Books, 1988. 167 pp. ISBN 0-8129-1727-6. Nonfiction.

This documentary recreates the concentration camp (called a relocation center) which existed at Manzanar, California, for two years during World War II. In 1942, all Japanese Americans who lived on the West Coast were forced to leave their homes and live in barracks in a desert surrounded by barbed wire and guard towers. The exceptional black-and-white photographs by Ansel Adams powerfully demonstrate the desolate conditions as well as the successful efforts made by the prisoners to improve their lives.

16.2 Banfield, Susan. **The Rights of Man, the Reign of Terror: The Story of the French Revolution.** J. B. Lippincott, 1989. 213 pp. ISBN 0-397-32354-9. Nonfiction.

Through glimpses of the daily lives of people from peasants to King Louis XVI and Queen Marie Antoinette, the causes, conflicts, and horrors of the French Revolution emerge. Short sketches of important figures in the Revolution, including Jean-Paul Marat, Madame Manon Roland, and Maximilien Robespierre, are interspersed throughout the chapters. In addition, many contemporary drawings, paintings, and portraits give life to the history.

16.3 Batchelor, John, and Julie Batchelor. **In Stanley's Footsteps: Across Africa from West to East.** Cassell/Blandford, 1990. 176 pp. ISBN 0-7137-2116-2. Nonfiction.

Wonderfully illustrated with drawings and photographs, this book tells the story of parallel adventures, that of explorer Henry Morton Stanley, who set out in 1887 to cross Africa on an expedition to rescue Emin Pasha, and that of the authors who retraced Stanley's footsteps a hundred years later. The book is a combination of history and travelogue as the authors remember Stanley's trip across Africa and delight in their own experiences that unveil the rivers, forests, and mountains of that vast continent.

16.4 Dalrymple, William. **In Xanadu: A Quest.** William Collins and Sons, 1989. 314 pp. ISBN 0-00-217948-2. Nonfiction.

In 1986, when the Karakoram Highway opened, linking Pakistan with China, William Dalrymple, a student at Cambridge University, and a few other students decided to retrace Marco Polo's twelve-thousand-mile journey from Jerusalem to Xanadu, the summer palace of Kubla Khan. Their summer journey took Dalrymple and his companions to Syria, Turkey, Iran, Pakistan, and China. He describes this event-filled expedition—battling sandstorms, boarding a packed Pakistani train through an open window, crossing the Indus River on inflated animal hides, traveling across China's forbidden territories hidden within a truckload of coal, and encountering bureaucratic red tape at nearly every step of the way. The trip was complete when Dalrymple, echoing Polo, emptied a vial of holy oil from Jerusalem onto the ground at the spot where the throne of the Khan used to stand. Black-and-white photographs, maps, notes, index.

16.5 Fogg, G. E., and David Smith. **The Explorations of Antarctica: The Last Unspoilt Continent.** Illustrated by David Smith. Cassell, 1991. 224 pp. ISBN 0-304-31813-2. Nonfiction.

What is the hope for Antarctica? The mysteries surrounding the seventh continent, its explorations, and untapped natural resources are the basis for continued study. The remote, almost hostile environment is difficult and expensive to explore, but the necessity for preserving this last unspoilt continent is imperative to the future of the United States. Political controversy overshadows the stark beauty of this continent and gives emphasis to the importance of the 1991 Antarctic Treaty to be reviewed by the United States. What will the future hold?

16.6 Frazier, Ian. **Great Plains.** Farrar, Straus and Giroux, 1989. 290 pp. ISBN 0-374-21723-8. Nonfiction.

The Great Plains are filled with stories, legends, and history, and Ian Frazier set out to explore each tale. Across ten states and over 25,000 miles of roads Frazier drove to find long-overlooked places like the site of Sitting Bull's cabin, a house where Bonnie and Clyde stayed, and a town of fifty people which was founded by black homesteaders over a century ago. Everywhere Frazier traveled, he talked to the people and learned the tales of the Native Americans who traveled the land and of the famous people who came from the Great Plains (including Teddy Roosevelt, Billy the Kid, and the Sioux Chief Crazy Horse). Frazier brings the forgotten history and people of America's Great Plains to life with vivid description and memorable details.

16.7 Gale, Robert Peter, and Thomas Hauser. **Final Warning: The Legacy of Chernobyl.** Warner Books, 1988. 230 pp. ISBN 0-446-51409-8. Nonfiction.

On April 26, 1986, in the midst of being shut down for routine maintenance, massive heat buildup in the reactor core of the Chernobyl nuclear power station in Soviet Ukraine triggered the explosion of the core in the world's worst nuclear accident. On May 2nd, Robert Peter Gale, chairman of the Advisory Committee of the International Bone Marrow Transplant Registry, was on his way to Moscow to assist in the treatment of individuals exposed to radiation. Several additional medical experts soon joined him, followed by a million dollars in scientific equipment airlifted from twenty countries. The bulk of this book is a personal memoir of Gale's several trips to the Soviet Union during 1986 and 1987. He and coauthor Thomas Hauser also provide a very simplified explanation of nuclear power reactors, discuss the profound social, political, and scientific consequences of nuclear technology, and recommend what we all can do to prevent nuclear accidents.

16.8 Gelman, Rita Golden. **Nicaragua: Young People's Dreams and Fears.** Franklin Watts, 1988. 189 pp. ISBN 0-531-15085-2. Nonfiction.

The author spent eight months in Nicaragua, most of the time living with the Rivera family in Managua, the capital. But she also visited peasant families of farmers in the war zone. She had come to interview young people (most of the population of the country is under fifteen) to try to understand their lives and to answer the question of whether the good government is fighting the bad guerrillas or the bad government is fighting the good guerrillas.

16.9 Haskins, James. **Black Dance in America: A History through Its People.** Thomas Y. Crowell, 1990. 232 pp. ISBN 0-690-04659-6. Nonfiction.

In this history of black dance, discover the origins of such popular dance forms as the Charleston and tap dance, which can be traced back to the rhythms and movements of the Africans. Gain insight into some of the best performers and choreographers in dance history, like Bill "Bojangles" Robinson and Katherine Dunham, and learn how African Americans have made an enormous contribution to dance styles in America, from break dancing to more classic forms.

16.10 Haskins, James, and Kathleen Benson. **The 60s Reader.** Viking Kestrel, 1988. 244 pp. ISBN 0-670-80674-9. Nonfiction.

What was called "The Killer Decade" comes alive through short biographies, letters, and essays of the prominent personalities of the time—John F. Kennedy, Martin Luther King, Jr., Jerry Rubin, the Berrigan brothers, and many others. The authors describe the Civil Rights, Black Power, Anti-War, Peace, and New Religious Movements and their influences on the music, the student uprisings on campuses across the nation, and the drug culture of the 1960s.

16.11 Hillel, Shlomo. **Operation Babylon.** Translated from Hebrew by Ina Friedman. Doubleday, 1987. 301 pp. ISBN 0-385-23597-6. Nonfiction.

This is the suspenseful story of the post-World War II rescue of Jews living in Iraq in a Jewish community dating back 2,500 years. Author Shlomo Hillel played an instrumental role in the largest air migration in history, in which 125,000 Iraqi Jews made a safe exodus to Israel between 1947 and 1952. The Iraqi operation started on a small scale with the Mossad for Illegal Immigration paying Arab truck drivers to conceal human cargo on their runs to the Mediterranean port of Haifa. At that time it was a twofold operation: the Jews had to be smuggled out of Iraq and then smuggled into Palestine, as the British had banned Jews from entering Palestine. When the State of Israel was created in May 1948, the new country welcomed the immigrants, but the turbulent state of affairs closed all overland routes into the country. The movement turned to air transport. Two years later, the Iraqi government permitted Jews to emigrate to Israel, and by 1952, fully 95 percent of the Jewish population in Iraq had left for Israel. Black-and-white photographs.

16.12 Kronenwetter, Michael. **The War on Terrorism.** Julian Messner, 1989. 130 pp. ISBN 0-671-69050-7. Nonfiction.

Terrorism is drama! The audience is the world; the plot is staged by the terrorists against a government or group of people to promote a "cause." This provocative, hostile game is examined, and we learn the history, the past and present players—Kuwait, the Ku Klux Klan, Army of the Red Star, and others.

16.13 Marrin, Albert. **Inca & Spaniard: Pizarro and the Conquest of Peru.** Atheneum, 1989. 211 pp. ISBN 0-689-31481-7. Nonfiction.

The Incan Empire was one of the most powerful in the Americas during the time of Columbus. It was also rumored to be one of the richest, a kingdom of gold. These rumors drew Hernando Pizarro, an aging Spanish adventurer, from his settlement in Panama, setting him and his brothers in search of the fabled empire. They found the Incas during a time of civil war, and the kingdom of gold fell to the ruthless Spanish invaders. Marrin details the life of Pizarro, the development of the Incan culture, and the inevitable conflict between conquerors and the conquered.

16.14 Maurer, Harry. **Strange Ground: Americans in Vietnam, 1945—1975: An Oral History.** Henry Holt, 1989. 634 pp. ISBN 0-8050-0919-1. Nonfiction.

The author discovers the Vietnam War's history through personal interviews with Vietnam veterans. Truthful, haunting accounts of Americans and their participation in the Asian conflict fill the pages. This book contains mature language for mature readers.

16.15 Meltzer, Milton, editor. **The American Promise: Voices of a Changing Nation, 1945–Present.** Bantam/Starfire Books, 1990. 184 pp. ISBN 0-553-07020-7. Nonfiction.

Much history is political history only, and the authentic voice of the people who lived that history is muffled. But Meltzer's *American Promise* shows the events from 1945 to the present through the eyes of men and women who lived through those years. The author documents his sources carefully and writes a readable history.

16.16 Meltzer, Milton. **Rescue: The Story of How Gentiles Saved Jews in the Holocaust.** Harper and Row, 1988. 168 pp. ISBN 0-06-024209-4. Nonfiction.

Milton Meltzer tells the heroic stories of the Gentiles who helped Jews survive during the Holocaust. In Berlin, the Nazi capital, Countess Marushka worked for the German resistance movement and allowed escaping Jews to stay in her apartment. Oskar Schindler ran a German war plant in Poland and eventually employed hundreds of Jews as skilled workers so that they would not be sent to concentration camps. These and many more are the stories of Gentiles from all over Europe who helped to rescue Jews from the Nazis.

16.17 Meyer, Carolyn. **Voices of Northern Ireland: Growing Up in a Troubled Land.** Harcourt Brace Jovanovich, 1987. 212 pp. ISBN 0-15-200635-4. Nonfiction.

Carolyn Meyer spent six weeks in 1986 touring Northern Ireland, a land of centuries-old hostility between Catholics and Protestants and their different cultural, political, economic, and religious backgrounds. The Catholics of Northern Ireland, descended from the original inhabitants of Ireland, tend to be powerless and economically inferior and to favor independence from the United Kingdom. The Protestants, descendants from the sixteenth-century colonizers from England and Scotland, hold the most power and look to the United Kingdom to maintain that power. Meyer's aim was to bring her readers a better understanding of the people of Northern Ireland and their problems in hopes that it would lead readers to examine their own values and prejudices. The voices from Northern Ireland convey the ever-present distrust, suspicion, and anger and describe a land where there is no compromise; both sides are too stubborn and too fearful of what they will have to give up, rather than what they might gain. Maps of Northern Ireland and Belfast, bibliography, index.

16.18 Monk, Lorraine. **Photographs That Changed the World: The Camera as Witness, the Photograph as Evidence.** Doubleday, 1989. 51 pp. ISBN 0-385-26195-0. Nonfiction.

From the oldest existing photograph of a blurry courtyard in France, taken in 1826, to the color image of the *Challenger* explosion in 1986, these fifty-one photographs capture significant faces, figures, and events which illuminate the history of our world during those one hundred and sixty years. The collection includes: "Chief Sitting Bull," 1885; "Raising the Flag at Iwo Jima," 1945; and "Marilyn Monroe," 1955.

16.19 Rosenblum, Mort. **Moments of Revolution: Eastern Europe.** Photographs by David and Peter Turnley. Stewart, Tabor, and Chang, 1990. 183 pp. ISBN 1-55670-167-5. Nonfiction.

David and Peter Turnley, twin American photographers based in Paris, have captured in brilliantly colored photographs such human emotions as hope, rage, joy, despair, and grief in the faces of Eastern Europeans during the dramatic events of the late 1980s and 1990—the dismantling of the Berlin Wall, the election of dissident playwright Vaclav Havel as president of Czechoslovakia, and the bloody overthrow of Romania's Stalinist regime headed by Ceausescu. Mort Rosenblum's text briefly traces the events taking place in Eastern Europe, but it is the stunning photographs, many of them spread across two pages, that tell the story of the rise of freedom and democracy in East Germany, Czechoslovakia, Romania, Hungary, Poland, Bulgaria, Lithuania, and Soviet Georgia.

16.20 Schurke, Paul. **Bering Bridge: The Soviet-American Expedition from Siberia to Alaska.** Pfeifer-Hamilton, 1989. 227 pp. ISBN 0-938586-31-9. Nonfiction.

In 1989, Paul Schurke and a group of eleven women and men began a trek across 1,000 miles of arctic tundra. They traveled along the Bering Strait by dog sled, braving unbelievable cold and wind, on a mission of international peace. The expedition led to the right of free travel across the Soviet-American border for the region's natives, and ultimately, "These dog sled diplomats helped build a bridge of peace that connects not only the natives of the Bering Strait region, but all citizens of the USA and the [former Soviet Union]."

16.21 Terkel, Studs. **The Great Divide: Second Thoughts on the American Dream.** Pantheon Book, 1988. 439 pp. ISBN 0-394-57053-7. Nonfiction.

Americans of the 1980s tell their stories, revealing the variety and the diversity in our country. The religious and the nonreligious, the old and the young, the yuppies and the farmers—people at the top, in the middle, and at the bottom all tell their tales. Their stories reflect the ways we have changed and the way we live now, at once celebrating our country's diversity and identifying some of our society's problems. Questions surface about the "American Dream" as these individuals candidly reveal their experiences, their beliefs, their hopes, and their fears.

16.22 Wolf, Bernard. **In the Year of the Tiger.** Photographs by Bernard Wolf. Macmillan, 1988. 124 pp. ISBN 0-02-793390-3. Nonfiction.

Over a three-month time period, Bernard Wolf lived with the Chen family in the Chinese village of Ai Shan. Through vivid black-and-white photography and insightful writing, Wolf examines the day-to-day life in China under Communist rule. Many things have changed since the revolution in 1949, but even more things have stayed the same. The Chen family is a living example of tradition—they grow their own food, work their own fields, and raise their children as Chinese families have for centuries. In the midst of all this tradition, they attend village meetings where the changes that Communism has made are felt the most.

17 Hobbies

17.1 Eden, Maxwell. **Kiteworks: Explorations in Kite Building and Flying.** Sterling, 1989. 288 pp. ISBN 0-8069-6712-0. Nonfiction.

Kite authority and enthusiast Eden presents not only the how-to's of kiting but also the history. Did you know that a kite was significant in our gaining independence from Great Britain? You will find also the basics of aerodynamics, as well as the science and the mystery of kiting explained. Beautiful color photographs and drawings illustrate the variety and versatility of kites and kite design. Plans for fifty kites are included, with detailed instructions suitable for the amateur.

17.2 Moscovich, Ivan. **Fiendishly Difficult Math Puzzles.** Sterling, 1991. 64 pp. ISBN 0-8069-8270-5. Nonfiction.

The math puzzles are based on two-color diagrams or sketches so that answers may come by close scrutiny or with paper and pencil. The assortment with creative titles—such as Husbands and Wives, The Octopus Handshake, Life or Death, and Jumping Coins—provides variety in the problems posed. The graphs provide hints to answers, but if the reader encounters real difficulty, answers are included in the back of the book.

17.3 Moscovich, Ivan. **Fiendishly Difficult Visual Perception Puzzles.** Sterling, 1991. 64 pp. ISBN 0-8069-8268-3. Nonfiction.

These more than forty challenging visual problems, all with color illustrations, have accompanying hints to solve the puzzles. Some of the answers can be found by using common sense; others will take concentration, time, and creative ways of looking at the problems posed. If all else fails, there are answers in the back of the book.

17.4 Obojski, Robert. **Coin Collector's Price Guide.** Sterling, 1990. 126 pp. ISBN 0-8069-6864-8. Nonfiction.

An introduction for beginning coin hobbyists and a resource for more advanced collectors, this handbook contains current prices for seven different conditions of coins with explanations of how to grade them for highest prices. The comprehensive guide covers all United States and Canadian coins, from the historic U.S. Continental issue of 1776 to the 1990 Eisenhower Centennial silver dollar and the Canadian 1990 silver dollar marking the 300th anniversary of the exploration of Canada's western prairies.

17.5 Schwartz, Perry. **How to Make Your Own Video.** Lerner, 1991. 72 pp. ISBN 0-8225-2301-9. Nonfiction.

Using simplified terminology and directions, the award-winning film-maker-turned-author presents the techniques for making a good video. Also included are the elements of effective storytelling, a necessity for a meaningful video according to the author. Information about camcorders and other equipment is outlined in this "how-to" book. Illustrated with full-color and black-and-white photographs, this informative text includes advice for young would-be video producers.

17.6 Townsend, Charles Barry. **World's Toughest Puzzles.** Sterling, 1990. 93 pp. ISBN 0-8069-6962-8. Nonfiction.

How would you divide a round cake into eight pieces of equal size by making just three cuts? What word contains five consonants in a row? These and many other puzzles are posed—and solved in this book. Each richly illustrated page presents a puzzle which is both challenging and fun. The solutions are listed in the back, but don't peek! Easy reading.

18 Horror, Witchcraft, and the Occult

18.1 Buffie, Margaret. **The Haunting of Frances Rain.** Scholastic, 1987. 196 pp. ISBN 0-590-42834-9. Fiction.

Fifteen-year-old Lizzie McGill has to get away from her family—they are constantly bickering and will not leave her alone. She seeks refuge on deserted Rain Island, but she keeps feeling like someone else is there. Then Lizzie finds an old pair of glasses. When she puts them on, she suddenly appears to be in a cabin. She realizes that she can see the past with these glasses, a time when Frances Rain and her daughter lived alone on the island. Frances Rain wants something from Lizzie, and the haunting will not stop until she gets it!

18.2 Buffie, Margaret. **The Warnings.** Scholastic Hardcovers, 1991. 245 pp. ISBN 0-590-43665-1. Fiction.

Rachel McCaw is shuffled off by her father to live with her Aunt Irene, an older lady who shares her home with a strange assortment of people. Rachel refers to the older people as "fossils," as they seem to live in the past. Yet they appear to be shielding her from some kind of strange goings-on in the house. Rachel misses her father, who told her he'd be back, and she wonders if he may desert her just as her mother did years ago. Then the warnings start again, and Rachel fears them and the ghost who once occupied her attic room. But Rachel has a boyfriend who cares enough about her to help her, and that may be her answer to a normal life.

18.3 Charnas, Suzy McKee. **The Golden Thread.** Bantam/Starfire Books, 1990. 209 pp. ISBN 0-553-28553-X. Fiction.

In this third book in the Sorcery Hall trilogy, fourteen-year-old Valentine Marsh discovers that she has inherited a magic power from her grandmother. Together with six friends, Valentine must fight the evil Bosanka Lonat, an alien witch from a dying planet. Valentine fears and despises Bosanka and her wicked spells until she learns compassion for all living things.

18.4 Cormier, Robert. **Fade.** Dell, 1989. 293 pp. ISBN 0-440-20487-9. Fiction.

Young Paul Moreaux lives a normal life until he discovers the unique power of what he calls "fade." His Uncle Abelard explains this power to Paul; it is passed down from one generation to another, and Abelard has learned to live with it. After one horrifying experience, Paul vows never to fade again, but his resolve weakens when he finally finds his aunt's illegitimate son who is wreaking havoc on his small town.

18.5 Hoh, Diane. **The Accident.** Scholastic/Point, 1991. 165 pp. ISBN 0-590-44330-5. Fiction.

Megan decides to trade a week with a ghost who appears in her mirror. She feels sorry for Juliet, the ghost who says that she died in a boating accident just before her sixteenth birthday. Little does Megan know how evil Juliet is and what dreadful things she will do to Megan, her family, and her friends as she lives in Megan's body. Luckily, Justin, Meg's best friend, is still able to "hear" Megan and to find holes in Juliet's final evil plan.

18.6 Katz, Welwyn Wilton. **False Face.** Dell/Laurel-Leaf Books, 1990. 196 pp. ISBN 0-440-20676-6. Fiction.

Two teenagers unearth a pair of Iroquois false-face masks in a meadow in downtown London, Ontario. Laney knows her parents would gladly latch onto the masks, each for different reasons, but her new friend Tom, one-half Iroquois himself, appreciates the value of the masks. Together they must solve the mystery of the masks' supernatural powers before Laney and her mother are taken over by the evil in the ancient relics. It is Laney's father and Tom who finally have the power to break the hold of the supernatural.

18.7 Katz, Welwyn Wilton. **Witchery Hill.** Dell/Laurel-Leaf Books, 1990. 244 pp. ISBN 0-440-20637-5. Fiction.

Mike Lewis accompanies his famous dad on a summer holiday to the island of Guernsey. From his first meeting with their host, Tony St. George, his wife, and his daughter, Mike knows this will be no ordinary visit. He discovers information about witchcraft and, after one chilling moment in a prehistoric tomb, he understands that witches are for real. He and his new companion, Lisa, work to uncover the real identity of the witch controlling Tony St. George, Lisa's father. Mike's father can't help because he has always been able to deal with logic only; he leaves his son to cope alone.

18.8 King, Stephen. **Four Past Midnight.** Viking, 1990. 763 pp. ISBN 0-670-83538-2. Fiction.

A blind girl wakes up on a red-eye flight from L.A. to Boston and senses the sighted aunt she was traveling with is gone. Figuring her aunt just went to the bathroom, Dinah doesn't worry, until she slowly realizes that the whole, once-filled plane now seems to be totally empty! In another story, fifteen-year-old Kevin Delevan gets a camera for his birthday, but when he takes the first picture, it is obvious that there is something wrong. The picture is of an outdoors scene Kevin has never seen, and he took the picture in his house! These and two other novellas bend and twist reality in a classically horrifying King way.

18.9 King, Stephen. **Misery.** New American Library/Signet, 1988. 338 pp. ISBN 0-451-15355-3. Fiction.

When Annie Wilkes "rescued" Paul Sheldon from the wreck of his Camaro on that snowy Rocky Mountain day, she knew just what to do; she was, after all, a nurse. She pulled him out, took him home, splinted his shattered legs, fed him intravenously, gave him just the "right" amount of pain-killing drugs, and even brought him back from death with artificial respiration. It was the least she could do because Paul was special, the author of a series of bestselling historical romances about a character named Misery Chastain; and Annie was his number-one fan. The least he can do in return is to write one more book just for her. That's what Annie says and Annie never takes "no" for an answer. Like Scheherazade in the *Arabian Nights,* Paul Sheldon has got to tell a good story or he's going to die—one little bit of him at a time. Building the horror step-by-step, Stephen King has created in psychopathic Annie Wilkes a creature as scary as anything in his supernatural thrillers.

18.10 Klause, Annette Curtis. **The Silver Kiss.** Delacorte Press, 1990. 198 pp. ISBN 0-385-30160-X. Fiction.

Zoe's mother is dying of cancer. When beautiful yet frightening Simon, who understands the pain of loneliness and death, appears, he helps Zoe come to terms with her mother's illness. But he also reveals his terrible secret: he is a vampire seeking revenge against his brother, Christopher, for the gruesome murder of their mother three hundred years before. Does Simon dare ask Zoe to help in his quest for revenge and to free him of his insufferable loneliness?

18.11 Martin, Valerie. **Mary Reilly.** Doubleday, 1990. 263 pp. ISBN 0-385-24968-3. Fiction.

If you've read *Dr. Jekyll and Mr. Hyde,* you'll enjoy this new twist on the story, written in diary form. Mary Reilly is a young housemaid in the employ of the strange but charming Dr. Henry Jekyll. Gentle and intelligent, Dr. Jekyll takes an interest in Mary, and she reciprocates with a reluctant but nevertheless strong affection. But she senses that something is wrong. When Dr. Jekyll's brutal "assistant," Mr. Hyde, starts making appearances at the house, Mary is filled with fear. She loves Jekyll, hates Hyde, and knows something terribly wrong is going on between the two of them, but can she stop it?

18.12 Nixon, Joan Lowery. **Whispers from the Dead.** Dell/Laurel-Leaf Books, 1991. 180 pp. ISBN 0-440-20809-2. Fiction.

When Sarah's father is transferred to Houston and her family moves into a new house, Sarah feels the tug of a spirit. It is a secret that Sarah keeps to herself. To the family's dismay, they learn that a murder had occurred in this house and although some clues pointed to the young boy of the family, no evidence could put the boy at home when the young pizza delivery girl was killed. The mystery brings unhappiness and concern to the family, especially Sarah, who vows she will help the spirit in the house.

18.13 Peterson, Keith. **The Scarred Man.** Bantam, 1990. 323 pp. ISBN 0-553-27860-6. Fiction.

Michael North, a young reporter, gets out of New York City for the Christmas holidays by visiting the Connecticut home of his boss. There he meets and falls in love with Susannah McGill. But one night, as he tells a ghost story by the fire, Susannah becomes hysterical. Michael, in telling his story, is describing the same scarred man that haunts her dreams! The two realize that the scarred man is not just a figment of their imaginations but is very much alive, and he is tracking them down. The scarred man wants them dead!

18.14 Pike, Christopher. **Witch.** Archway Paperbacks, 1990. 225 pp. ISBN 0-671-69055-8. Fiction.

Julia, a high school student, has the power to heal people by touching them and when she looks in water, she can see events taking place miles away. Julia is a witch. Her mother, who was also a witch, had warned her against looking into water when moonlight is shining on it. However, Julia does look into moonlit water and sees a horrifying vision of a young man dying in her arms. Does he really have to die? Can Julia change the future? In using her supernatural powers to try to prevent that horrible event from happening, she risks her own life and the lives of her friends.

18.15 Riddell, Ruth. **Shadow Witch.** Atheneum, 1989. 202 pp. ISBN 0-689-31484-1. Fiction.

Drew MacCaslim can't tell whether or not the Shadow Witch is real or simply a figment of his imagination, the result of LSD "flashbacks." Whichever she is, she poses a real threat to Drew, who lies in his bedroom in Rossmoor, the family house, unable to walk after an LSD-induced fall from a rooftop. Over and over he finds himself confronted with the evil Shadow Witch and her wild dogs, and it seems that only Angus Corkum, the old caretaker, can save him. Angus knows about a secret hidden deep inside Drew which even Drew doesn't know about. It may be that secret which can keep the Shadow Witch from destroying Drew.

18.16 Saul, John. **Creature.** Bantam Books, 1989. 377 pp. ISBN 0-553-28411-8. Fiction.

Mark Tanner is your average scrawny high school kid. When his ex-football jock father relocates the family, Mark is faced with all sorts of pressure to be a jock, too. In this new town, sports are a mania. The football team never loses and all the guys at school are large and athletic. In fact, if a guy isn't on a sports team, he can't even get a job in town! Poor Mark knows he's going to be a big disappointment to his dad. Then, his ambitious dad is convinced to try something that will help Mark grow, help him become stronger. It's been tried before on the kids in town and has worked as planned—most of the time. . . .

18.17 Saul, John. **Second Child.** Bantam, 1990. 341 pp. ISBN 0-553-05877-0. Fiction.

Thirteen-year-old Melissa Holloway is a shy and troubled youngster when she comes to the secluded town of Secret Cove, Maine. There, behind a locked attic door, she discovers a horrifying secret that has lain hidden for a hundred years, since the night a young servant girl committed an act of violence so shocking that its legacy lives on. Now Melissa is having nightmares, but are they just dreams, or is the evil that has waited for so long ready to live again and wreak its vengeance on Secret Cove?

18.18 Springer, Nancy. **The Hex Witch of Seldom.** Baen Books, 1988. 276 pp. ISBN 0-671-65389-X. Fiction.

Bobbi Yandro does not realize that she has the Sight until she sees the ghostly image of the Trickster Shane in the eyes of the black stallion on her grandfather's ranch. But this realization is more than just

Sight—it plunges her into the dark and mysterious world of the Circle of the Twelve, witches and warlocks who are the human manifestations of primal, raw emotions. Bound to Shane by deepening affection, Bobbi pursues her magical heritage into a hidden society within our own, where ghosts from the past wait and prophesies can come true.

18.19 Stewart, Mary. **Thornyhold.** William Morrow, 1988. 207 pp. ISBN 0-688-08425-7. Fiction.

When Gilly's cousin, Geillis, dies, it is Gilly who inherits the old house, Thornyhold, as well as Geillis' reputation—as a witch! The local people believe that Gilly is one of their kind and that she is ready to join their coven. While it's true that Gilly sometimes experiences moments of incredible yet unbelievable magical powers, she is shy and insecure. Is it the house, or maybe the ghost of her cousin Geillis, that gives her these powers? As the mystery begins to unravel, Gilly finds herself coming out of her shell and allowing people like Christopher John into her life. Magic and romance go hand-in-hand as Gilly learns more about the enchanted world of magic surrounding Thornyhold.

18.20 Stine, R. L. **The Stepsister.** Archway Paperbacks, 1990. 165 pp. ISBN 0-671-70244-0. Fiction.

When Emily gains a new stepsister, Jessie, she learns the terror of Jessie's mistrust. Emily confides in Josh only to later doubt his good intentions as well. Who can Emily trust? Who can explain the mysterious, dark secrets that haunt her life? Does anyone understand her?

18.21 Vance, Steve. **Spook.** Soho Press, 1990. 234 pp. ISBN 0-939149-38-9. Fiction.

MaryAnn Nelson, at sixteen, lives alone with her mother, isolated on a patch of land the townspeople avoid. She has never been to school and has never had friends. Almost no one has seen her face, since she never goes out in the daytime and at night she wears a hood. People have heard her, though, baying at the moon. Kids call her "Spook," and when macabre incidents occur in the county, the townspeople are sure MaryAnn is responsible for them. The new school administrator, however, has seen MaryAnn's disturbing but brilliant artwork, and she is determined to dispel the mystery surrounding MaryAnn Nelson. She is sure MaryAnn is not evil, but what is the secret that keeps MaryAnn and her mother so chillingly isolated from human contact?

18.22 Wescott, Earle. **Winter Wolves.** Yankee Publishing, Inc., 1988. 192 pp. ISBN 0-89909-160-1. Fiction.

Fran Thomas returns to Maine to recover from a nervous breakdown, a failed marriage, and a high-pressure job at the Los Angeles *Herald*. His job at the Riverston *Republic* seems to be just the antidote that he needs. Then he starts covering a story in nearby Steel Harbor: the town drunk suffers a fatal heart attack, and his body is disfigured by scratches and bites. At first no one believes the local recluse's claim that wolves are responsible. But next a young biologist at the local university starts investigating whether wolves might be in the area, and her body is found horribly mutilated. Fran finds himself caught up in a terrifying struggle for life.

18.23 Windsor, Patricia. **The Hero.** Delacorte Press, 1988. 225 pp. ISBN 0-385-29624-X. Fiction.

The premonitions just come to him; Dale doesn't know from where or why, just that they exist. The fact that he is a psychic is something he used to know how to deal with. Now, afraid that he is making the future instead of seeing it, Dale has had to reveal his little secret so that someone can help him to find answers. That someone is Dr. Louis Airman, but Dale doesn't trust Airman—Airman has connections to the military. Is it possible that the government wants to use Dale's psychic abilities as a secret weapon? The more questions Dale asks, the more endangered his life and the lives of his new friends at Airman's institute become.

19 Human Rights

19.1 Cagin, Seth, and Philip Dray. **We Are Not Afraid: The Story of Goodman, Schwerner, and Chaney and the Civil Rights Campaign for Mississippi.** Macmillan, 1988. 500 pp. ISBN 0-02-520260-X. Nonfiction.

Step-by-step you will share the experiences of the murdered civil rights workers Andrew Goodman, Michael Schwerner, and James Chaney, killed in June 1964. The history of the Civil Rights Movement and the background of the three martyrs are interwoven with details of the crime. All three were working to encourage blacks to register to vote and to draw the attention of the country to Mississippi, which was then the stronghold of prejudice.

19.2 Coil, Suzanne M. **The Poor in America.** Julian Messner, 1989. 126 pp. ISBN 0-671-69052-3. Nonfiction.

Are you writing a research paper and needing the latest information about the poor in America? Well, here is help. The chronic poor and the "new" poor are examined in this book, which includes statistics for rural and urban areas as of 1989. Resource agencies are listed in the detailed bibliography.

19.3 Cowell, Alan. **Why Are They Weeping? South Africans under Apartheid.** Photographs by David C. Turnley. Stewart, Tabori and Chang, 1988. 198 pp. ISBN 1-55670-044-X. Nonfiction.

David Turnley, a foreign photojournalist for the *Detroit Free Press,* selected one hundred of his color photographs of the people of South Africa for his book. He moved in both the white and black worlds and took photos of people in their everyday lives. Ever-present is the reality of the definite black and white conflicts which dominated the mid-1980s when Turnley shot these pictures. The text by Alan Cowell provides the background and facts of apartheid which have separated this country for years. He also explains more current history which brought on the state of emergency, with its repercussions for the government and for the groups demanding change.

19.4 Frankel, Marvin E., with Ellen Saideman. **Out of the Shadows of Night: The Struggle for International Human Rights.** Delacorte Press, 1989. 257 pp. ISBN 0-385-29752-1. Nonfiction.

People all over the world are in revolt; they seek their basic rights as "human beings on the planet." Is it a governmental or individual responsibility to ensure the right to live with dignity? Many heroes are featured—Eleanor Roosevelt, Nelson Mandela, Corazon Aquino, Andrei Sakharov, Dr. Martin Luther King, Jr. as well as others—and their struggles to meet the challenges of human rights are detailed.

19.5 Ho, Minfong. **Rice without Rain.** Lothrop, Lee and Shepard Books, 1990. 236 pp. ISBN 0-688-06355-1. Fiction.

Seventeen-year-old Jinda's village in Thailand is plagued by drought. There are no crops, and the rent collector has yet to come to take away two-thirds of their precious harvest. Then a group of idealistic young students from Bangkok come to the village with revolutionary new ideas. Among them is Ned, an activist Jinda falls in love with, who convinces her to come to Bangkok for a student uprising. What she witnesses there makes her question the effectiveness of what Ned is doing. While she believes in the changes he is trying to bring about, she abhors the violence that seems unavoidable in the fight for political reform. In a rapidly changing world, Jinda is forced to make a decision about who she is and what she wants to be.

19.6 Human Rights in China. **Children of the Dragon: The Story of Tiananmen Square.** Macmillan/Collier Books, 1990. 224 pp. ISBN 0-02-033520-2. Nonfiction.

Human Rights in China is the nonprofit organization that published this detailed history, through both text and photographs, of the tragedy in Tiananmen Square during the summer of 1989. After giving some necessary background information, the book goes on to describe the key people involved in the incident, the hunger strike, the imposition of martial law, and, finally, the brutal killings. It ends with a description of the aftermath of the massacre and with optimism for China in the future.

19.7 Kozol, Jonathan. **Rachel and Her Children: Homeless Families in America.** Crown, 1988. 252 pp. ISBN 0-517-56730-X. Nonfiction.

By interviewing homeless people and researching facts collected by governments, Kozol focuses on the people as individuals. Interested in homeless families, he finds their answers to why they are without permanent shelter. He uncovers facts on how private, municipal, state, and federal agencies are spending money to combat the hunger and other physical needs of these people, but what they're doing is ineffective. Oftentimes these efforts are only deterrents for the homeless people to get out of these "hotels" and out on their own. The conversations with parents and children are honest and painful as they tell how and why they are there in the streets. Rachel and other mothers like her are trying to hold their families together, but it seems that governmental economic restrictions, combined with rental lords' demands, drive them apart. This book, written in the 1980s, is a foreteller of what may happen in the 1990s as more people lose their jobs, their homes, and possibly their families.

19.8 Mathabane, Mark. **Kaffir Boy: The True Story of a Black Youth's Coming of Age in Apartheid South Africa.** Plume Books, 1986. 354 pp. ISBN 0-452-25943-6. Nonfiction.

In this autobiography, Mark Mathabane recalls his childhood in Alexandra, a black township in South Africa, where he fought the oppression of apartheid which kept him in poverty. His story is one of hardships, from the segregated public restrooms to the midnight raids by the white police, raids designed to humiliate and degrade the black citizens. Mathabane fought these conditions, rising from a "Kaffir" (a cruel expression used by whites in South Africa to refer to blacks) to a person, until he was able to escape to an education in the United States. His recollections provide insight into the legalized racism that continues to exist in South Africa, where his family still struggles to survive.

19.9 Naidoo, Beverley. **Chain of Fire.** Illustrated by Eric Velasquez. J. B. Lippincott, 1989. 245 pp. ISBN 0-397-32427-8. Fiction.

Fifteen-year-old Naledi, her friends, and her brother are swept up into a political whirlwind when their South African village is sold off by their chief. When the villagers protest being moved to a "homeland" their schools are shut down, the water supply is cut off, and the church is bulldozed. Naledi becomes involved with a student demonstration to protest these developments. The brutality that these children are treated with brings home the horrors of apartheid while, for the villagers, that same brutality firms the bonds in the chain of resistance that is forged.

19.10 Nelson, George (Ed.) for the National Urban League. **Stop the Violence: Overcoming Self-Destruction.** Pantheon Books, 1990. 79 pp. ISBN 0-679-72782-5. Nonfiction.

Stop the Violence is an effort by rap stars and the music industry to address the problem of violence at rap concerts and in the black community. Such rap music stars as Chuck D and Flavor Flav of Public Enemy, and Kool Moe Dee urge young blacks to "arm yourself—not with a knife or a gun, but with the arsenal of your mind." The book provides interviews, pictures, letters from young people about their experiences, lyrics, and an Afrocentric reading list, reflecting "a black view of the world, as written by African American writers." The message is simple and powerful: maintain ethnic pride, "fight the powers that be," but stop the self-destruction.

19.11 Reaver, Chap. **Mote.** Delacorte Press, 1990. 217 pp. ISBN 0-385-30163-4. Fiction.

Chris Miller and his best friend, Billy, are high school students. Mote, a mysterious Vietnam veteran, becomes their friend and father figure. When a sadistic schoolteacher is murdered and Mote becomes the principal suspect, Chris and Billy decide to do everything they can to clear his name. They, along with two police detectives, sift through the incriminating evidence, following the evidence to a white supremacist group and then to a black supremacist group, all in hopes of solving the horrible crime.

19.12 Scott, Elaine. **Choices.** Morrow Junior Books, 1989. 186 pp. ISBN 0-688-07230-5. Fiction.

Football fever, Texas-style, turns rival high school students to ugly vandalism. Beth O'Connor enters into pranks to rile her school's arch-rival, never dreaming that the entire course of her senior year, and even her college plans, would be destroyed. Beth's family fights for her civil rights, but the old community system does not change easily. How will Beth's life be changed?

19.13 Tolan, Stephanie S. **Plague Year.** Morrow Junior Books, 1990. 198 pp. ISBN 0-688-08801-5. Fiction.

With his long braided hair and gold earring, the new student, Bran Slocum, seems weird to the other high school students in Ridgewood. The students' cruel taunts become more vicious after they discover a secret Bran's been carefully concealing. This maliciousness spreads like a contagious disease until the entire town is infected.

20 Humor and Satire

20.1 Adamson, Joe. **Bugs Bunny: Fifty Years and Only One Grey Hare.** Henry Holt/Donald Hutter Books, 1990. 175 pp. ISBN 0-8050-1190-0. Nonfiction.

Not just a history of Bugs Bunny's life, this book also provides a detailed account of the beginning of cartoons and the artists who created them. But Bugs is the star, and his creators discuss his character's evolution from his first cartoon, a 1940 production called "A Wild Hare," to his most recent, made in 1990, entitled "Box Office Bunny." Photographs and illustrations on nearly every page show the intricacies of animation and how Bugs Bunny has changed over fifty years. Written for the serious student of animation.

20.2 Bisson, Terry. **Voyage to the Red Planet.** William Morrow, 1990. 236 pp. ISBN 0-688-09495-3. Fiction.

NASA becomes a subsidiary of Disney, and a bankrupt U.S. government sells off its divisions to private interest. The Nixon Orbital Space Station becomes a family-oriented theme park. In this humorous novel, set in the future, an ambitious renegade producer decides that he wants to provide the public with the ultimate movie-going experience—a film shot on location on Mars. Assembling a motley crew aboard the highly secret Mars ship *Mary Poppins,* he sets out for the Red Planet, little suspecting what he has gotten them into!

20.3 Borns, Betsy. **Comic Lives: Inside the World of American Stand-Up Comedy.** Fireside Books, 1987. 304 pp. ISBN 0-671-62620-5. Nonfiction.

While this book won't teach you how to become a stand-up comic, it will show you what it's like to be one. Author Betsy Borns looks at the recent growth of the comedy club, where acts are live and there is direct contact between comedian and audience. She explores the reasons why someone turns to comedy and looks at how comedians handle a life of travel and odd hours. She combines her own knowledge with spicy comments from nearly fifty of today's hottest comics, including Jay

Leno, George Carlin, and Rita Rudner. Black-and-white photographs. Mature language.

20.4 McManus, Patrick F. **The Night the Bear Ate Goombaw.** Henry Holt, 1989. 184 pp. ISBN 0-8050-1033-5. Nonfiction.

In a series of humorous essays, McManus relates many of his hunting and fishing escapades, introduces relatives and friends, and passes along many so-called words of wisdom. The Troll (his sister), Goombaw (Eddie Muldoon's grandmother), and Retch Sweeney are only a few of the crazy characters who populate his tales. He admits that he's "out of sync"—especially when he tries to meet a fishing buddy at 5:00 a.m. in front of a brown farmhouse—and he even explains how having a runny nose can be a blessing if you're a kid brother.

20.5 Schulz, Charles M. **There Goes the Shutout.** Henry Holt/Owl Books, 1990. 128 pp. ISBN 0-8050-1344-X. Fiction.

America has loved Charlie Brown and his dog Snoopy since they first appeared nearly forty years ago. Included in this four-book series of Peanuts gang cartoons are some of Charles M. Schulz's original Charlie Brown comic strips. Material in this first book was originally published in the early 1950s, and the characters' appearances differ from what they are today. But the warmth, the pathos, and the wit has remained consistent, making it easy to understand why everyone still loves Charlie Brown.

20.6 Schulz, Charles M. **Things I Learned After It Was Too Late (And Other Minor Truths).** Henry Holt/Owl Books, 1989. 121 pp. ISBN 0-8050-1202-8. Fiction.

"Nothing echoes like an empty mailbox," says Charlie Brown. And the wry echoes of lessons learned too late come from all of Charlie Brown's friends. Snoopy tells us that no matter how hard he tries, he can't steer a dog dish down a snowy slope, and we can all relate to Lucy's comment that being crabby all day makes you hungry.

20.7 Schulz, Charles M. **Things I've Had to Learn Over and Over and Over (Plus a Few Minor Discoveries).** Henry Holt/Owl Books, 1989. 125 pp. ISBN 0-8050-1203-6. Fiction.

The whole Peanuts gang share lessons learned about life. Pigpen is philosophical; Lucy is cranky as usual ("What are friends for if you can't forget them?"); Snoopy, Woodstock, and Charlie Brown himself add their own kind of twisted comment ("You know it's cold when you hear your feet coughing").

20.8 Schwartz, Joel L., Aidan Macfarlane and Ann McPherson. **Will the Nurse Make Me Take My Underwear Off? and Other Mysteries of Life as Revealed by Eric Mason.** Illustrated by John Astrop. Dell, 1988. 195 pp. ISBN 0-440-20636-7. Fiction.

Fourteen-year-old Eric Mason is a self-proclaimed hypochondriac and general nervous wreck who, luckily for us, keeps a diary. In it, he compiles the answers he finds to teenagers' most pressing questions about health, their bodies, and life in general. Questions such as, Will I ever grow body hair? Should I call her? How many different words are there for throwing up? and more are answered in these pages. The answers come from such reliable sources as parents, doctors, teachers, and Eric's eleven-year-old sister's diary (when he can get it!).

20.9 Wyss, Thelma Hatch. **Here at the Scenic-Vu Motel.** Harper and Row, 1988. 154 pp. ISBN 0-06-022250-6. Fiction.

How would you like to spend your senior year in high school staying four nights a week at a motel? That's what Jake Callahan and six other students from Bear Flats, Idaho, have to do. The school board can't afford to send a school bus on the three-hour round-trip every day; so the four males and three females call the Scenic-Vu home from Monday to Friday. Jake is in charge because he is the oldest, and he keeps a journal of his trials with an unusual landlady, junk food, snobbish town girls, and visitors.

21 Mysteries, Spies and Crime

21.1 Abrahams, Peter. **Hard Rain.** E. P. Dutton, 1988. 374 pp. ISBN 0-525-24581-2. Fiction.

Jessie Shapiro is initially annoyed when her former husband, Pat Rodney, is late in bringing their ten-year-old daughter, Kate, back after a weekend together. Her anger turns to terror, however, when no trace of the two can be found. A sweepstakes ticket leads Jessie from California to a nearly deserted sixties commune in Vermont and to a small college town in Massachusetts. Jessie begins to realize that there is a horrible secret involved in Pat's disappearance, a secret that traces back to the 1960s' Woodstock festival, which symbolized peace and brotherhood to her generation. But this secret is sinister, and soon Jessie's and Kate's lives are in danger.

21.2 Bennett, Jay. **Sing Me a Death Song.** Fawcett/Juniper Books, 1990. 131 pp. ISBN 0-449-70369-X. Fiction.

Jason Feldon's mother is to be executed on his eighteenth birthday. Although separated from her for eight years, he knows he is the only one who believes in her innocence, in her inability to take another's life. From his death bed, a police detective contacts Jason and gives him the awesome responsibility of bringing forward documents which prove Marion Feldon's innocence. Flying to Florida from New York City, Jason begins a thirty-six-hour trip during which he experiences fears and adventures while searching for papers which can insure his mother's freedom. He must act bravely and coolly without thinking of the consequences to himself.

21.3 Bode, Janet. **The Voices of Rape.** Franklin Watts, 1990. 138 pp. ISBN 0-531-10959-3. Nonfiction.

Did you know that one out of every four women experiences sexual intercourse for the first time through rape? Bode, herself a survivor of rape, has compiled interviews with the various people involved in a rape incident, from the survivors, to the offenders, hospital staff, the police, and legal advisors. The book also deals with both date and stranger rape, the rape of teens, and male survivors of rape. Bode has tried to pave the way for more open and honest discussions of this cultural epidemic, dispelling some of the myths surrounding the brutal act of rape.

21.4 Campbell, Robert. **Thinning the Turkey Herd.** Thorndike Press, 1988. 261 pp. ISBN 0-89621-236-X. Fiction.

Amateur sleuth Jimmy Flannery works for the Chicago Sewer Department and is a Democratic precinct captain. At the request of Alderwoman Janet Canarias, he starts looking into the disappearance of Joyce Lombardi, the beautiful blond model with whom Janet was involved. Jimmy discovers that several young would-be models, or "turkeys," as they are called in the trade, have been murdered recently, so he is fearful that Joyce, too, may be involved in this thinning of the turkey herd. But his only real clues to solving the case are things that are not there—a hairdryer and a pair of rhinestone earrings. A Jimmy Flannery mystery.

21.5 Cebulash, Mel. **Carly and Co.** Fawcett, 1989. 201 pp. ISBN 0-449-14555-7. Fiction.

Who could have dreamed that living in Tuscon, Arizona, would land Carly and her friend, Sandy, in so much trouble? A fat security guard, a pit bull, and a stolen bicycle start things off—but Carly's a policeman's daughter, and she smells trouble. Before Carly and Sandy know it, they are involved with a dangerous drug ring. A *Carly and Co.* mystery.

21.6 Cebulash, Mel. **Part-Time Shadow.** Fawcett, 1990. 219 pp. ISBN 0-449-14557-3. Fiction.

Mysteries are not new to supersleuth duo Carly Simon and her friend, Sandy. Carly meets Chris Adams, a newcomer in town, who is very handsome but difficult to know and like. She spots a man who is following him and another suspicious character who darts behind a parked car. Together Carly and Sandy set out to discover the mystery surrounding Chris. A *Carly and Co.* mystery.

21.7 Chambers, Aidan. **NIK: Now I Know.** Charlotte Zolotow Books, 1987. 308 pp. ISBN 0-06-021208-X. Fiction.

Author Aidan Chambers uses prose, poetry, journal entries, tape-recorded messages, letters, and dialogue to weave together three separate plots, all set in England. In one, seventeen-year-old Nicholas Frome, an admitted nonbeliever, reluctantly agrees to serve as a researcher for a group making a film about what would happen if Christ returned to Earth today. In the second, nineteen-year-old Julie, completely swathed in bandages, lies in a hospital bed recovering from a near-fatal accident and wondering if her damaged eyes will ever see again. In the final plot, young constable Thomas Thrupp is hoping to advance his career by solving the mystery of a young man who is found crucified on a rusty metal cross and who then disappeared. All three plots focus on the characters' coming to terms with their own sense of religion and faith in God.

21.8 Cohen, Barbara. **Tell Us Your Secret.** Bantam/Starfire Books, 1990. 171 pp. ISBN 0-553-28768-0. Fiction.

Crunch Oliver and eleven other high school students take part in a summer writing project where they learn hidden truths or mysterious secrets about each other. Crunch gets background material from the underground cellars of the mansion they are staying in for the ghost story he wants to write. He also learns from the others about evil and about human nature.

21.9 Cook, Robin. **Mortal Fear.** G. P. Putnam's Sons, 1988. 364 pp. ISBN 0-399-13318-6. Fiction.

When Alvin Hayes, a famous biomedical geneticist, begins to explain a recent medical breakthrough to Jason Howard, an internist at Boston's Good Health Plan Clinic, Hayes suddenly dies in a violent manner. Then one after another, patients at the clinic develop serious medical problems and die. As Jason tries to discover just what Hayes was researching at the time of his death and to pinpoint what is causing his patients to die, he discovers an ominous connection between the two. This suspenseful story of his search for answers involves an exotic dancer, a brawny bodybuilder, and a police detective who warns him to stop playing private investigator and to stick to medicine. But Jason is determined to get to the truth.

21.10 Cusick, Richie Tankersley. **Teacher's Pet.** Scholastic/Point, 1990. 214 pp. ISBN 0-590-43114-5. Fiction.

While attending a writers' conference at a secluded camp, Kate enjoys receiving special attention from Gideon, who teaches classes about writing horror stories. However, when she receives strange warnings, death threats, and sees grisly clues dragged in by a cat, she realizes her life is in danger.

21.11 Davidson, Nicole. **Crash Course.** Avon/Flare Books, 1990. 217 pp. ISBN 0-380-75964-0. Fiction.

Spend the entire Thanksgiving vacation at an isolated mountain cabin? No phones, no electricity, no hot water, and too cold for swimming? No way! That was the first reaction to Mr. Porter's plan, but each of the eight specially selected juniors from Thomaston High School had compelling reasons for needing a high SAT score, and that was the payoff. Mr. Porter, the school's toughest teacher, guaranteed to show them how to raise their scores on the test which would be their key to college entrance as well as to scholarships. So they went. The first night one of them died, his dreams drowned forever, and for the rest the nightmare has just begun. Now they're not laughing at the scary legends of Deep Creek Lake. Now they know that someone or something is out there lurking, just waiting to strike again.

21.12 Davidson, Nicole. **Winterkill.** Avon/Flare Books, 1991. 181 pp. ISBN 0-380-75965-9. Fiction.

Karen Henderson is immediately befriended by four classmates when she enters a new school in Vermont. Having dreaded the move from New York City to a small village, she does not count on having such a busy social schedule. And from the first day's skiing lesson with Matt, she knows her life is changing. Little does she realize that within weeks she will be the key witness to a murder which the local police will brush off as a hit-and-run accident. Joining up with a new friend, she works to solve the mystery of the murder, and her involvement almost causes more deaths.

21.13 Davis, Lindsey. **Silver Pigs.** Crown, 1989. 258 pp. ISBN 0-517-57363-6. Fiction.

Marcus Didius Falco gives a colorful commentary on his life and times—he is a private detective in Ancient Rome. He tries to help Sosia Camillina, who is running away from two men who tried to kidnap her. She leads Falco to a "silver pig" (a lead ingot containing silver) which is very valuable. When he discovers that it and others have been stolen, Sosia's uncle, a senator, hires Falco to find the thieves.

21.14 Duncan, Lois. **Don't Look behind You.** Delacorte Press, 1989. 178 pp. ISBN 0-395-29739-4. Fiction.

In one quick afternoon, April Corrigan's life is turned upside down. She learns that her father, who she thought was a mild-mannered man working an ordinary job for an airline, is really an undercover agent for the FBI working against a drug ring. After testifying for the government, he finds that he and his family are all in danger. They must be relocated and given new identities under the Federal Witness Protection program. She finds herself restricted to a little Florida town with few real friends and a mother who has turned to alcohol. Missing her boyfriend, her home, and her tennis team, April sends a letter to her boyfriend and goes in search of him and her grandmother. Then the family is threatened by an assassin who is waiting at every turn.

21.15 Ferguson, Alane. **Show Me the Evidence.** Avon/Flare Books, 1990. 164 pp. ISBN 0-380-70962-7. Fiction.

Three babies are dead, three babies were buried, and now three babies are missing from their tombs. Lauren can hardly believe it isn't all a nightmare. The police think that her best friend, Janann, is a killer, and Lauren doesn't know what to do. How can she turn her back on her best friend no matter how strangely she's been acting? Janann is begging Lauren to believe in her and help her look for the real killer, but neither girl realizes how much danger the search will bring or how terrifying the whole truth will be. Winner of the Edgar Award for the best Young Adult Mystery of 1989.

21.16 Gilman, Dorothy. **Incident at Badamyâ.** Doubleday, 1989. 204 pp. ISBN 0-395-24760-5. Fiction.

Genevieve Ferris is sixteen when her missionary father kills himself, and she finds herself alone in Burma in 1950 at the outset of the Korean War. Upon seeing how little savings her father had left, she realizes that there was not enough money for both fares back to the United States and recognizes the sacrifice that he made for her. As Gen makes plans to get aboard a steamer to Rangoon and then to travel on to New York, where an aunt lives, she is taken captive by soldiers of the Red Army, who are holding an odd assortment of other hostages as well: the widow of an English peer, a beautiful murderer, the mystical wife of a famous archeologist, an Armenian American, a greedy travel writer, and a Burmese puppetmaster. In meeting their dangerous situation, the captives remove their masks and reveal themselves as they struggle to win their freedom.

21.17 Grafton, Sue. **"F" Is for Fugitive.** Henry Holt, 1989. 261 pp. ISBN 0-8050-0460-2. Fiction.

Bailey Fowler, convicted and confessed killer of Jean Timberlake, escapes from prison and disappears. Bailey is suddenly in the limelight, and Kinsey Millhone, private eye, takes on his case. If Bailey didn't kill Jean, then who did? Kinsey aims all of her skills toward solving this old case while more murders and threats to her own life occur all around her. A Kinsey Millhone mystery.

21.18 Grafton, Sue. **"G" Is for Gumshoe.** Fawcett Crest, 1990. 327 pp. ISBN 0-449-21936-4. Fiction.

Kinsey Millhone, private investigator, is turning thirty-three. Her birthday activities include moving back into her apartment, reconstructed after it was blown sky-high during one of her earlier cases; being hired to find Mrs. Clyde Gersh's mother in the Mojave Desert and persuading her to return to California; and making it to the top ten on Tyrone Patty's hit list. She reluctantly hires a bodyguard and embarks on one of her toughest cases yet. A Kinsey Millhone mystery.

21.19 Grant, Charles L. **Fire Mask.** Bantam Books, 1990. 202 pp. ISBN 0-553-07167-X. Fiction.

Cliff Abbott draws his friend Del into solving the mystery of the burnt hotel. They discover a badly burned body, thought to be that of the arsonist, in the front yard of the wealthy hotel owner, Kelvin Nunn. The last words of the arsonist plague Cliff, especially after his unusual encounter with Nunn and his daughter. Then a mysterious man in a white suit and a golden mask chases Cliff and his new friend, Cindy; in fact, he takes a shot at them, which adds to Cliff's determination to get to the bottom of this strange mystery. His experiences include an excursion into a fiery pit of evil.

21.20 Guy, Rosa. **And I Heard a Bird Sing.** Dell/Laurel-Leaf Books, 1988. 232 pp. ISBN 0-440-20152-7. Fiction.

Set in modern Brooklyn, this story centers on eighteen-year-old Imamu Jones, who is living with his recovering-alcoholic mother. Imamu's foster family is supportive, so all seems to be well until a rich and beautiful older woman mesmerizes him. Add to this odd romance the horrifying murder of a young woman, and Imamu may be in over his head.

21.21 Hall, Lynn. **A Killing Freeze.** Avon/Flare Books, 1988. 120 pp. ISBN 0-380-75491-6. Fiction.

Harmon Falls, Minnesota, is the setting for this horrifying mystery in which people are dying left and right. Tangled in the center of the web of mystery is Clarie Forrester, the daughter of the local skimobile salesman and the discoverer of the first body, who finds herself drawn to the killings despite the exciting Winterfest that's going on in town. The murders are unusually vicious—one person seemed to be frozen alive—and for Clarie, the closer she finds herself to solving the mystery, the more dangerous it becomes. Can Clarie find the culprit before he finds her?

21.22 Hambly, Barbara. **Those Who Hunt the Night.** Ballantine/Del Rey Books, 1988. 296 pp. ISBN 0-345-34380-8. Fiction.

James Asher finds a vampire sitting at his desk when he returns to his home in Oxford, England in 1907. His wife, Lydia, and their servants are in a deep sleep—a sleep induced by the vampire, Don Simon Ysidro. Don Simon wants to hire James (who had been a spy for the British government) to find out who has been destroying other vampires. If James does not agree to work for him, Don Simon will kill Lydia.

21.23 Hammer, Jeff. **Dying to Know.** Avon/Flare Books, 1991. 171 pp. ISBN 0-380-76143-2. Fiction.

Writing a gossip column for her high school newspaper is all in fun, or so Diane Delany thinks until a young classmate dies. Diane is asked to investigate because the dead girl's family does not believe it was suicide. Before long, Diane uncovers information which leads to five suspects, including Diane's boyfriend. However, leads keep returning to the victim's best friends who, as a threesome, Diane had labeled the Evil Sisters because of their destructive, malicious gossip. There seems to be some evil hovering just out of Diane's reach, so she sets a trap to catch the murderer.

21.24 Hillerman, Tony. **Coyote Waits.** Harper and Row, 1990. 292 pp. ISBN 0-06-016370-4. Fiction.

Officer Jim Chee is shocked to find his friend and fellow police officer Delbert Nez in a burning car on the road. He is even more shocked to find that, after being burnt himself getting Nez out of the car, Nez is already dead—he was shot. When Ashie Pinto, an old Navaho shaman, is found staggering drunk along the same road with the murder weapon in hand, Chee figures he has an open-and-shut case. But there are others investigating the case, and they are not as convinced that things are as simple as they seem. . . .

21.25 Hillerman, Tony. **Talking God.** Harper and Row, 1989. 239 pp. ISBN 0-06-016118-3. Fiction.

Tribal Police Officer Jim Chee of the Navajo arrests Henry Highhawk, who is accused of sending bones of Anglo ancestors to their descendants at the Smithsonian as a protest against the museum's policy of not returning the remains of Native Americans to the earth. Nearby, Lieutenant Joe Leaphorn begins an investigation into the murder of an unidentified victim: the body has been stripped of identification. When the two cases begin to overlap, Leaphorn and Chee join forces to uncover the mysteries surrounding Henry Highhawk, who, it seems, is wanted for more than just grave-robbing.

21.26 Hillerman, Tony. **A Thief of Time: A Novel.** Harper and Row, 1988. 209 pp. ISBN 0-06-015938-3. Fiction.

Dr. Eleanor Friedman-Bernal is an archaeologist. While searching for ancient Indian pottery in the canyons of a Navajo reservation in Arizona, she makes an unusual discovery. Later, when she disappears and three men are killed, Lieutenant Joe Leaphorn of the Navajo Tribal Police wonders if there is a connection between the pottery, the archaeologist, and the murdered men. Did Dr. Friedman-Bernal kill the men or is she dead as well, making someone else the killer he is looking for?

21.27 Jaspersohn, William. **Grounded.** Bantam Books, 1988. 234 pp. ISBN 0-553-05450-3. Fiction.

Joe Francis feels misunderstood. So when he is grounded, he decides to run away. After he meets Nan and she hides him, they attempt to solve a deadly mystery. By the end of the story Joe starts to regain his self-confidence and to appreciate his self-worth. Easy reading.

21.28 Johnston, Norma. **Whisper of the Cat.** Bantam Starfire Books, 1987. 183 pp. ISBN 0-553-26947-X. Fiction.

Sixteen-year-old Tracy Fairbrother is on her way to spend the summer with a father she's never really known. He and Tracy's stepmother have settled down at the family mansion, Bonne Espérance, on Dorr Island. Tracy has an uneasy feeling during the whole trip, and when she arrives at the mansion, located near swamps and quicksand, the feeling that something weird is going on intensifies. Then she finds a body in the swamp. Who or what is behind the evil on Dorr Island?

21.29 Kennedy, William P. **Toy Soldiers.** St. Martins Press, 1988. 376 pp. ISBN 0-312-01478-3. Fiction.

Sharif is a fanatical terrorist from the Middle East who is called "the Flaming Sword from the Desert." He and his men capture the students and teachers of Saint Anselm's School in Rome and hold them hostage inside the school. The students are all sons of wealthy and influential Americans, and Sharif is sure that the government, unwilling to gamble with the lives of these children, will have to give in to his demands. Sharif, however, does not know fifteen-year-old Billy Tepper. Mature language and situations.

21.30 Knight, Kathryn Lasky. **Mortal Words.** Summit Books, 1990. 316 pp. ISBN 0-671-68446-9. Fiction.

Calista Jacobs, illustrator and makeshift sleuth, is immediately intrigued when an author of children's books on evolution is murdered in Calista's hometown of Cambridge, Massachusetts. Along with her computer genius thirteen-year-old son Charley, and a handsome archeologist, Archie, Calista dashes off on the trail of the murderer. Before the case is solved, the three intrepid detectives will run into fundamentalist preachers, a "biological emperor with Nazi dreams," and a whole lot of trouble!

21.31 Landau, Elaine. **Teenage Violence.** Julian Messner, 1990. 113 pp. ISBN 0-671-70153-3. Nonfiction.

America's teens are angry! Have they lost hope for their dreams? Yusuf K. Hawkins was a victim of teenage violence. The New York City's Central Park jogger fell victim to a "wilding" attack. Gang rape, drug rings, school violence, and date rape appear in the media daily. What is the catalyst?

21.32 Lantigua, John. **Heat Lightning.** G. P. Putnam's Sons, 1987. 288 pp. ISBN 0-399-13300-3. Fiction.

Chicano homicide detective David Cruz is investigating the murder of a beautiful young Latina woman in the Mission District of San Francisco. He learns that Gloria Soto had come to the United States illegally to escape the bloodshed in her native El Salvador. David is struck by the look of fear frozen in her eyes, fear like the flash of heat lightning. He has some theories about who might have killed Gloria—her Salvadoran guerilla lover, whom she recently rejected; her new lover, a giant of a man who smuggled her into the country; or a Salvadoran death squad operating in the United States. In solving the case, David finds himself looking at his own past.

21.33 Levin, Betty. **The Keeping-Room.** Greenwillow Books, 1989. 247 pp. ISBN 0-688-80300-8. Fiction.

Hal's social studies project is to get old Mrs. Titcomb to tell about the Titcomb farm. Imagine how you might feel if you were Hal and found yourself face-to-face with a child who had disappeared over a hundred years ago. Hal learns about history (including the Candlewood curse) and about the present and gains a better understanding of the people who inhabit both.

21.34 Malcolm, Jahnna N. **Get the Picture.** Bantam Books, 1990. 149 pp. ISBN 0-553-28191-7. Fiction.

High school junior Pepper Larson has been chosen as one of the four teen finalists in San Francisco's Picture the City Contest. But when her photos are stolen, Pepper and her best friend, Amanda Hart, suspect a jealous fellow contestant. Suddenly the situation becomes more sinister as the girls are followed, Pepper's house is ransacked, and the friends fear for their lives. They must ask Mick Soul for help. He's tough, street-wise, and he soon links Pepper's photos to an unsolved murder and killer druglords. Can these teenagers beat the mob and escape with their lives? A *Hart and Soul* book.

21.35 Malcolm, Jahnna N. **Play Dead.** Bantam Books, 1990. 166 pp. ISBN 0-553-28006-6. Fiction.

Amanda Hart is the editor of her high school newspaper. When she attends the dress rehearsal of a play her friend, Kitty, has a part in, an on-stage accident convinces her that someone is trying to sabotage the play by harming the performers. In order to investigate, she accepts a minor part in "Murder at Midnight" and her handsome friend, Mick Soul, shows up to protect her. Will they be able to solve the mystery, and will the play go on as scheduled? A *Hart and Soul* book.

21.36 Malcolm, Jahnna N. **Speak No Evil.** Bantam Books, 1990. 165 pp. ISBN 0-553-28077-5. Fiction.

Amanda Hart turns seventeen and her parents, who travel worldwide, buy her a private telephone so that they can reach her more easily. Amanda loves the phone but almost immediately she begins to receive threatening calls. The caller seems to know where she is at all times. Worry and suspicion begin to affect her relationships with everyone until she can't trust anyone. Having the number changed does no good, and the phone company thinks she is making up the whole story! A *Hart and Soul* book.

21.37 Mosher, Howard Frank. **A Stranger in the Kingdom.** Doubleday, 1989. 421 pp. ISBN 0-385-24400-2. Fiction.

In Kingdom County, Vermont, in 1952, a seventeen-year-old girl is found murdered. The man most strongly suspected of the crime is Reverend Walter Andrews, a black Presbyterian minister and a newcomer to Kingdom County. Told from the viewpoint of Jim, a sensitive young boy, the mystery unfolds, revealing hidden racism and intolerance in a once-quiet community, and climaxes in the trial of Reverend Andrews which will change Kingdom County forever.

21.38 Moyes, Patricia. **Black Girl, White Girl.** Henry Holt, 1989. 217 pp. ISBN 0-8050-1148-X. Fiction.

Tampica, a small unspoiled Caribbean island, is being ruined by the importing of White Girl—the local name for cocaine. Emmy and Henry Tibbett pass themselves off as rich, stupid tourists and visit

Tampica to drive out the druglords. But can they confront murderers and corrupt officials while politely having tea and crumpets like good British tourists?

21.39 Muller, Marcia. **The Legend of the Slain Soldiers.** New American Library/Signet, 1987. 223 pp. ISBN 0-451-15050-3. Fiction.

As director of the Santa Barbara Art Museum, Elena Oliverez meets many interesting people. She has a sideline of solving murders. Enlisting the aid of her mother and her boyfriend, she goes to work with Police Lieutenant Dave Kirk to uncover the latest murder which relates back to an unsolved murder of long ago.

21.40 Paretsky, Sara. **Blood Shot.** Dell, 1989. 376 pp. ISBN 0-440-20420-8. Fiction.

Victoria I. Warshawski grew up in south Chicago, but her life as a lawyer and private investigator, specializing in financial crime, has led her to the more affluent North Side. Now, twenty years later, V. I. returns to her blue-collar neighborhood to attend a reunion of her championship basketball team. She is asked by former neighbor Caroline Djiak to take on a case. Caroline's mother, Louisa, was an unmarried, pregnant girl shunned by her parents when she moved into the house next door to V. I.'s family. She would never reveal the identity of Caroline's father. Now Louisa is dying, and Caroline is determined to know her father and her past, and perhaps begin a new life with a new family. As V. I. searches to reveal Louisa's secret, she uncovers more than she bargained for. A corrupt politician, witnesses who clam up, a multibillion-dollar chemical company, a mob figure, a murdered friend, and an attempt on her own life are all parts of the puzzle that V. I. must piece together.

21.41 Paretsky, Sara. **Burn Marks.** Dell, 1990. 340 pp. ISBN 0-440-20845-9. Fiction.

V. I. Warshawski, Chicago-based sleuth, is less than delighted to be awakened by the arrival of her wacky aunt, Elena, in the pre-dawn hours. Elena, who used to pass out at family Thanksgiving dinners, has a drinking problem, in addition to her numerous personality flaws, so when she tells V. I. that something strange is happening at her sleazy, old residence, V. I. is more than a little skeptical. However, she decides to do some investigating and finds herself embroiled in a case that extends from the world of Chicago's homeless to bedroom politics with some of the city's biggest players. If she can't get to the bottom of the case, it could literally be the end of her.

21.42 Pickard, Nancy. **Bum Steer.** Pocket Books, 1990. 240 pp. ISBN 0-671-68040-4. Fiction.

Jenny Cain is flying to Kansas, leaving behind her Cape Cod vacation with her husband, but for what? To find out why the Port Frederick Civic Foundation has been bequeathed a four million dollar Kansas cattle ranch! But when she arrives, the benefactor of the Foundation, Charles W. Benet IV, is dead—murdered in his hospital room. Wading through suspicious police, Benet's ex-wives, and their jealous second husbands wasn't how she had planned to spend this vacation time. Neither was dodging bullets and strategically placed rattlesnakes. Who is so eager to get rid of her? A Jenny Cain mystery.

21.43 Pike, Christopher. **Die Softly.** Archway Paperbacks, 1991. 248 pp. ISBN 0-671-69056-6. Fiction.

A girl is murdered, but this has nothing to do with Herb Trasker—or does it? Herb has one talent and that is photography. Taking pictures of cheerleaders in the shower is the beginning of his days of uncertainty and mystery. He is awed when head cheerleader Alexa Close seems interested in him, but this new relationship jeopardizes his longstanding friendship with Sammie. Alexa drops hints about who murdered Lisa, but Herb has the whole scene on film. His infatuation with Alexa brings him in on the murder of two people, and he uncovers the real Alexa but at great personal expense.

21.44 Pople, Maureen. **A Nugget of Gold.** Henry Holt, 1989. 183 pp. ISBN 0-8050-0984-1. Fiction.

A century-old brooch found in a mine shaft provides the catalyst for two teenagers a century apart to unravel its mystery: Sally, from this century, who found the gold nugget and is determined to know its story; and Ann, from the previous century, who tells a memorable love story. Although Sally comes to understand more about her family's heritage, only Ann and the reader know the true story behind the inscription on the brooch.

21.45 Pullman, Philip. **Shadow in the North.** Alfred A. Knopf/Borzoi Sprinters, 1989. 331 pp. ISBN 0-394-82599-3. Fiction.

Sally Lockhart's promise to recover her client's investment leads her from danger to danger in the Victorian era in England. An unscrupulous businessman warns Sally that he will destroy her, her business, and her friends if she continues her investigation. But she will not relent and soon her good friends, Frederick and Jim, are also involved in uncovering an evil plot to control the world. A sequel to *The Ruby in the Stone.*

21.46 Rosen, Richard. **Saturday Night Dead.** Viking, 1988. 274 pp. ISBN 0-670-81977-8. Fiction.

When murder occurs at the cast party for "Last Laughs," the once trend-setting late-night live comedy show which has since fallen from grace, ex-baseball player turned private detective Harvey Blissberg is asked to find the killer. Blissberg finds himself digging into well-kept secrets, old vendettas, alibis, and distrust behind the scenes of the "Last Laughs" show. Was it the reclusive (somewhat deranged) writer? The embittered bit player? The Joke Doctor? The script writer with the dead dog? Or one of the other dozen neurotic suspects, each with a motive and an opportunity? Opening with a list of possible culprits—the cast and crew "credits" for "Last Laughs"—this sequel to *Strike Three You're Dead* and *Fadeaway* is filled with the unique characters and startling revelations that make for a wonderful whodunit set in a world of cutthroat television.

21.47 Schneider, Joyce Anne. **Darkness Falls.** Pocket Books, 1989. 310 pp. ISBN 0-671-67317-3. Fiction.

On a beautiful June morning, the body of eighteen-year-old Kelly Payne washes up in the surf—was it suicide, an accident, or murder? That's what Doctor Amanda Hammond has to find out, but no one in the wealthy community of Grand Cove, Connecticut, is talking. Brian Kirkley, Kelly Payne's boyfriend, might know something because he was the last person to see her alive. But Brian's father, a candidate for the senate, doesn't want his son involved with dead girls and medical investigations. Even the medical examiner, Peter Barron, might be involved in covering up important clues to what happened to Kelly Payne. And Doctor Amanda Hammond just might have to consider herself a suspect as secret memories of another body floating ashore come back from her childhood to haunt her. Could these secret memories lead to another death? And could Amanda Hammond be the next victim?

21.48 Schultz, Marion. **Hotline to Terror.** Fawcett/Juniper Books, 1991. 136 pp. ISBN 0-449-70371-1. Fiction.

Is a werewolf stalking the halls of Abbie Lane's high school, or is it all a prank? Abbie doesn't think so and begins her own investigation, but soon she receives warnings to cease. She can't convince her high school newspaper editor, Conway Davis, to let her write articles that might help find clues to the mysterious werewolf. He stands in her way and continues to pay attention to Tara, who Abbie sees as real competition for Con's attention. Abbie forges ahead, getting into tight and dangerous situations in pursuit of answers to this mysterious unhuman ghost.

21.49 Southall, Ivan. **The Mysterious World of Marcus Leadbeater.** Farrar, Straus and Giroux, 1990. 180 pp. ISBN 0-374-35113-9. Fiction.

Marc is looking forward to a visit with his grandmother—it's the first time he has been back since his grandfather died. He plans to show Gran all of the places he enjoyed with Gramps. He arrives in town early and goes to the old home. He remembers all the times that he helped Gramps work on it and how lovingly they had cared for it. The first thing he sees on the lawn is the real estate sign, "Auction Here," and the sale is set for tomorrow. Gran is gone! This house was to be Marc's someday. How could it be for sale?

21.50 Spruill, Steven. **Painkiller.** St. Martin's Press, 1990. 278 pp. ISBN 0-312-03905-0. Fiction.

Dr. Sharon Francis's mother is a schizophrenic. Therefore, Sharon, a young resident at Adams Memorial Hospital, doesn't take it very seriously when her mother claims that other psychiatric patients are being forced to discharge themselves and are then disappearing. But when Sharon starts looking into the matter, she becomes the target of some very unsubtle murder attempts. Then she herself is committed to the hospital as a schizophrenic by an unscrupulous doctor. Sharon and the two men who are attracted to her must discover what's going on and prove Sharon's sanity before it is too late!

21.51 Steiner, Barbara. **The Photographer.** Avon/Flare Books, 1989. 138 pp. ISBN 0-380-75758-3. Fiction.

Megan Davidson, a senior and a reporter for her school newspaper, befriends Derrick Ames, even though her best friend, Cynthia Harlow, finds Derrick scary. Gradually Megan, too, feels uncomfortable around Derrick—especially after there seems to be a strange connection between homecoming photos Derrick took and a strange illness at Boulder High. Only the girls Derrick has photographed become ill, and Megan grows more and more suspicious. Is Derrick responsible?

21.52 Stine, R. L. **The Boyfriend.** Scholastic/Point, 1990. 165 pp. ISBN 0-590-43279-6. Fiction.

Joanna is rich and spoiled and doesn't allow herself to really care about other people. After she breaks up with her boyfriend, Dex, he is killed in an accident. She is not upset about Dex's death because it wasn't her fault and she never loved him. But then Dex comes back from the dead for revenge.

21.53 Stine, R. L. **Curtains.** Archway Paperbacks, 1990. 139 pp. ISBN 0-671-69498-7. Fiction.

Julie convinces Rena to accompany her to theater camp. Rena is chosen for the lead in the camp production of *Curtains.* At first, she is elated by her big break, but soon has doubts when Hedy, another aspiring actress, threatens her, and Julie, her best friend, is acting strangely. The director uses various exercises designed to "open everyone up." As his techniques become increasingly strange, Rena realizes that he will do anything to bring out emotions that could lead even to murder. When practical jokes become spiteful and the stage blood turns out to be real, Rena knows that the most terrifying challenge of her life has just begun.

21.54 Stine, R. L. **The Snowman.** Scholastic/Point, 1991. 181 pp. ISBN 0-590-43280-X. Fiction.

After Heather's parents die, her aunt and uncle become her guardians. Uncle James is demanding and makes life difficult for Heather by controlling her money, her time, and her social life. When she meets a young man at work, she is immediately interested in the handsome, white-haired teenager. They begin dating and, before long, she has shut out her longtime friend, Ben. "The Snowman," as her new friend prefers to be called, comes to dinner with Heather, her aunt, and her uncle, and after an embarrassing time together, he tells Heather he can deal with her uncle. Little does Heather realize the depths he will go to cope with Uncle James. Only later does she see the true "Snowman" for what he is, and it comes after she finds herself buried in snow struggling for every breath.

21.55 Stine, R. L. **Halloween Party.** Archway Paperbacks, 1990. 147 pp. ISBN 0-671-70243-2. Fiction.

Terry and Nikki are part of the special group invited to Justine's Halloween party. Unusual events start as they cross the cemetery on Fear Street to get to the "haunted house." At the party they find other vengeful surprises, all planned by Justine. Will they be able to stop her plot before she goes too far?

21.56 Stine, R. L. **Ski Weekend.** Archway Paperbacks, 1991. 165 pp. ISBN 0-671-72480-0. Fiction.

Ariel and her friends, Shannon and Doug, are returning from a fun ski weekend in Vermont when they become stranded in a blizzard with Red, a boy they met back at the lodge. They take refuge in a desolate farmhouse. The owner of the house is strange and frightening, and soon Ariel realizes that she and her friends have walked into a trap. Doug's car is gone. The phones are dead. And the house is full of guns. They steal one and attempt to escape, and that's when the real terror begins.

21.57 Stoll, Clifford. **The Cuckoo's Egg: Tracking a Spy through the Maze of Computer Espionage.** Doubleday, 1989. 323 pp. ISBN 0-385-24946-2. Nonfiction.

Clifford Stoll—astrophysicist, systems manager of a lab, and James Bond of the computer world—gained international attention when he tracked down an elusive intruder in American research and military computer systems. The trail of espionage led to West Germany, then back to Pittsburgh, where Stoll and half a dozen national agencies discovered a spy ring which was dealing with the KGB for money and cocaine. A real-life spy story with a very contemporary twist.

21.58 Strasser, Todd, with Dennis Freeland. **Moving Target.** Fawcett/Juniper Books, 1989. 135 pp. ISBN 0-449-70324-X. Fiction.

Angelo's life is totally changed when his father enters into the Witness Protection Program. Angelo hates leaving his girlfriend, but through his efforts, criminals from the past are caught. Suspense builds as Angelo searches for answers to the riddles surrounding him.

21.59 Strieber, Whitley. **Billy.** G. P. Putnam's Sons, 1990. 317 pp. ISBN 0-399-13584-7. Fiction.

Billy Neary is a normal, video game-playing, suburban, twelve-year-old boy. Unfortunately, Billy also becomes the target of the maladjusted Barton Royal who, at forty-four, is looking for his own lost childhood and decides kidnapping Billy is how he will regain it. As the story unfolds, Billy realizes that he is in the hands of a dangerous psychopath with no grip on reality. Will Billy ever escape the black room in Barton's basement?

21.60 Tate, Eleanora E. **The Secret of Gumbo Grove.** Bantam/Starfire Books, 1988. 199 pp. ISBN 0-553-27226-8. Fiction.

Raisin Stockhouse is curious to learn black history. But when she questions her teacher about black heroes from her hometown, Gumbo Grove, South Carolina, Miz Gore says there are none. However, while Raisin is helping Miz Effie Pfluggins clean the church cemetery, Miz Effie tells her about the lives of some of the black people buried there, many of whom lived heroic lives. Her parents' anger over her repeating of Miz Effie's stories only increases Raisin's interest in discovering more about the black history of Gumbo Grove.

21.61 Westall, Robert. **The Watch House.** Alfred A. Knopf/Borzoi Sprinters, 1990. 229 pp. ISBN 0-679-80129-4. Fiction.

Anne is sent off to a small seaside village for the summer. Added to her worry about her parents' pending divorce, she encounters spirits in the old Watch House and involves two new friends. With their help, she is drawn into the supernatural and a murder committed years ago. Only a strong will and help from the village priests can put everything in proper perspective.

21.62 Whelan, Gloria. **The Secret Keeper**. Alfred A. Knopf/Borzoi Books, 1990. 186 pp. ISBN 0-679-90572-3. Fiction.

She shouldn't have kept the secrets of the Beaches—Annie knew that now, but at first it had all seemed so perfect. On the shore of Lake Michigan, the Beaches is a private community, beautiful and elegant, summer retreat for a small group of rich and powerful families. Here for the first time as a companion to one of the children, Annie is enchanted. Wanting so much to belong, she at first ignores the small signs that the Beaches has a dark side. But as Annie learns more and more about the past, she realizes that something terrible threatens the Beaches, and she may be the next victim. For the people of the Beaches have created their own special world, one they will do anything to protect.

21.63 Whitney, Phyllis A. **Mystery on the Isle of Skye.** Fawcett/Juniper Books, 1991. 184 pp. ISBN 0-449-70364-9. Fiction.

Cathy MacLeod's grandmother becomes ill and plans to send Cathy to live with her Aunt Bertha. But first, her grandmother sends Cathy on a surprise trip to the Isle of Skye in Scotland, where Cathy is to travel with unfamiliar relatives from Philadelphia. Cathy's grandmother sends messages and clues along with Cathy, challenging her to solve puzzles involving strange folklore and fairy legends of the Scottish isle. When her grandmother takes a turn for the worse, and Cathy is invited to make a big decision, is it ancient magic that helps her make the decision? Does that magic work in positive ways?

21.64 Whitney, Phyllis A. **Mystery of the Golden Horn.** Fawcett/Juniper Books, 1990. 180 pp. ISBN 0-449-70363-0. Fiction.

When fourteen-year-old Vicki Stewart fails school, everything changes. When her mother is hospitalized, she is sent to Istanbul, Turkey, to stay with her father. Little does she know that she will encounter gypsies, a mysterious castle, and face frightening danger to herself and her new friends.

21.65 William, Kate. **No Place to Hide.** Bantam Books, 1988. 217 pp. ISBN 0-553-27-554-2. Fiction.

When Barbara, the girl Nicholas Morrow falls in love with, tells him that they must keep their relationship a secret because she is frightened for their safety, Nicholas asks twins Jessica and Elizabeth Wakefield for help. During their investigation, they find their lives threatened. What will the twins do? Save Barbara at risk of their lives or give up, leaving Barbara in danger?

21.66 Wormser, Richard. **Lifers: Learn the Truth at the Expense of Our Sorrow.** Photographs by Richard Wormser. Julian Messner, 1991. 203 pp. ISBN 0-671-72548-3. Nonfiction.

The author, a filmmaker, takes readers behind the barbed wire and maximum security of East Jersey State Prison in Rahway, New Jersey, to a group of men serving life sentences. Known as the Lifers' Group, these men use their histories to persuade young offenders to avoid similar criminal mistakes before those mistakes take over their lives. Through photos and personal accounts, the book explores the Lifers' program as depicted in the 1979 TV documentary "Scared Straight," explaining how the program began and how it helps the teenagers and their families, as well as the men who are spending their lives behind bars. Communication between prisoners and young offenders can continue beyond the initial visit by youngsters to the prison. Telephone calls and letters are used to keep the relationship open. This book gives an inside view of prisoners who face years of confinement, though hopes for freedom show through.

22 Myths, Legends, and Folklore

22.1 Cohen, Daniel. **Southern Fried Rat and Other Gruesome Tales.** Illustrated by Peggy Briar. Avon/Flare Books, 1989. 128 pp. ISBN 0-380-70655-5. Fiction.

Twenty-one short stories drawn from contemporary tales which range from premature burial through haunted prom dresses to bloodthirsty maniacs will live up to expectation. Many of them are topped off with short histories of the origin of the myths. This is a book written for campfire readers.

22.2 Fife, Graeme. **Arthur the King.** Sterling, 1991. 200 pp. ISBN 0-8069-8344-2. Nonfiction.

Graeme Fife attempts for the first time to discover the explanations behind the mysteries of the Arthurian legend and its enduring fascination. He traces the origins of these tales to the early twelfth century and reconstructs their development through their major themes of chivalry, courtly love, hunting, heraldry and pageantry, magic, and the Holy Grail.

22.3 Hamilton, Virginia. **In the Beginning: Creation Stories from around the World.** Illustrated by Barry Moser. Harcourt Brace Jovanovich, 1988. 161 pp. ISBN 0-15-238740-4. Nonfiction.

"In the beginning, all was darkness forever. Night covered the earth in a great tangle." So starts this creation story from the Australian Northern Aranda aborigines. There are twenty-four more tales from all over the world here—each one with a full-page color illustration. Hamilton offers comments and explanations at the end of each myth, and at the end of the book she writes "More About These Myths."

22.4 Hoover, H. M. **The Dawn Palace: The Story of Medea.** E. P. Dutton, 1988. 244 pp. ISBN 0-525-44388-6. Fiction.

In this retelling of the Greek myth, Medea, the daughter of King Aeëtes, grows up in the Dawn Palace. She learns secret powers of healing and destruction from her aunt, Circe the sorceress. Medea falls in love with Jason at first sight and uses her powers to help him become King of

Corinth. When they marry, Jason swears that he will never betray her, and it is ten years before Medea discovers that he will not keep his promise.

22.5 Lewis, Naomi, translator. **Proud Knight, Fair Lady: The Twelve Laëis of Marie de France.** Illustrated by Angela Barrett. Viking Kestrel, 1989. 100 pp. ISBN 0-670-82656-1. Fiction.

These twelve stories from the twelfth century are tales of knights and ladies, chivalry and treachery, as well as love and hate. Here readers will find magical wolves, swan messengers, life-giving blossoms, and cities of ancient splendor where princes are hawks and houses are made of silver. These poetic fairy tales are translated from the writings of Marie de France, a twelfth-century French woman who collected oral fables and put them down on paper so that they might be shared with everyone.

22.6 Pankake, Marcia, and Jon Pankake. **A Prairie Home Companion Folk Song Book.** Foreword by Garrison Keillor. Illustrated by John Palmer Low. Viking, 1988. 316 pp. ISBN 0-670-82159-4. Nonfiction.

"The Department of Folk Song" was a popular segment on the "Prairie Home Companion" radio program between 1983 and 1987. Listeners were encouraged to submit their favorite songs, following the ground rules that host Garrison Keillor laid out: the songs were to be those that "you have heard from someone else" (not original songs and not from a definitive written or recorded source) and those "to which you remember the words mostly" (implying that songs change over time). The more than three hundred songs in this collection, selected by Marcia and Jon Pankake from the nearly 1,800 submissions, include sea chanteys, lullabies, traditional ballads, parodies of old popular tunes, and nonsense songs. Some of the songs contain musical scores, but in most cases only lyrics are needed because the songs are sung to well-known tunes, such as "The Battle Hymn of the Republic." Featured are "Mine Eyes Have Seen the Glory of the Burning of the School," "From the Halls of School's Dark Prison," and the ever-popular "Greasy Grimy Gopher Guts." Indexes.

22.7 Severin, Tim. **The Ulysses Voyage: Sea Search for the Odyssey.** Drawings by Will Stoney and photographs by Kevin Fleming, Nazem Choufeh, and Rick Williams. E. P. Dutton, 1987. 253 pp. ISBN 0-525-24614-2. Nonfiction.

Are the events which Homer related in the epic poem "The Odyssey" true? If so, where are the exotic places that Ulysses visited? Tim

Severin decided to find out by traveling the same route from Troy to Ithaca outlined in "The Odyssey." He began at the site of ancient Troy (confirmed by archaeologists) on the ship *Argo* which was built according to descriptions of the galleys used 3,000 years ago in the time of Ulysses. Are Homer's places fact or fantasy, and is his Ithaca the site of present-day Ithaca?

22.8 Skutch, Robert. **The Day the World Forgot: A Tale for All Times.** Celestial Arts, 1988. 74 pp. ISBN 0-89087-536-7. Fiction.

A single, gentle idea about peace occurs in the world; logic and truth abound in all nations. Russians and Americans approach the negotiation table without fear, without consideration of past promises broken. Israeli and Arab students attend classes together in their homeland. The message of peace is universal for people as they live singularly and together as nations.

22.9 Switzer, Ellen and Costas. **Greek Myths: Gods, Heroes and Monsters—Their Sources, Their Stories and Their Meanings.** Photographs by Costas. Atheneum, 1988. 208 pp. ISBN 0-689-31253-9. Nonfiction.

Some 3,000 years ago the Greeks were telling stories about gods, the monsters that the early Greeks believed inhabited the world, and the heroes who were able to deal with both the gods and the monsters. Although these gods were human in appearance, character, moral values, and behavior, they had special powers. For example, Zeus could throw thunderbolts and could turn himself into a human, animal, vegetable, or mineral being. The monsters were particularly frightening. Medusa, "the world's ugliest monster," had bulging eyes, a swollen black tongue, yellow fangs, and live snakes in place of hair. It was the heroes' part to get rid of such monsters. These ancient Greek myths and legends represent one way by which our ancestors tried to explain the workings of the universe and the fortunes and misfortunes in their own lives. By retelling these stories, the authors help bring an ancient culture into the present and give readers a look at the whole of Western civilization.

22.10 Visser, Margaret. **Much Depends on Dinner: The Extraordinary History and Mythology, Allure and Obsessions, Perils and Taboos, of an Ordinary Meal.** Grove Press, 1987. 351 pp. ISBN 0-8021-0023-6. Nonfiction.

How much do you think the food you eat affects you? What does your dinner have to do with the economics of the world? Why is chicken such a popular food in America? These and other unusual questions are answered in this book, which focuses on a variety of edibles—chicken, rice, salt, corn flakes, ice cream, and others—and how they relate to the world around us. Did you know that it was once believed that ice cream could be dangerous if eaten after a heavy meal because it supposedly slowed digestion? Many other fascinating facts are included in this examination of the history and the mythology of food.

22.11 Weinreich, Beatrice Silverman. **Yiddish Folktales.** Translated from Yiddish by Leonard Wolf. Pantheon Books, 1988. 413 pp. ISBN 0-394-54618-0. Fiction.

From the vivid world of East European Jews come these two hundred entertaining tales which have never before been published. Sections on Allegory, Magic, Everyday Morals, Humor, and the Supernatural are presented in this volume. These tales present a look at history not presented in most history books.

23 Poetry and Drama

23.1 Adoff, Arnold. **Chocolate Dreams.** Illustrated by Turi MacCombie. Lothrop, Lee and Shepard Books, 1989. 63 pp. ISBN 0-688-06823-5. Fiction.

Arnold Adoff, who believes that poetry is making music with words and space, celebrates chocolate in all its forms and variations. In forty-eight poems, ranging in mood from ridiculous to sublime, from gently humorous to nostalgic, from wistful to melancholic, he explores every possible nuance of the cacao bean and its derivatives. Chocolate is used as a basis for such activities as writing math word problems, reflecting on the nature of true love, speculating on the possibility of extraterrestrial life, and poking fun at Stephen King. With a nod to the practical, even the dentist is not forgotten. Mouthwatering watercolor paintings accompany the poems, but readers are cautioned not to lick, bite, or chew the pages.

23.2 Agard, John, compiler. **Life Doesn't Frighten Me at All.** Henry Holt, 1990. 95 pp. ISBN 0-8050-1237-0. Nonfiction.

These eighty-five "fun" poems are for teenagers who are "allergic to poetry" but who want to know how to better cope with life's loves, injustices, and disappointments. They are written by Maya Angelou, W. B. Yeats, Attila the Stockbroker, Zinzi Mandela, and other poetry lovers throughout the world.

23.3 Carson, Jo. **Stories I Ain't Told Nobody Yet: Selections from the People Pieces.** Orchard Books, 1989. 84 pp. ISBN 0-531-05808-5. Nonfiction.

"I lived off old 42, / up Cook's Holler, / through the gap, / and down Limestone Creek a ways. . ." This is where Jo Carson hears the stories which make up her poetry. The people she encounters in east Tennessee and in the Appalachian region speak about their lives, their thoughts, and their friends and families. "I've got whole lives of stories that belong to you. / I could fill you up with stories, / stories I ain't told nobody yet."

23.4 Glenn, Mel. **Back to Class.** Photographs by Michael J. Bernstein. Clarion Books, 1988. 95 pp. ISBN 0-89919-656-X. Nonfiction.

High school students and staff are candidly exposed by the author, who captures their dreams, fears, and realities in the free verse form. Photographs of students and teachers add to the visual imagery. These sixty-five poems of the students' day are fresh and haunting.

23.5 Janeczko, Paul B. **Brickyard Summer.** Illustrated by Ken Rush. Orchard/Richard Jackson Books, 1989. 53 pp. ISBN 0-531-08446-9. Nonfiction.

Two teenagers, the speaker and friend, use poetry to express their thoughts about the people in their neighborhood. They talk about ordinary happenings, describe commonplace buildings, and praise ordinary people who show strength and courage in everyday life. From the first "tearing and crumpling of pages" at the end of school to "The kiss started when I danced with Molly Burke," Janeczko captures moments of a small-town summer. Illustrations by Ken Rush add to the poetic walk.

23.6 Janeczko, Paul B., compiler. **The Music of What Happens: Poems That Tell Stories.** Orchard Books, 1988. 188 pp. ISBN 0-531-05757-7. Nonfiction.

The stories in these poems tell of love, of war, of ghosts, of animals, of moments, and of lifetimes. Some will make you see things in a different way: "But the woods seem richer with a snake in them / yellow and black, a sliding night / that carries the day on its back, / lighting up some of the dark places" Some will describe real people—but not just famous people. As one poem says, "The purpose of poetry is to tell us about life."

23.7 Janeczko, Paul B., compiler. **Preposterous: Poems of Youth.** Orchard/Richard Jackson Books, 1991. 127 pp. ISBN 0-531-08501-5. Nonfiction.

Janeczko has selected poems by eighty-two American poets who have recorded their memories of being teenagers. Problems and concerns experienced during those adolescent years fill page after page as individual incidents come alive. There are also moments of deep reflection when some poets picture specific persons who helped them through times of unhappiness, especially the deaths of friends and relatives. "Remembered" youth is Janeczko's aim.

23.8 Komunyakaa, Yusef. **Dien Cai Dau.** University Press of New England/Wesleyan University Press, 1988. 63 pp. ISBN 0-8195-2163-9. Nonfiction.

These are poems about Vietnam and what it was like for Americans who were fighting there. The poems describe the life of soldiers and the experiences of war. For example: "he goes, the good soldier, / on hands and knees, tunneling past / death sacked into a blind corner, / loving the weight of the shotgun / that will someday dig his grave."

23.9 McCullough, Frances, compiler. **Earth, Air, Fire and Water.** Harper and Row, 1989. 140 pp. ISBN 0-06-024207-8. Nonfiction.

According to Frances McCullough, the poems in this collection were selected for "their specific gravity: the pull they exert on the readers." The poets are old and young, famous and not-so-famous, including James Joyce, Ogden Nash, and Tom Clark. The poems have conventional and unconventional titles: "Song," "There's a Little Ambiguity Over There Among the Bluebells," and "Hair On Television." This is a revised edition of the original title published in 1971.

23.10 Morgan, Robert. **Sigodlin.** Wesleyan University Press, 1990. 64 pp. ISBN 0-8195-1180-3. Fiction.

Robert Morgan's poetry is about the things around us which we no longer notice: the colors of late summer, the jet trails across the clear sky, and the view in a rearview mirror. His memories of children shaking hands in a contest of power or of a child exploring grandma's forbidden bureau are powerful and exact, and they reflect the innocence and magic of youth.

23.11 Pike, Frank and Thomas G. Dunn. **Scenes and Monologues from the New American Theater.** New American Library/Mentor, 1988. 301 pp. ISBN 0-451-62547-1. Fiction.

This anthology of contemporary scenes and monologues is ideal for auditions and showcases. It consists of scenes for two men, two women, one man and one woman, and nineteen monologues. You'll find both comedy and tragedy here in the works of Christopher Durang, August Wilson, Beth Henley, and many others.

23.12 Ratliff, Gerald Lee, and Suzanne Trauth. **On Stage: Producing Musical Theatre.** Rosen, 1988. 108 pp. ISBN 0-8239-0697-3. Nonfiction.

Consult this book for ideas on performing, directing, and producing musicals. It defines the musical as a medium and gives exercises in breath support, vocal mechanics, body flexibility, and communication. Suggestions are given for choreography and for publicizing the production. Appendixes list primary rental agencies and musicals recommended for production. From The Theatre Student series.

23.13 Rylant, Cynthia. **Soda Jerk.** Paintings by Peter Catalanotto. Orchard/ Richard Jackson Books, 1990. 47 pp. ISBN 0-531-05864-6. Nonfiction.

The narrator is a kid who works as a soda jerk in the small town's only drug store. Everyone comes in—the jocks, the rich kids, the popular and not-so-popular, the old and the young, the hopeful and the desperate. He watches them all, and he really sees, listens, and hears. Then, in a series of connected poems, he tells about them. And it's incredible how much he really knows, most of all about himself. Impressionistic paintings by Peter Catalanotto add visual appeal, but don't judge *Soda Jerk* by its cover. It looks like a picture book and it looks like poetry, but it sounds like real life.

23.14 Sears, Peter. **Gonna Bake Me a Rainbow Poem: A Student Guide to Writing Poetry.** Scholastic, 1990. 143 pp. ISBN 0-590-43085-8. Nonfiction.

Using student poems, like the one that gives this book its title, Peter Sears takes the reader on a creative journey where all the signposts read, "you can be a poet." Chapters include "Choosing a Subject," "Associations," "Fantasy," and "Imagery, Simile, Metaphor." For anyone who enjoys poetry and/or writing poems, Sears demonstrates through his student examples and commentary that poetry belongs to everyone.

23.15 Simon, Neil. **Biloxi Blues.** New American Library/Signet, 1988. 101 pp. ISBN 0-451-15392-8. Fiction.

It is the summer of 1943 in Biloxi, Mississippi, and Eugene Norris Jerome is bound for Army basic training. This play recounts Eugene's experiences with the tough Sergeant Toomey and his company of colorful young recruits. Eugene pledges not to beat the German and Japanese, but to "become a writer, not get killed, and lose his virginity." Mature language and situations.

24 Politics and Law

24.1 Ashabranner, Melissa, and Brent Ashabranner. **Counting America: The Story of the United States Census.** G. P. Putnam's Sons, 1989. 101 pp. ISBN 0-399-21747-9. Nonfiction.

Did you know that it cost ten dollars per person to take the 1990 census? Did you know that in spite of the tremendous effort made to find everyone, it is estimated that 5.9 percent of young black males were not counted? Did you know that not even the FBI or the IRS can look at an individual census questionnaire? Mandated by the Constitution in order to distribute representation to Congress, the census has been taken every decade since 1790. Attempting to explain the importance of this giant project, the Ashabranners trace the history of the census, explain the how and why of the process, and examine how the information is used by the government, as well as by business and industry. While the basic goal is to count every man, woman, and child living in the United States, the census also takes a picture of the nation at a given moment in time showing who we are, what we need, and where we need it.

24.2 Chancellor, John. **Peril and Promise: A Commentary on America.** Harper and Row, 1990. 176 pp. ISBN 0-06-016336-4. Nonfiction.

John Chancellor, commentator for the NBC Nightly News, fears that America is in a rapid social, political, and economic decline from which it may not recover unless the way we operate and manage our affairs is reconsidered. He addresses issues such as foreign competition, the national debt, and the challenges facing the educational system. Although he is very worried about the path the country is taking, he remains optimistic, providing an interesting analysis of why we are in our current predicament and how we can work to improve the future.

24.3 Kavanaugh, Michelle. **Emerald Explosion.** Pineapple Press, 1988. 191 pp. ISBN 0-910923-46-9. Fiction.

Patrick Kendal, a seventeen-year-old from Miami, whose mother, a top scientist, is reported killed in Russia, decides to find out what really happened. He succeeds in getting to Russia where he discovers that his mother is alive and that she has defected. With the help of his computer-genius brother, Patrick becomes involved in stealing scientific theories. Romance between Patrick and Rina, a Russian citizen, provides a glimpse into real life in Russia.

24.4 Landau, Elaine. **Armed America: The Status of Gun Control.** Julian Messner, 1991. 128 pp. ISBN 0-671-72386-3. Nonfiction.

Beginning with facts and stories about incidents of gun-related deaths in America, the author gives a historical perspective of how and why gun ownership has increased dramatically in the past few years. Reasons for and against gun control are illustrated with real-life stories in which people have been killed or saved by the use of guns. A listing and views of interest groups on both sides of the issue are given in this fact-filled book.

24.5 Meltzer, Milton. **American Politics: How It Really Works.** Illustrated by David Small. Morrow Junior Books, 1989. 185 pp. ISBN 0-688-07494-4. Nonfiction.

If you are growing up in the United States, do you need to know how politics works? Our schools, our workplaces, our government, and our lives are all influenced by politics. You can learn how politics works and how to bring about change in this clear and understandable analysis of the political system.

24.6 Nixon, Joan Lowery. **A Candidate for Murder.** Delacorte Press, 1991. 210 pp. ISBN 0-385-30257-6. Fiction.

Cary Amberson's life is changed dramatically when she overhears two men talking at a party. Although she does not understand what she hears, she senses foul play. Then she knows something is going on when she receives mysterious late-night phone calls suggesting that her life is in danger. Her father, a wealthy oilman, is running for governor of Texas, and she is certain that it is all tied in together. Her friends begin to tease her, newspapers draw cartoons of her father, and the family walks a tightrope not knowing who wants to harm him. Will these events make her father drop out of the race?

24.7 Polovchak, Walter, with Kevin Klose. **Freedom's Child: A Courageous Teenager's Story of Fleeing His Parents—and the Soviet Union—to Live in America.** Random House, 1988. 246 pp. ISBN 0-394-55926-6. Nonfiction.

Walter Polovchak was only twelve when he arrived in Chicago from a small city in the Ukraine, yet he was immediately attracted by the freedoms and fast pace of American life. Just six months later, in July 1980, when his disillusioned parents wanted to return to the Soviet Union, Walter defiantly announced his decision to remain in Chicago. His bewildered parents had him brought in to the police station as a runaway, and soon the U.S. State Department, the Immigration and Naturalization Service, and the American Civil Liberties Union were involved in his legal battle to remain in the U.S. It took six years for Walter's case to go through the legal system, but in the end he was victorious. Walter describes his impressions of his early years in the Ukraine (where there were constant food shortages and where his father sometimes sold on the black market the gifts sent to the family by American relatives) and of the United States (where Walter was amazed to see a supermarket aisle devoted to dog food and where it appeared to him that everyone had a car).

24.8 Reedy, George E. **The U.S. Senate: Paralysis or a Search for Consensus.** New American Library/Mentor, 1988. 220 pp. ISBN 0-451-62608-7. Nonfiction.

Insider George Reedy writes about the Senate and its productivity during the 1950s. His purpose in examining the powerful senators, their cooperation, their disagreements, and how they worked out compromises is to shed some light on what was done right and what was done wrong. He explains how the Senate works and what he sees as its function in balancing the presidency and the House of Representatives.

24.9 Richardson, Robert O. **The Weird and Wondrous World of Patents.** Edited by Timothy Nolan. Sterling, 1990. 160 pp. ISBN 0-8069-7250-5. Nonfiction.

A device for producing dimples, a guard that prevents food from lodging in your moustache, a face fly mask for dairy cows, and a unique device for waking people from sleep are among patents illustrated, as well as more serious inventions like the internal combustion engine, aerial railway and car, and the teeth protector on a football helmet. Patents, patent law, and the Patent Office requirements are explained. Almost all patents stem from inventions by people who had an idea on how to improve an existing article, or by people who, from necessity, invented something new. All it takes is an idea. This book may stimulate more ideas—and patents. Ideas, anyone?

24.10 Romney, Ronna, and Beppie Harrison. **Momentum: Women in American Politics Now.** Crown, 1988. 229 pp. ISBN 0-517-56890-X. Nonfiction.

Politics is not just a realm for men, and such women as Geraldine Ferraro, Jeanne Kirkpatrick, and Elizabeth Dole, among others, prove that both sexes can play the political game. Drawing on the biographies of these and other women, the authors present an insider's look at American politics and the role women play in it. From fundraisers to campaign managers and from the local to the federal level, all aspects of the political machine are dissected to explore what makes them work and how today's women work within the structure, as well as how women are breaking the boundaries long held sacred by the men at the top.

24.11 Weiss, Ann E. **Who's to Know? Information, the Media and Public Awareness.** Houghton Mifflin, 1990. 182 pp. ISBN 0-395-49702-7. Nonfiction.

A devastating Chinese earthquake is reported eighteen years later, for the first time in Western newspapers. It takes forty years to learn about radioactive waste dumped in Ohio. Who decides what news we get, and what gets covered and what doesn't in the media? Using contemporary examples, Weiss discusses such vital issues as the public's right to know, freedom of speech, censorship, who is controlling the information we receive, and what that may mean to us.

25 Reference

25.1 Darnell, Jane. **Rhyme Your Way to a Powerful Vocabulary.** Henry Holt/Owl Books, 1990. 329 pp. ISBN 0-8050-1258-3. Nonfiction.

Author Darnell has arranged two hundred and fifty-eight groups of four synonyms each into rhyming and/or rhythmic patterns to aid the growth of vocabulary. The book's main purpose is preparation for SAT exams, but obviously vocabulary enrichment is a lifetime achievement.

25.2 Gilbert, Sara. **Go for It: Get Organized.** Morrow Junior Books, 1990. 100 pp. ISBN 0-688-08852-X. Nonfiction.

This author has some very practical ideas on time management. Her nine-step plan begins with the SOS (Simplify, Order, Steps) system, a basic "first-aid kit" or set of principles for organizing anything. This is followed by strategies for defining and prioritizing goals, and then techniques for finding, making, and using time to accomplish them. Lots of examples and a helpful, easy-to-use Go Chart are included. Although the system is flexible enough to be useful to different types of teenagers, the key to improvement with this or any other self-help system is not in the reading but in the honest self-evaluation and subsequent action taken by the reader.

25.3 Hendrickson, Robert. **The Henry Holt Encyclopedia of Word and Phrase Origins.** Henry Holt/Owl Books, 1990. 581 pp. ISBN 0-8050-1251-6. Nonfiction.

Explanations of some 7500 words and phrases are offered in an easy-to-read and humorous style. Surprising, little-known facts about our lively language make this an encyclopedia that's fun to read, as do the amusing contradictions often present in our phrases and expressions. For example, the phrase " 'I wouldn't know him from Adam' doesn't make much sense, because Adam had no navel, wore only a fig leaf, and shouldn't have been hard to identify at all."

25.4 Higgins, George V. **On Writing: Advice for Those Who Write to Publish (or Would Like To).** Henry Holt, 1990. 226 pp. ISBN 0-8050-1180-3. Nonfiction.

George Higgins has written a readable, hands-on manual for writers. This is not a handbook of punctuation and grammar but an entertaining and useful discussion any writer would enjoy. Higgins offers a running commentary on changes in the writing profession in recent years.

25.5 Kohn, Alfie. **You Know What They Say . . . The Truth About Popular Beliefs.** HarperCollins, 1990. 236 pp. ISBN 0-06-016040-3. Nonfiction.

You know what they say . . . chocolate causes acne, boys are better at math than girls, blondes have more fun, breakfast is the most important meal of the day. . . . There is no end to what "they" say! But brunettes, chocolate lovers, and those who feel ill at the mere sight of food before noon may rejoice, as this carefully researched and clearly-written book points out, what "they" say often has no basis in reality. Once you read this book, you can attack math class with new confidence, feel free to swim right after a meal, and refuse those candied carrots if you want to—they won't do anything for your eyes!

25.6 Lutz, William. **Doublespeak: From "Revenue Enhancement" to "Terminal Living".** Harper and Row, 1989. 290 pp. ISBN 0-06-016134-5. Nonfiction.

What do you think a "previously distinguished car" is? A used car, of course! How about "negative patient care outcome" or "terminal living"? What they are trying to say is that the patient is dead. In this entertaining and yet sobering analysis of how language is used to camouflage reality, Professor William Lutz offers many such examples of organizational mumbo-jumbo. Although the book's material is inherently funny, his more serious consideration is how language is routinely being used to deceive us, by government, businesses, and advertisers.

25.7 Paxson, William C. **The Mentor Guide to Writing Term Papers and Reports.** New American Library, 1988. 240 pp. ISBN 0-451-62612-5. Nonfiction.

Students who need to write term papers and reports will find this book to be a useful tool. Researching, narrowing topics, revising, and proofreading the first draft are all included in a step-by-step format. This book also provides help in developing appropriate writing styles, as well as assistance with punctuation and other technicalities. If you want to learn how to evaluate sources, take better notes, and avoid plagiarism, this may be just the book for you.

25.8 Rawson, Hugh, and Margaret Miner. **The New International Dictionary of Quotations.** New American Library/Signet, 1988. 485 pp. ISBN 0-451-15153-1. Nonfiction.

"Ask not what your country can do for you; ask what you can do for your country." Who said it? The *Dictionary of Quotations* can answer that and many other questions. More importantly, perhaps, a reader can browse and find snappy quotations on many subjects from advertising to zeal.

26 Romance

26.1 Aks, Patricia. **Impossible Love.** Fawcett/Juniper Books, 1991. 133 pp. ISBN 0-449-70297-9. Fiction.

Friends are important at the girls' boarding school, but they become much less so for Kim as she becomes the assistant to the new English teacher. Before she realizes it, she is shutting out her friends and rationalizing her long work hours as a way of earning more money. Her parents barely have enough money to meet the bills while her father is sick. Carrie, her best friend, tries to help Kim see the foolishness of falling in love with a teacher who is at least ten years older than Kim, but Kim has to come to grips with her own feelings by herself.

26.2 Ashley, Ellen. **Barri, Take Two.** Fawcett, 1991. 156 pp. ISBN 0-449-14584-0. Fiction.

Barri and her best friend, Melanie, are in New York, guests of Barri's aunt, Laura. Laura, a soap opera star, has arranged an audition for both of them for her soap opera. Barri and Melanie are given the star treatment and go to a cast party, where Barri meets a handsome daytime star who takes an interest in her. But is a national heartthrob the kind of boyfriend Barri really wants? This is the second book in the Center Stage series.

26.3 Ashley, Ellen. **Lights, Camera, Action.** Fawcett, 1991. 168 pp. ISBN 0-449-14586-7. Fiction.

This book, fourth in the Center Stage series, continues the high school acting adventures of Barri Gillette and her friends Melanie and Joel. This time, Barri is thrilled when her drama teacher, Mr. Heifetz, announces that a real Hollywood movie will be filmed at Fillmore High. Not only will it star Barri's favorite teen actor, Reed Spencer, but there will be a few small parts for local actors, too. Barri desperately wants a part to start her acting career. But conflicts develop when she begins dating Joel, and her family wants her to spend more time at home. Just when she thinks she has a part, Barri discovers some surprises about being a movie actress.

26.4 Ashley, Ellen. **Star Struck.** Fawcett, 1990. 148 pp. ISBN 0-449-14583-2. Fiction.

Barri Gillette has to decide between the leading role in the high school production written by her friend, Joel, and auditioning for the community theater production of *Romeo and Juliet.* She wants to appear in *Romeo and Juliet* because Ward McKenna, a television star, will be playing the part of Romeo. Barri's problems increase when she finds out that she will be in competition with her best friend, Melanie, for the part of Juliet. The conflicts force Barri to consider the price of fame and the value of loyalty. This is the first book in the Center Stage series.

26.5 Bloss, Janet Adele. **Two Boys Too Many.** Bantam Books, 1988. 152 pp. ISBN 0-553-27552-6. Fiction.

Jack Arnold is so popular and such a good athlete. On the other hand, Paul Zepperelli is so much fun. Bonnie Jean Tyler likes them both, and all goes well until she makes the same date with both boys for the Christmas dance. Forced to decide between them, she turns for advice to the bookish Brian Macklin, who helps her see through her confusion with a new perspective.

26.6 Boies, Janice. **Crossed Signals.** Bantam Books, 1988. 168 pp. ISBN 0-553-27593-3. Fiction.

Laura Newman is Amy Tyler's best friend, and all is fine until Laura's date to the concert, Ben Richardson, shows an interest in Amy. What is Amy to do? She cares for Laura, although Laura insists Amy never see Ben again, but she cares more and more for Ben. These new-found interests provide a real test for everyone involved in this friendship.

26.7 Boies, Janice. **Love on Strike.** Bantam Books, 1990. 168 pp. ISBN 0-553-28633-1. Fiction.

Do opposites attract? Lillie Evans asks classmate Jay Carson to help her with a promotional poster campaign to benefit a fundraiser for homeless children. As they work together, they grow to care for each other. Yet while dating, they notice the many disagreements they have. Can they agree to disagree?

26.8 Bracale, Carla. **Puppy Love.** Bantam Books, 1990. 136 pp. ISBN 0-553-28830-X. Fiction.

Jason Waring is the boy Wendy Thomas had always dreamed of—handsome and charming. They fall in love. There's one problem, however: Jason doesn't want her to go out with anyone else, including her friend, Scott, who she's been dating for many years. Can she retain Scott's friendship and keep Jason's love?

26.9 Buchan, Stuart. **Guys Like Us.** Dell/Laurel-Leaf Books, 1989. 149 pp. ISBN 0-440-20244-2. Fiction.

"First we meet them, then we worship them, then we fight, then we break up; then we write about them." So Harry summarizes his mother's romances and she ought to know; she's written forty romance novels. And from her, Harry may find answers about love. Harry and his friend, Zack, have much in common: both have one-parent families and both live on houseboats. Can the friendship survive both boys falling in love with a lovely, rich girl? The same lovely, rich girl? And is it true that guys like them don't belong with and never get such girls?

26.10 Busselle, Rebecca. **A Frog's-Eye View.** Orchard Books, 1990. 191 pp. ISBN 0-531-08507-4. Fiction.

When Nick, Neela's boyfriend, takes a day job and plays in a band, the new situation causes Neela to have too much time to herself, time she had planned to spend with Nick. Can she compete for Nick's attention against the attractive new girl who joins his band?

26.11 Campbell, Joanna. **True Love.** Bantam/Starfire Books, 1991. 199 pp. ISBN 0-553-25295-X. Fiction.

Caitlin's tragic secret haunts her. Jed Michaels has refused to see her since she let Diana Clausen take the blame for an accident that crippled a child. Caitlin resolves to make atonement and does find Diana's forgiveness, but she can't reunite with Jed unless she is completely honest with everyone. The final book in the Caitlin series.

26.12 Campbell, Joanna. **Loving.** Bantam/Starfire Books, 1991. 200 pp. ISBN 0-553-24716-6. Fiction.

Caitlin is beautiful, charming, rich, intelligent, and very clever. Caitlin, who has been told she is an orphan, is being raised by her wealthy grandmother. She has everything she could want—except love. She falls in love with a new student, Jed Michaels, and plots how she can win him. Then a tragedy occurs which changes her life. The first book in the Caitlin series.

26.13 Campbell, Joanna. **Love Lost.** Bantam/Starfire Books, 1991. 198 pp. ISBN 0-553-25130-9. Fiction.

Beautiful, rich, charming Caitlin seems to have everything. But there is a secret which haunts her life. She loves Jed Michaels, a fellow student at her exclusive Virginia boarding school, but can't find the courage to tell Jed her tragic secret. The second book in the Caitlin series.

26.14 Cooney, Caroline B. **Camp Reunion.** Bantam/Starfire Books, 1988. 180 pp. ISBN 0-553-27551-8. Fiction.

Can teens who were counselors at a summer camp for children resume their friendship several months later? This is the question Vi asks herself when she receives an invitation to a camp reunion over Thanksgiving weekend. As much as she wants to go, she considers staying away. There's no guarantee that her best camp friend, Marissa, will still feel close to her, and how should she feel about Jamie, her summer boyfriend?

26.15 Cross, Gillian. **Chartbreaker.** Dell/Laurel-Leaf Books, 1989. 181 pp. ISBN 0-440-20312-0. Fiction.

Janis Mary droops over her coffee cup until Christy and his rock band explode into her life. Christy knows how to force Janis to show her intense anger and turn it into song. He helps her create a tough public image called Finch, but under the Finch persona Janis can both love and hate Christy. It's like a love affair between two tigers, played out at rock concerts. Can love overcome anger?

26.16 Curtis, Stefanie. **Mr. Perfect.** Bantam Books, 1988. 152 pp. ISBN 0-553-27553-4. Fiction.

Popular, confident, and self-assured—Ned Taggert is everything Randi Hinton wishes to be. Being painfully shy, she is surprised and delighted when he takes an interest in her and offers to coach her with her speech for the student body. The lessons lead to dating, until the Christmas dance makes Randi doubt herself and Ned. Is Randi's shyness her own worst enemy? She'll need a special jolt of confidence to keep Mr. Perfect.

26.17 Danziger, Paula. **Remember Me to Harold Square.** Dell/Laurel-Leaf Books, 1988. 145 pp. ISBN 0-440-20153-5. Fiction.

Fourteen-year-old Kendra is bored with the idea of a long empty summer, when suddenly she has a house-guest, a fifteen-year-old boy. She and Frank spend the summer exploring culturally rich New York City. Can teenage love bloom during these comic and frantic dashes through the Big Apple?

26.18 Farish, Terry. **Shelter for a Seabird.** Greenwillow Books, 1990. 163 pp. ISBN 0-688-09627-1. Fiction.

Embittered by a teenage pregnancy, Andrea Tagg verbally attacks tourists and outsiders who invade her island home off the New York coast. The seabirds—terns—are her only love until she meets a young

AWOL deserter. Can she love a man as she loves these seabirds? Can she give up her angry denunciation of life and learn to accept and to love?

26.19 Feil, Hila. **Between Friends.** Fawcett, 1990. 167 pp. ISBN 0-449-14609-X. Fiction.

Tessa and Justine are friends spending a summer of work and fun on Cape Cod. When Keith, a college student, shows interest in first one girl and then the other, the girls learn important lessons about friendship and loyalty.

26.20 French, Michael. **Soldier Boy.** Bantam/Starfire Books, 1990. 173 pp. ISBN 0-553-28609-9. Fiction.

B.J. has joined the army after failing at college; Cliff has joined to fulfill his family's dream by becoming an officer. Nina and Melanie are friends attending high school in a small town near the army base. Each suffers disappointment as their plans for the future fail, and they turn to each other to decide what to do with their lives.

26.21 Gabhart, Ann. **Wish Come True.** Avon/Flare Books, 1988. 137 pp. ISBN 0-380-75653-6. Fiction.

Little did fifteen-year-old Lyssie know that the mirror she selected from Aunt Riva's attic had magical powers, until she wished for something and discovered that it had happened. It was wonderful—being prettier, having the most popular girl in school as a friend, and being noticed by the cutest boy in school—until Aunt Riva warned that a careless wish could cause something really terrible to happen.

26.22 Gorman, Susan. **The Game of Love.** Bantam Books, 1988. 150 pp. ISBN 0-553-27476-7. Fiction.

Cory Hughes is a popular, athletic junior at Glenbrook High School. She is dating Clark Williams, the school's star football player. Clark also coaches the girls' Powder Puff football team for which Cory plays. The boys' team has been struggling and the student body seems unconcerned; the girls' team, on the other hand, is having a winning season. Cory comes up with great ideas to win student support for the boys and to make money for the girls' uniforms. But all of her popularity, clever ideas, and athletic abilities seem to be causing problems in her relationship with Clark.

26.23 Greenberg, Joanne. **Of Such Small Differences.** Henry Holt, 1988. 262 pp. ISBN 0-8050-0902-7. Fiction.

John wants a normal life but obstacles stand in his way, all because he is blind and deaf. He reaches out to Leda, an aspiring young actress who returns his love. She wants to be his eyes and ears, and their everyday adventures bring joy into their lives. John records his thoughts of life, love, frustration, and pain into poetry which he sells for extra pocket money. Living independently is important to John and others like him, but neighbors reject those who are different. This is a real burden for John to carry alone, as Leda realizes her inadequacies in living with John in his limited world.

26.24 Grimes, Frances Hurley. **Love Lines.** Bantam Books, 1988. 149 pp. ISBN 0-553-27414-7. Fiction.

Dark-haired, blue-eyed Padraic McKennon is the first poet Anne Margaret Thorton has ever met. Scheming carefully, she joins a poetry workshop, hoping to interest the handsome young instructor. Tall, funny Tommy is one of Annie's oldest friends until he joins the workshop, threatens to disturb Annie's scheme, and develops a special interest in another girl in their class. Annie must decide what's imaginary and what's real, even if it means confusion, jealousy, and the disappointment of learning that life is not all romance.

26.25 Keene, Carolyn. **Going Too Far.** Archway Paperbacks, 1990. 152 pp. ISBN 0-671-67761-6. Fiction.

Carolyn Keene has always written stories about memorable teens and this book is a continuation of the River Heights series, based in Nancy Drew's hometown. Brittany Tate is delighted to be dating Jack Reilly and just can't wait for him to ask her to the country club dance. Complications arise as Jeremy Pratt tries to use Brittany to get close to her friend, Kim Bishop. But the gossip and the boy trouble are just beginning.

26.26 Laskin, Pamela. **Music from the Heart.** Bantam Books, 1990. 154 pp. ISBN 0-553-28551-3. Fiction.

Tone-deaf Madline Davis stays in the high school band to be near popular George Held, who plays saxophone. Jeff Lang, another talented band member, agrees to tutor Maddy, leading her to discover new feelings about her music and about the boys in her life.

26.27 Makris, Kathryn. **A Different Way.** Avon/Flare Books, 1989. 182 pp. ISBN 0-380-75728-1. Fiction.

Steve Lansing-Ames, a transfer student from back East, has to decide how to get into the "popular" crowd at Texas' Sam Houston High

School. Steve works part-time at a greenhouse where he meets Addy Florio, an "in-crowd" girl. His efforts to win her and rise to popular status are the novel's focus. Will he succeed, and will it be worth it?

26.28 Mango, Karin N. **Just for the Summer.** Charlotte Zolotow, 1990. 204 pp. ISBN 0-06-024038-5. Fiction.

At seventeen, Jenny Smith is a warm and caring girl, working as a summer camp counselor in New Hampshire. She notices a boy in the cabin next door who is about her age, but moody, withdrawn, and with a noticeable aura of tension around him. In her typical bubbly way, Jenny decides to befriend him and finds herself falling in love with a boy deeply tormented by the death of his father. The two become close friends and help each other work out some very painful incidents from their pasts. Jenny realizes that there are different expressions of courage in life, and she begins to reevaluate her attitude toward a deaf boy at home whom she hurt very badly.

26.29 Matthews, Phoebe. **The Boy on the Cover.** Avon/Flare Books, 1988. 154 pp. ISBN 0-380-75407-X. Fiction.

Love strikes fifteen-year-old Cyndi Carlisle as she looks at a picture of a boy on the cover of a book. She enlists her friend's help in finding out who the boy is. Belinda is quick to help Cyndi but only in exchange for Cyndi's help in snaring an excellent debate partner for herself. Much to Cyndi's surprise and dismay, she sees the boy on the cover one day in her high school. Using all of her ingenuity to keep her true feelings from him, she finally meets him, only to discover he has some secrets of his own—about her.

26.30 Mauser, Pat Rhoads. **Love Is for the Dogs.** Avon/Flare Books, 1989. 134 pp. ISBN 0-380-757230. Fiction.

How could fourteen-year-old Janna fall for Bramwell Hamilton, who neglects his dog, Pepper? To an animal lover, this is unforgivable. How can Janna rescue Pepper? She never thought her concern would lead to a nearly fatal drowning of Pepper and an attraction for Bramwell, the boy she was certain she hated.

26.31 Miller, Sandy. **Allegra.** New American Library, 1988. 205 pp. ISBN 0-451-15413-4. Fiction.

When Allegra Stephenson loses both her parents, she seems to have more than her share of sorrow. She will gain strength and courage from unexpected sources during her years in high school, but her dream of a career in music seems impossible. Allegra's first romance with Matt may be the road to her dreams—or is it?

26.32 Oldham, June. **Grow Up, Cupid.** Dell/Laurel-Leaf Books, 1989. 182 pp. ISBN 0-440-20256-6. Fiction.

When Mag decides to go to technical school, her teachers are delighted. Bored with boys as well as school, she writes three chapters of a romance novel, and the publishers are definitely interested. But how can you write authentically about romance if you've sworn off it? Perhaps, she decides, you have to keep your options open!

26.33 Pfeffer, Susan Beth. **Meg at Sixteen.** Bantam/Starfire Books, 1990. 182 pp. ISBN 0-553-05854-1. Fiction.

Five years after their father's death, the Sebastian Sisters gather for the marriage of their mother to another man. As the girls sort out their feelings, Meg spends a few hours alone to put the past behind her and to look to a happy future. This is Margaret Windore Sebastian's story—the year Meg turned sixteen and fell madly in love with charming, unpredictable Nicholas Sebastian. The author explores family ties and separations as individuals learn to take responsibility for their own lives and happiness.

26.34 Pfeffer, Susan Beth. **Thea at Sixteen.** Bantam/Starfire Books, 1988. 166 pp. ISBN 0-553-05498-8. Fiction.

Thea, the second oldest of the four Sebastian girls, hopes that her sixteenth birthday will mark the beginning of a wonderful year. Her father suggests that she volunteer at the local hospital, and she becomes a Friendly Visitor to twelve-year-old Gina, a cancer victim with little hope for recovery. Thea has no idea that her life is to change so much. Her weekly visits to Gina and the relationship she develops with Kip become important to her. And soon thereafter, Thea is unprepared for a family crisis; her loyalty is tested as she realizes the complexities of relationships and love. This second novel of the Sebastian Sisters series is a thoughtful exploration of family ties, at once tender and intense.

26.35 Pringle, Terry. **A Fine Time to Leave Me.** Algonquin Books of Chapel Hill, 1989. 293 pp. ISBN 0-945575-16-5. Fiction.

When Lori Lynn Connor breaks a soda bottle and cuts her foot in the grocery store where Chris Grey works, he knows it's fate: she is his woman! Unfortunately, she is a senior in college and he's a freshman; she is wealthy and he is poor. Saying to hell with it, Chris and Lori break class and age barriers, her mother's heart, and his bank account while giving in to their mutual passion. Things are confusing from the start, though, when Chris calls Lori and tells her he wants to "love her whole body," but it turns out to be Mrs. Connor he is propositioning! Things only get weirder, especially after the baby! As these two madcaps work out love, marriage, parenting, and growing up—all at once—you'll laugh at their hare-brained, passionate, and always well-meaning exploits.

26.36 Quin-Harkin, Janet. **Just Desserts.** Fawcett, 1990. 170 pp. ISBN 0-449-14535-2. Fiction.

Deborah and Joe's final summer is filled with both fun and disappointment when they find out that Heartbreak Café is to be replaced by a fancy resort, Paradise Inn! This fast romantic and adventurous novel explores feelings of all sorts. A *Heartbreak Café* book.

26.37 Quin-Harkin, Janet. **No Experience Required.** Fawcett, 1990. 186 pp. ISBN 0-449-14530-1. Fiction.

Deborah Lesley faces a new life when her parents unexpectedly divorce. Ultimately, working at the Heartbreak Café provides extra money and a more fulfilling lifestyle than the rich world she knew before. Teens having to make home adjustments will get a morale boost from this novel. A *Heartbreak Café* book.

26.38 Richards, Ann. **Cross-Country Match.** Bantam Books, 1988. 168 pp. ISBN 0-553-27413-9. Fiction.

Liz Martin is the only girl on Edenvale's cross-country team, and running is the most important part of her life—until she meets Tyler Haynes. Tyler is new in school and is on the team, too. Captain Steve Keller and Liz's dad are eager supporters of Liz's athletic efforts, but she sometimes feels pressured. When she becomes confused about her relationships with Tyler and Steve, her cross-country times suffer, as do her hopes of becoming a champion.

26.39 Schultz, Mary. **Fortunes of Love.** Bantam Books, 1988. 154 pp. ISBN 0-553-27358-2. Fiction.

Karen Daly has just broken up with Jeremy, who is overly possessive. Her family throws a wonderful sixteenth birthday party for Karen, and among the entertainment, a strange fortuneteller appears to Karen only. Her words about the future and a "mysterious match" lead Karen to seek out the right man for her.

26.40 Simbal, Joanne. **Long Shot.** Bantam Books, 1988. 134 pp. ISBN 0-553-27594-1. Fiction.

Ariel is interested in art and when she hears about the school's Winter Festival film contest, she decides to enter. Patty and Fudge agree to help. However, when they receive their subject, the ice hockey team, it is not what Ariel wanted at all. In fact, she hates jocks! As she begins work on the film, she realizes her old junior high boyfriend, Eddie, is on the team. She's still bitter about the past, and her feelings extend to all jocks, including Cooper Garris, co-captain of the hockey team, who finds her attractive.

26.41 Simpson, Holly. **Dream Time.** Fawcett, 1989. 138 pp. ISBN 0-449-14592-1. Fiction.

Casey Benson dreams of the Olympics, and she really is a great gymnast, though still a freshman at Fairfield High. The new girl, Sarabeth, is also a talented gymnast, but the competition that bothers Casey is not athletic but romantic. Will Brett follow Sarabeth's lead? And how can the team excel if Sarabeth will not be a serious athlete?

26.42 Smith, Anne Warren. **Blue Denim Blues.** Avon/Flare Books, 1988. 117 pp. ISBN 0-380-70379-3. Fiction.

Near the end of her freshman year, shy Janet Donovan feels like a fifteen-year-old failure. She is determined to change, so she gets a summer job as a teaching assistant at a nearby preschool. Mrs. Bailey, the teacher, recognizes her musical talent and puts her in charge of the children's music sessions. This gives Janet confidence, and soon she is performing in a bluegrass quartet that includes her father and the boy she has a crush on, Darrell. She finds that bringing others happiness through music helps her overcome her shyness.

26.43 Strasser, Todd. **Wildlife.** Dell/Laurel-Leaf Books, 1988. 180 pp. ISBN 0-440-20151-9. Fiction.

The Coming Attractions' worldwide tour was the most successful yet, but the band is falling apart. Gary Specter seems to be the only one who's got it together, especially after the other members take off on their own. Turning to his high school love, Allison, he tries to keep the band alive, his manager happy, and his own mental balance. Has too much already been destroyed and can he really count on Allison's friendship for help?

26.44 Thesman, Jean. **Couldn't I Start Over?** Avon/Flare Books, 1989. 170 pp. ISBN 0-380-75717-6. Fiction.

Life is good for Shiloh until she meets Lovey Sullivan, a new sophomore student at North Seattle High. If only she could have been warned about Lovey's true character and intentions! She steals Shiloh's best friend, Emily, as well as the boy she wanted for her boyfriend. Why was Shiloh so naive as to be tricked by Lovey's charms?

26.45 Weyn, Suzanne. **The Makeover Summer.** Avon/Flare Books, 1988. 121 pp. ISBN 0-380-75521-1. Fiction.

Best friends Rissa, Sara, and Marsha eagerly anticipate the upcoming summer vacation, one sure to be full of boys, summer jobs, and plenty of makeover club meetings. What they don't anticipate is the arrival of Lena Laffleberger, a clumsy exchange student from Zurich who is staying with Sara. After some makeover moves, the girls transform Lena into a pretty, almost too-popular type. Find out how the makeover club deals with the new Lena.

26.46 William, Kate. **The Love Bet.** Bantam Books, 1990. 151 pp. ISBN 0-553-28618-8. Fiction.

Dana Larson and Aaron Dallas are both fed up with love. But Elizabeth has a plan to make them fall in love with each other, even though they are opposites in almost every way. With help from Todd, Elizabeth bets it will be either a disaster or the match of the year.

26.47 William, Kate. **Ms. Quarterback.** Bantam Books, 1990. 150 pp. ISBN 0-553-28767-2. Fiction.

A female on the football team? Sweet Valley High needs a new quarterback, so Claire Middleton vies for the position. But ex-quarterback Ken Matthews, recently recovered from a head injury, is also competing. Can Ken's girlfriend, Terri Adams, find a way for him to resume his place on the team?

26.48 William, Kate. **Enid's Story.** Bantam Books, 1990. 213 pp. ISBN 0-553-28576-9. Fiction.

Enid Rollins seems to have her life together; she no longer runs with a wild crowd. Then something happens. She becomes interested in Jeffrey French, her girlfriend's ex-boyfriend, but she soon discovers that he hasn't gotten over Elizabeth yet. To make matters worse, Enid's alcoholic father appears, and she and Elizabeth have a disagreement. What should she do to feel wanted?

26.49 William, Kate. **Troublemaker.** Bantam Books, 1988. 166 pp. ISBN 0-553-27359-0. Fiction.

Julie Porter, a shy student at Sweet Valley High, is in love for the first time—with the most conceited jerk senior, Bruce Patman. Julie is the only one who can't see what everyone else can—that Bruce doesn't really care about her and that he has a nasty fraternity prank up his sleeve. Josh Bowen, Julie's friend and neighbor who is trying to get into Bruce's fraternity, sees Bruce for what he really is. Can he convince Julie he's the one for her and save his fraternity chances at the same time?

26.50 William, Kate. **Slam Book Fever.** Bantam Books, 1988. 137 pp. ISBN 0-553-27416-3. Fiction.

Slam books, do-it-yourself prediction lists about students at Sweet Valley High, are all the dangerous rage. They're dangerous because they cause trouble. Elizabeth and Jessica Wakefield, twins at Sweet Valley, start showing up on slam books everywhere. Elizabeth's been paired up as a future love of AJ Morgan, the boy her sister's fallen hard for. And Jessica has been branded the girl most likely to flirt. Suddenly, friends are turning friends against each other and slam books become the basis for a lot of trouble at school. Can friends straighten out the trouble, and will Elizabeth and Jessica work out theirs?

26.51 William, Kate. **Playing for Keeps.** Bantam Books, 1988. 165 pp. ISBN 0-553-27477-5. Fiction.

Jessica Wakefield, the spicy half of a twin set, wishes she could be more studious like her sister, Elizabeth. Why? She's in love with AJ Morgan, whom she's convinced likes the studious type. Yet just as she's contemplating turning herself into a shy, quiet type, she finds out about a promotional fashion show to pick the representative for Nadine's fashions. She'd love to enter but it might jeopardize her new image with AJ. Can she enter and still win AJ's love?

27 Science and the Environment

27.1 Baker, David. **The Henry Holt Guide to Astronomy.** Illustrated by David A. Hardy. Henry Holt/Owl Books, 1990. 280 pp. ISBN 0-8050-1197-8. Nonfiction.

What are the names of five constellations or of the nine planets in our solar system? What's the difference between a meteor and a meteorite? These and countless other questions about the universe are answered in this guide to astronomy. Color illustrations on nearly every page add to the reader's understanding.

27.2 Baldwin, J., editor. **Whole Earth Ecolog.** Crown/Harmony Books, 1990. 128 pp. ISBN 0-517-57658-9. Nonfiction.

The editors have compiled a list of environmentally conscious products and books, organized them into categories, and provided reviews and ordering information for them. The types of concerns they deal with are far-flung, from traditional issues like global warming and the rainforests, to more esoteric ones such as solar aquatics, the electromagnetic environment, and biospheres. There is sure to be something to catch your eye in this catchall compilation of environmentally correct consumables!

27.3 Bornstein, Sandy. **What Makes You What You Are: A First Look at Genetics.** Illustrated by Frank Cecala. Julian Messner, 1989. 115 pp. ISBN 0-671-63711-8. Nonfiction.

Where did you get those eyes, those ears, that nose, etc.? This book provides a clear understanding of genetics, the study of inherited traits and how they are transmitted. Helpful illustrations and interesting activities such as "building your own family tree" help the reader grasp this fascinating and complex subject. The roles that cells, genes, and chromosomes play in the mystery of life and growth are clearly explained.

27.4 Brennan, Richard P. **Levitating Trains & Kamikaze Genes: Technological Literacy for the 1990s.** John Wiley & Sons, 1990. 262 pp. ISBN 0-471-62295-8. Nonfiction.

A large number of Americans think that prehistoric people fought dinosaurs. They couldn't have—humans evolved much later—but this underscores Brennan's point about how little we know about science and technology. What will we use for energy in the not-so-distant future? What can computers really do? Can we clone humans already? Brennan provides clear and interesting explanations for many of the issues that we will soon have to face. As he notes, at our current level of technological ignorance, we compare to a fishing community which hasn't yet figured out that clouds bring rain!

27.5 Brown, Bruce, and Lane Morgan. **The Miracle Planet.** Gallery Books, 1990. 257 pp. ISBN 0-817-5999-2. Nonfiction.

Based on the PBS television series, this book is full of beautiful photographs and fascinating information about our planet. It explores the history of the planet and probes the question of whether or not the major periods of mass extinction will recur, eliminating humankind. It accompanies pilots who fly to the stratosphere to monitor the ozone layer, and delves to the depths of the ocean to investigate the "chimneys" that bubble there. The book touches on some of the most puzzling aspects of the Earth's 4.6 billion year history.

27.6 Feldman, David. **Why Do Clocks Run Clockwise? and Other Imponderables.** Illustrated by Kas Schwan. Harper and Row, 1987. 251 pp. ISBN 0-06-015781-X. Nonfiction.

Readers of David Feldman's book *Imponderables* suggested the subjects for this companion book. Feldman explores what he calls "Imponderables," those little nagging mysteries that appear to have no answer but which we ponder just the same. He provides solutions to a wide range of age-old mysteries: why people don't get goosebumps on their faces, why whips "crack," why one side of aluminum foil is shiny and the other dull, and why there are more brown M&M's than any other color. Feldman also invites readers to solve the top ten "Frustables," or frustrating Imponderables (such as why yawning is contagious) and to suggest more Imponderables for his next book. Black-and-white illustrations.

27.7 Flanagan, Dennis. **Flanagan's Version: A Spectator's Guide to Science on the Eve of the 21st Century.** Borzoi Books, 1988. 272 pp. ISBN 0-394-55547-3. Nonfiction.

Author Dennis Flanagan, who served as editor of *Scientific American* for four decades, describes for the nonscientist the major scientific discoveries during these years. Flanagan, a nonscientist himself, explains exciting innovations in the areas of physics, astronomy, geology, biology, and technology. For example, he discusses the physicists' search for their Holy Grail, a mathematical theory unifying and describing matter and energy, and the astronomers' exploration of the origin and evolution of the universe. Throughout, the focus is on the systematic, trial-and-error research of scientists that has led to these amazing discoveries.

27.8 Gibbons, Bob. **The Secret Life of Flowers: A Guide to Plant Biology.** Cassell/Blandford, 1990. 160 pp. ISBN 0-7137-2168-5. Nonfiction.

Flowers, in their many shapes, sizes, and colors, have always fascinated us. We enjoy wildflowers and cultivate flowers for their fragrance and beauty. This book shows how the flowering plant fits into the plant kingdom, how each separate part of the plant functions, and explains how and why flowers are produced. Using line drawings and color photographs, the book describes how a plant gets food and water, as well as the processes of respiration, transpiration, vegetative and sexual reproduction, pollination, and seed dispersal. There are also discussions of classification, evolution, and ecology.

27.9 Gorman, James. **The Man with No Endorphins and Other Reflections on Science.** Viking Penguin, 1988. 174 pp. ISBN 0-670-81842-9. Nonfiction.

The lighter side of science is featured in this collection of twenty-eight columns from *Discover* magazine. We learn that the toothpaste pump is the solution for sloppy tube-squeezers in need of "low-tech" help and that dogs are superior to cats because of their sense of humor (cats don't tell jokes, and when you tell one, they don't laugh). Additional essays discuss toilet tank valves, the problem of droppings from nonmigrating geese, and the positive impact on the economy caused by the fleas on our cats and dogs.

27.10 Hamilton, W. R., A. R. Woolley and A. C. Bishop. **The Henry Holt Guide to Minerals, Rocks and Fossils.** Photographs by Peter J. Green. Illustrated by Valerie Jones. Henry Holt/Owl Books, 1989. 320 pp. ISBN 0-8050-1118-8. Nonfiction.

This complete, accurate guide is designed to help you identify rocks, minerals, and fossils from all over the world. It is arranged as a practical field guide to provide both amateurs and experts with relevant information for identifying specimens. Many drawings and photographs accompany the explanations.

27.11 Hartmann, William K. **Cycles of Fire: Stars, Galaxies and the Wonder of Deep Space.** Illustrated by William K. Hartmann and Ron Miller, with Pamela Lee and Tom Miller. Workman Publishing, 1987. 189 pp. ISBN 0-89480-510-X. Nonfiction.

William K. Hartmann combines scientific explanation with brilliantly colored paintings to look at the universe beyond our solar system. The illustrations are based on astronomical research, geologic knowledge, artistic knowledge of light and landscape, and some intuition and imagination. Hartmann begins with an examination of stars and star systems and then looks at the galaxies in our universe. Many of the illustrations depict otherworldly landscapes on planets that astronomers believe may orbit many stars. The final chapter speculates about the possibilities of life forms existing on other planets. Third in a trilogy about the universe *The Grant Tour, Out of the Cradle.*

27.12 Hawking, Stephen W. **A Brief History of Time: From the Big Bang to Black Holes.** Illustrated by Ron Miller. Introduction by Carl Sagan. Bantam, 1988. 198 pp. ISBN 0-553-05340-X. Nonfiction.

This is an unusual book by an unusual author. Stephen W. Hawking, a brilliant theoretical physicist, is a victim of ALS, or motor neuron disease, and is unable to walk or talk, but he can communicate by means of a communications program that allows him to write books and to speak with a speech synthesizer. His topic is the nature of time and the universe. Was there a beginning of time? Will there be an end? Does the universe have boundaries? Hawking traces humankind's view of the world back to Aristotle and his belief that the earth was a round sphere rather than a flat plate. Hawking discusses Galileo's and Newton's discoveries and then explains, step-by-step, Einstein's general theory of relativity and the theory of quantum mechanics. Finally, he explores efforts to combine these two theories into a single quantum theory of gravity and its implications for the role of God.

27.13 Horner, John R., and James Gorman. **Digging Dinosaurs.** Illustrated by Donna Braginetz and Kris Ellingsen. Workman, 1988. 210 pp. ISBN 0-89480-220-8. Nonfiction.

In Montana in 1978, John Horner was the first to discover the fossils of a nest of baby dinosaurs. Nests of eggs had been discovered before but not ones with babies in them. It meant that this was a different kind of dinosaur. Unlike other reptiles, these dinosaurs did not just lay the eggs and leave them; these babies had been fed in the nest. Horner and James Gorman clearly explain what paleontologists do, the history of dinosaurs, and his other digs of discovery.

27.14 Kettelkamp, Larry. **Computer Graphics: How It Works, What It Does.** Morrow Junior Books, 1989. 144 pp. ISBN 0-688-07504-5. Nonfiction.

Today animation, mapmaking, and video games all depend on computer graphics, a combination of technology and art. Computer graphics have dramatically changed the ways in which illustrations can be drawn and expanded the ways in which illustrations can be used. This book explains the how and why of the many applications of computer graphics.

27.15 Kronenwetter, Michael. **Managing Toxic Wastes.** Julian Messner, 1989. 118 pp. ISBN 0-671-69051-5. Nonfiction.

Toxic waste is a contemporary plague of our world. How can we help to keep our world from becoming a garbage dump? This book talks about the challenges presented by chemicals, ash, gases, ozone depletion, landfills, and dumping waste in the ocean. It shows how we can meet these challenges by all working together. From the Issues for the 90s series.

27.16 Martin, Laurence W. **Nuclear Warfare.** Illustrated by Tony Gibbons, Peter Sarson, and Tony Bryan. Lerner, 1989. 48 pp. ISBN 0-8225-1384-6. Nonfiction.

Peace-keeping around the globe is serious business. Nuclear weapons, because of their capability for such catastrophic damage, present a great danger. This advancement in warfare technology has demanded an equal advancement in defense technology. Professor Laurence Martin discusses a number of missiles (air-to-surface, sea-launched, and land-based) as well as ways of controlling these nuclear forces. These tools, their uses, and their evolution are described and detailed in text, drawings, and diagrams. Glossary and index included.

27.17 McKibben, Bill. **The End of Nature.** Random House, 1989. 226 pp. ISBN 0-394-57601-2. Nonfiction.

We have reached "the end of nature." Bill McKibben does not mean the end of the world but "the end of a certain set of human ideas about the world and our place in it." We are generating global warming and are destroying the ozone layer by the carbon dioxide, methane, and chlorofluorocarbons (CFCs) we release into the atmosphere. We have taken nature for granted and misused it; and now, McKibben says, we must rethink our relationships with the land, animals, plants, water, and air which share this world with us.

27.18 Naar, Jon. **Design for a Livable Planet: How You Can Help Clean Up the Environment.** Harper and Row/Perennial Library, 1990. 338 pp. ISBN 0-06-055165-8. Nonfiction.

Did you know that evidence shows "radon in the home is the most deadly environmental hazard in America today"? Or that spider plants are "superior at removing carbon monoxide" while elephant ear philodendron "absorb large quantities of formaldehyde" from the air in your home? Naar's book provides descriptions of some of the biggest environmental problems facing us, and then suggests simple ways in which we can do our part to make our homes, communities and, eventually, the planet, happier, healthier places to live.

27.19 Rifkin, Jeremy, editor. **The Green Lifestyle Handbook.** Henry Holt/ Owl Books, 1990. 198 pp. ISBN 0-8050-1369-5. Nonfiction.

What shampoos contain animal by-products? Which bath soaps contain toxins? To protect ourselves and our environment, we all need to be aware of potentially harmful products, and to protect our pocketbooks, we need to know our rights as consumers. This guide offers you the knowledge of over twenty contributing authors to help you make wise choices. Specific name-brand products are examined, and lists of catalogue services, newsletters, consumer guide manuals, and individual stores providing environmentally safe products are provided.

27.20 Vare, Ethlie Ann, and Greg Ptacek. **Mothers of Invention: From the Bra to the Bomb: Forgotten Women and Their Unforgettable Ideas.** William Morrow, 1988. 256 pp. ISBN 0-688-06464-7. Nonfiction.

Many women do not receive credit for their inventions or discoveries. Dr. Lise Meitner, for example, discovered nuclear fission but refused to work on the atom bomb; her co-worker for thirty years, Dr. Otto Hahn, received the Nobel Prize, while Dr. Meitner did not. Did you know that Beatrix Potter, the author of the Peter Rabbit stories, discovered that lichen was not a variety of plant? Other women celebrities, including Lillian Russell and Hedy Lamarr, were also inventors.

27.21 Wilford, John Noble. **Mars Beckons.** Alfred A. Knopf, 1990. 244 pp. ISBN 0-394-58359-0. Nonfiction.

John Noble Wilford, *New York Times* science correspondent and two-time winner of the Pulitzer Prize, traces our fascination with Mars from the earliest written Babylonian records 3,000 years ago to today. He speculates on the fact that Mars is a planet capable of supporting a life form such as ours, considers colonization, and examines the natural resources that Mars offers. He describes the attempts to reach Mars, the eventual success of such spacecrafts as Viking I, and he dwells on the possibility of humans going to Mars in the twenty-first century. With full-color Viking I photographs, Wilford provides us with a thorough look at this mysterious red planet.

27.22 Xiyang, Tang. **Living Treasures: An Odyssey through China's Extraordinary Nature Reserves.** Bantam Books, 1987. 196 pp. ISBN 0-553-05236-3. Nonfiction.

When journalist Tang Xiyang was named editorial director of a Chinese nature magazine, he began exploring the network of nature reserves established some thirty years ago by the People's Republic of China. These reserves, currently numbering over 300 and scheduled to increase to 500 by the end of the century, cover five different climatic zones, from the tropical rain forests harboring gibbons in the south at Bawangling Nature Reserve on Hainan Island to the Swan Lakes in the northwestern province of Xinjiang, where there are only twelve frost-free days each year. Tang describes the more than 300 color photographs depicting the amazing plants, animals, ecosystems, and geological sites contained within the 42 million acres of China's nature reserves. The book concludes with a portrait gallery of 140 rare animals under government protection and 40 rare plants. Color photographs, map, black-and-white diagrams.

28 Science Fiction

28.1 Alton, Andrea I. **Demon of Undoing.** Baen Books, 1988. 308 pp. ISBN 0-671-65413-6. Fiction.

Fenobar is a crippled semi-pariah, his life spared because his father is a clan King in the rigid Imkairan society. But Fenobar adopts a legendary demon as his ally. Long ago, many demons had been on the planet, but they left voluntarily after realizing that their radical thinking was upsetting the way of life on the planet. However, now is Fenobar's hour of need, and to his astonishment, a furless, two-legged demon does appear to him. Despite the creature's annoying habit of referring to himself as "human," the little demon is Fenobar's greatest hope for winning respect and his own kingdom.

28.2 Apostolou, John L., compiler, and Martin H. Greenberg. **The Best Japanese Science Fiction Stories.** Dembner Books, 1989. 176 pp. ISBN 0-942637-06-2. Fiction.

This first anthology of Japanese science fiction translated to English should put to rest the notion of Godzilla as the best sci-fi Japan has to offer. Here are thirteen tales of universal appeal, exploring such common bonds as the desire to hide the bad things in the world, feelings of self-contempt, and the need to understand what's happening around us before we are destroyed. As the author notes in his introduction, these Japanese writers use the science fiction of the future to examine the science fact of the past. Set against the backdrop of Japanese culture, these stories look at where we've been and where we're going with clarity and insight.

28.3 Appel, Allen. **Till the End of Time.** Doubleday, 1990. 405 pp. ISBN 0-385-24944-6. Fiction.

Alex Balfour, a history teacher, has an unfortunate genetic predisposition to losing his place in the space-time continuum. In his latest time-traveling adventure, Alex finds himself in the middle of a world war and in a position to prevent the American bombing of Hiroshima! As he agonizes over whether he should change history or not, he runs into some interesting people, including Albert Einstein, Betty Grable, and Franklin Delano Roosevelt.

28.4 Asimov, Isaac. **Nemesis.** Doubleday/Foundation, 1989. 364 pp. ISBN 0-385-26619-7. Fiction.

Nemesis: a star, very much like our own sun, on which the future of Earth depends. In 2236, the galaxy has become a very crowded place. Earth's one hundred space colonies are nearly out of control, a sign that society is degenerating. Commissioner Janus Pitt sees the Nemesis star system as the chance for Utopia, a chance for Earth's people to start again, and he will fight to see that Utopia created. But even as he and his band of followers secretly make their way to Nemesis with their plans for ruling the galaxy, fifteen-year-old Marlene learns a terrible truth about the new star: it could destroy Earth and all of its colonies. This may not be enough to deter Commissioner Pitt, who will stop at nothing to achieve his dreams of power. Marlene finds herself and all of humankind hurtling toward a future of certain doom—and there may not be anything she can do to stop it.

28.5 Asprin, Robert. **Phule's Company.** Ace Books, 1990. 232 pp. ISBN 0-441-66251-X. Fiction.

Captain William Phule, mega-millionaire, is the galaxy's only commander whose military career *began* with his court-martial. Included in his company of military rejects are Brandy, an Amazonian terror; Super Gnat, the smallest and toughest Legionnaire; Beeker, the butler; and Tusk-Annini, an alien with the face of a warthog but a heart of gold. Phule's company is sent to a distant planet where Earth's military leaders hope they can do no damage. Unfortunately for Earth, hostile enemies are marauding the galaxy, and Phule's company is their target!

28.6 Bear, Greg. **Eternity.** Popular Library, 1988. 366 pp. ISBN 0-445-20547-4. Fiction.

A visitor from the end of time comes to post-nuclear war Earth to take a handful of voyagers into space-time. Their mission is to destroy the ultimate marvel of science, The Way, an "infinite corridor that slices across universes both human and inhuman." The voyagers are told that the existence of The Way "threatens to abort the ultimate goal—and purpose—of all creation." This space opera is the sequel to the bestseller, *Eon.*

28.7 Bedard, Michael. **Redwork.** Atheneum, 1990. 261 pp. ISBN 0-689-31622-4. Fiction.

Teenager Cass and his mother move into the upper floor of an old house while their reclusive old landlord, Mr. Magnus, lives on the ground floor. Cass is confused by a feeling of familiarity he has about the house and is curious about Mr. Magnus, who always seems to be doing something in the garage. Although the neighborhood is unfriendly, Cass finally finds a friend in Maddy, a girl he meets through work. The two of them slowly begin to discover what Mr. Magnus is up to and get involved in a supernatural search for "true meaning"!

28.8 Bell, Clare. **People of the Sky.** Tom Doherty Associates, 1989. 344 pp. ISBN 0-312-93131-X. Fiction.

When her plane is forced down into a canyon during a storm, Kesbe Temiya, a restorer of antique aircraft, discovers the lost colony of a Pueblo tribe which vanished two hundred years earlier. Kesbe is rescued by a villager and his Aronan, one of the flying alien creatures the Indians need for their survival. However, the villagers refuse to help her unless she is initiated into the tribe and bonds with her own Aronan, things no one from outside the tribe has ever done before!

28.9 Benford, Gregory. **Great Sky River.** Spectra Books, 1987. 326 pp. ISBN 0-553-05238-1. Fiction.

When the mech civilization destroys the Citadel, Killeen's father and wife are killed, but he and his son, Toby, escape with nearly three hundred other members of the Family Bishop. This small band of people is probably the last remnant of humanity still alive, and it sets off on a desperate flight from extinction, crossing the ruins of the once-lush planet Snowglade. But can the group avoid takeover by the artificial minds that now rule Snowglade and that are able to control the images in the humans' minds?

28.10 Bova, Ben. **Welcome to Moonbase.** Illustrated by Pat Rawlings. Ballantine Books, 1987. 254 pp. ISBN 0-345-32859-0. Fiction.

You have signed a contract to spend one year at Moonbase, the first permanent settlement on the moon. You are given a handbook to help you learn about life there. The manual has four main sections: the history of Moonbase, living conditions, the major lunar industries, and future expectations. You will live underground, but you can enjoy a swimming pool, use a large-screen TV as a window on the base, and take moonwalks. Welcome to Moonbase, your future.

28.11 Bull, Emma. **Falcon.** Ace, 1989. 281 pp. ISBN 0-441-22569-1. Fiction.

Teenager Niki Falcon loses his family and, in fact, his whole planet, through the schemes of an agent of the Central Worlds Concorde—a man whom he once considered a friend. Now Niki is a heroic star-pilot, a man with a mechanical nervous system, an altered metabolism, and connect ports on his wrists and the back of his skull. But the drug he must take to keep himself in superhuman condition is also systematically destroying his immune system!

28.12 Caraker, Mary. **The Faces of Ceti.** Houghton Mifflin, 1991. 201 pp. ISBN 0-395-54698-2. Fiction.

The dangers and challenges facing the early colonists to Ceti, a small planet in the Tau Ceti system, increase as they look for a food source. The jade plant, which grows abundantly, is their first disappointment—it is poisonous and unsafe to eat. Death, mystery, and a foreign colony become the enemies of the colonists. Maya, although interested in Brock as a future mate, has too many responsibilities in helping her mother care for her baby sister and serving as her mother's lab apprentice to make any long commitment to Brock. She worries about his return after an enemy steals their rocket equipment and their food, then departs for another living site. Maya matures into womanhood in this strange place.

28.13 Caraker, Mary. **The Snows of Jaspre.** Houghton Mifflin, 1989. 234 pp. ISBN 0-395-48292-5. Fiction.

In a dazzling atmosphere of ice and snow, on an exotic planet named Jaspre, there lives a mystery man, Anders Ahlwen, who possesses extraordinary abilities. Is the source of his power good or evil? During the twenty-fourth century Morgan Farraday, an administrator from earth, arrives on Jaspre with her teenaged daughter, Dee, to begin a new job. What she finds are conflicts and dangers. To survive and succeed, she must get Ahlwen's help and has to decide whether to risk seeking him out in the ice caves of Lumisland.

28.14 Clarke, Arthur C., and Gentry Lee. **Cradle.** Warner Books, 1988. 293 pp. ISBN 0-446-51379-2. Fiction.

Miami Herald reporter Carol Dawson is filming a story about beached whales off Key West, Florida—or so it seems. In fact, the whales are a cover for her investigation of the U.S. Navy. Carol is trying to locate a top-secret cruise missile that vanished off the Florida coast on its way to a target near the Bahamas. But the Navy is also frantically trying to track down the missile before anyone learns of its existence, and Commander Vernon Winters knows that his military career depends on locating the missile. When Carol discovers whales behaving in a bizarre manner, underwater tank tracks, and a strange hole in the sea bed, she and the crew of the *Florida Queen* are suddenly caught up in a terrifying battle with killers, military police, and an alien force, and the survival of the human race seems in doubt.

28.15 Crispin, A. C. **Starbridge.** Ace Books, 1989. 309 pp. ISBN 0-441-78329-5. Fiction.

"We are not alone. . . . Across the galaxy, there are eleven known intelligent races. Humankind is the twelfth. We are about to meet our neighbors. . . ." And when we do, the encounter inexplicably becomes violent. It's up to a young human woman, an "alien" male, and a reluctant, grouchy human physician to travel the galaxy looking for salvation!

28.16 Dickinson, Peter. **Eva.** Dell/Laurel-Leaf Books, 1990. 219 pp. ISBN 0-440-20766-5. Fiction.

In the world of the future, great strides have been made in medical technology. Following an automobile accident, thirteen-year-old Eva is in an irreversible coma. Then doctors decide to try an experiment. They put her memory and brain patterns into a new body—that of a chimpanzee named Kelly. The new Eva/Kelly must learn to live in two worlds at once—the animal world and the human world.

28.17 Dickson, Gordon R. **Wolf and Iron.** A Tom Doherty Associates Book, 1990. 468 pp. ISBN 0-312-93214-6. Fiction.

America is on the brink of another Dark Ages, and young scientist Jeebee decides to brave the journey across the lawless and desolate post-Collapse country to find the one place where he can keep scientific thought alive. What keeps *him* alive, however, is Wolf, the huge animal, raised by humans, whose survival instinct is much more developed than Jeebee's. Together they teach one another how to survive, hope, and work for the future of life on the planet.

28.18 Duane, Diane. **Spock's World.** Pocket Books, 1988. 310 pp. ISBN 0-671-66851-X. Fiction.

In this *Star Trek* novel, the inhabitants of the planet Vulcan are moving toward secession from the Federation of hundreds of planets in the galaxy. The U.S.S. *Enterprise* is summoned to Vulcan from a twenty-third century Earth, halfway across the galaxy. Commander Spock and Captain James T. Kirk are to give testimony at the proceedings regarding the Referendum on repeal of the Vulcan Articles of Federation, testimony reinforcing the favors that the Federation has performed for Vulcan, Spock's home planet. On the other side is a strong proponent—Sarek, Spock's father. As Spock and Kirk struggle to preserve the future of the Federation, readers learn more about Spock's origins and about the innermost secrets of Vulcan, from merciless tribal warfare to medieval court intrigue, from exploration of space to the development of *c'thia,* the ruling ethic of logic.

28.19 Felice, Cynthia, and Connie Willis. **Light Raid.** Ace, 1989. 229 pp. ISBN 0-441-48311-9. Fiction.

Seventeen-year-old Hellene Ariadne, the daughter of a distinguished scientist, is evacuated from her home as a fierce war rages between the eastern and the western portions of North America. Her safety is short-lived, however, for when she finds out that her hometown was bombed and that her parents have disappeared, she sets out to discover what happened to them. Although she finds out that they are not dead, her relief is quickly replaced with horror by the situation they are in and the knowledge of what she must face in order to make things right again.

28.20 Foster, Alan Dean. **To the Vanishing Point.** Warner Books, 1988. 310 pp. ISBN 0-446-51338-5. Fiction.

A drive across the Mojave Desert in a motor home turns from boring to frightening when Frank Sonderberg, his wife, Alicia, and his children, sixteen-year-old Wendy, a rock music addict, and ten-year-old Steven, a junk-food addict, give a ride to a stranded young singer with violet eyes and dressed in a flowing, multi-hued silk gown. Once Mohostosocia, or Mouse, is aboard, the desert landscape becomes strange and ominous, and when huge rats wielding axes jump onto the motor home and try to force their way inside, the Sonderbergs are terrified. Mouse reveals that she is on a mission to save the cosmos from the evil Lord of Chaos by using her song to heal the Spinner, the entity who spins and weaves the fabric of existence. Together the Sonderbergs and Mouse struggle to reach the universe's Vanishing Point, the place where Mouse's magic can soothe the Spinner and restore its natural rhythm.

28.21 Gibson, William. **Mona Lisa Overdrive.** Bantam, 1988. 260 pp. ISBN 0-553-05250-0. Fiction.

In a future where world-dominating multinational corporations battle for power with high-tech outlaws, Mona, a young woman with a murky past and an uncertain future, is on a collision course with the internationally famous Sense/Net star Angie Mitchell. Angie has the ability to travel into the bizarre, hallucinatory, computer-generated universe known as cyberspace, and she can enter this artificial universe of hoodoos, loas, and mambas without a computer. From inside the matrix a phantom being, an entity that trades vast accumulations of stored data to get what it wants, is masterminding a kidnapping plot. What the entity wants now is Angie—and the rest of humanity.

28.22 Ingrid, Charles. **Lasertown Blues.** Donald A. Wollheim/DAW Books, 1988. 288 pp. ISBN 0-88677-260-5. Fiction.

The sole Dominion Knight survivor of The Sand Wars, Jack Storm, seeks out the traitor who caused the annihilation of his army at Milos. He secures a position in the Guard of Emperor Pepys to see how far the enemy has penetrated. With the help of his sentient battle armor and a beautiful psychic named Amber, he makes plans to defeat the evil force dedicated to the destruction of the human Dominion Empire. Can he overcome the enemy who will fireburn a planet to destroy him? Sequel to *Solar Kill.*

28.23 Ingrid, Charles. **Solar Kill.** Donald A. Wollheim/DAW Books, 1987. 301 pp. ISBN 0-88677-209-5. Fiction.

A forty-two-year-old mind in a twenty-year-old body gives a revenge-filled man certain advantages; so does a knight's suit of armor. The combination makes a killing machine. Jack Storm is determined to follow the code of honor he pledged to when he became a knight—seventeen years of deep-sleep ago. But Jack is no machine. Can he really fight evil in the Empire and not be beset by longing for love, loneliness, and other human emotions? Followed by *Lasertown Blues.*

28.24 Lichtenberg, Jacqueline. **Dreamspy.** St. Martin's Press, 1989. 335 pp. ISBN 0-312-03327-3. Fiction.

Kyllikki is a powerful Teleod telepath working with the Metaji. The two groups, however, are at war, a war which threatens to destroy the space-time continuum and render space travel impossible forever. Kyllikki is desperately trying to reconcile the two groups, and her only hope is to utilize the unique feature that humans have, the capacity to dream. She must unlock the powers buried in the mind of Elias, the human man she is beginning to love, in order to save the galactic governments from crumbling.

28.25 Lichtenberg, Jacqueline. **Those of My Blood.** St. Martin's Press, 1988. 402 pp. ISBN 0-312-02298-0. Fiction.

Astrophysicist Titus Shiddehara fights to maintain his composure when he recognizes the late-arriving final passenger in their compartment for the flight to the moon. It is Abbot Nandoha, his "father," who previously awakened Titus to the life of a vampire by giving of his own blood. Now the two are on a collision course. While both are lurens, a race of extraterrestrial vampires, Titus is a Resident and considers Earth his home. Abbot is a Tourist and looks on humans solely as food. An alien spaceship has crashed on the moon, and Titus's Project Hail hopes to identify the homestar of the spaceship and beam back a message of friendship from Earth to the aliens. Abbot's mission is to send out an SOS to the luren homeworld along with the humans' message, an SOS that would reveal Earth's location and ask for rescue, thus leading to the subjugation of all humanity. A possible source of help is a survivor of the lunar crash who is a luren, but neither Tourist nor Resident. However, no one knows his or her identity.

28.26 MacAvoy, R. A. **The Third Eagle: Lessons along a Minor String.** Doubleday/Foundation, 1989. 301 pp. ISBN 0-385-24919-5. Fiction.

Wanbli, a young warrior, sets out to find new worlds by sailing among the galaxies, going from ship to ship. Finally he comes in contact with the Earth colony ship *Condor,* which left Earth long before Wanbli's people did. The *Condor* traveled slowly, being overtaken by faster ships and losing its place in the universe. The only remaining mission for the *Condor* and its people is to scavenge the stars for debris; to seek out other ships wandering through the ages and to try to save them from their fate. When Wanbli stumbles across the colony ship *Commitment,* he feels a special kinship with those aboard it and begins to realize his mission in life.

28.27 Maguire, Gregory. **I Feel Like the Morning Star.** Harper and Row, 1989. 275 pp. ISBN 0-06-024021-0. Fiction.

Fifteen-year-old Sorb has been a resident of the Pioneer Colony for almost five years. The colony is located four thousand feet below the surface of the earth. An atomic explosion has closed the tunnels leading out. Sorb wonders why no one questions the strict rules of the Elders. He also wonders why no one tries to find a way back to the surface. When Sorb asks these questions of others, he is punished by a chemical "treatment." Can he and his two friends escape?

28.28 McCaffrey, Anne. **Dragonsdawn.** Ballantine/Del Rey, 1988. 431 pp. ISBN 0-345-33160-5. Fiction.

After a voyage of fifteen years, the 6,000 colonists of the Pern Colonial Expedition reach their destination. Pern is a planet similar to Earth in appearance, yet far enough from the center of the galaxy that it has not been ravaged by industrial development or interstellar warfare. All goes well with the colony for nearly eight years, but then disaster strikes. Deadly spores fall like silver threads from gray storm clouds and consume anything organic, leaving behind writhing masses of engorged sluglike forms. The colonists cannot possibly repel the onslaught of the Thread themselves, especially when they determine that the siege may last up to fifty years. Inspired by watching small dragonlike lizards, called dragonets, shoot flames that incinerate the Thread, the colonists set eminent geneticist Kit Ping to work at creating creatures which might save their planet from the thread—dragons. A *Dragonriders of Pern* book.

28.29 McCaffrey, Anne. **The Rowan.** Ace/Putnam, 1990. 335 pp. ISBN 0-399-13570-7. Fiction.

There is only one survivor of the tragic mudslide at the small Rowan mining camp on the planet Altair. The whole planet knows about the three-year-old girl who escapes because she is projecting her distress so strongly on a psychic level that it can even be heard off-world. Even in a future which has learned to accept, value, train, and utilize Talents, the Rowan child, as she comes to be called, is a unique power. The unusual girl, with her strange silver hair and big brown eyes, grows up to be a lonely woman, inhibited by her Talent from having normal relationships with others—that is, until the wild Talent, Jeff Raven, psychically storms into her life one day. Unfortunately, his planet is under attack from aliens, and the powers that be are reluctant to send him aid. Has she finally found a man she can love, only to lose him?

28.30 McIntyre, Vonda N. **Starfarers.** Ace, 1989. 280 pp. ISBN 0-441-78053-9. Fiction.

Victoria Fraser MacKenzie believes it is humankind's destiny to explore the depths of space and to make first contact with alien beings. It's been attempted before—but the first research ship never returned to earth. Now it's the starship *Starfarer*'s turn to try, and Victoria is team leader of what might be the most important voyage in history. But the government has other ideas; it wants to turn *Starfarer* over to the military. Will Victoria and her determined team allow their dreams to be taken from them? Or will they do something desperate, like hijack the *Starfarer*?

28.31 Moore, Alan, and David Lloyd. **V for Vendetta.** Warner Books, 1990. 286 pp. ISBN 0-446-39190-5. Fiction.

London in the late 1990s is a controlled state. The nuclear war of a few years earlier has left behind a society ruled by the military, where concentration camps and midnight raids of homes are once again commonplace. It is in this place that "V," a former prisoner of a medical experimentation camp, sets out to destroy not just the people who held him prisoner, but the rest of society as well. It is his vendetta. A graphic novel.

28.32 Murphy, Pat. **The City, Not Long After.** Doubleday/Foundation Books, 1989. 244 pp. ISBN 0-385-24925-X. Fiction.

Only about one hundred people are living in San Francisco fifteen years after the plague killed almost everyone. Teenagers like Danny Boy and Jax cannot remember what life was like before. Now all they know is the looted, empty stores and homes, the artists' colony, the threat of war, and the monkeys. The monkeys were brought from Nepal to many cities of the world as a symbol of peace. The monkeys brought with them the plague—and so a kind of peace. Now war threatens again.

28.33 Pike, Christopher. **See You Later.** Archway Paperbacks, 1990. 226 pp. ISBN 0-671-67657-1. Fiction.

Time travel, intrigue, and death are parts of this story, whose plot resembles a computer game. Mark has a crush on Becky, a clerk in a record store that carries the games he has created. But because Becky already has a boyfriend, she won't date Mark. Later in the same shop, Mark meets Vincent, a quiet young man also interested in computer games. Vincent and his roommate Kara change the course of Mark's and Becky's lives in this adventure.

28.34 Preuss, Paul. **Starfire.** Tom Doherty Associates, 1988. 310 pp. ISBN 0-312-93056-9. Fiction.

Travis Hill, a petroleum geologist and an astronaut, is inside a small satellite when it ruptures the Euclid space station's air lock and is unable to dock. His air supply is sufficient to wait on docking, but the Euclid's orbit will expose him to enough solar radiation to prevent him from flying in space again. Boldly disobeying NASA's orders, Hill decides to be the first astronaut to try out the emergency escape pod and parachute device, similar in size to a portable toilet, that can take him directly to Earth. Although Hill survives the harrowing descent and becomes a public hero, NASA's response to such insubordination is to ground him. He leaves NASA and starts a private center for asteroid study, but he is determined to get into space one more time. Coincidentally, the first manned flight to the inner solar system is being planned for the spaceship *Starfire.* Is it possible for Hill to be named to that flight? Perhaps his wealthy, influential Texas family will come in handy.

28.35 Robinson, Kim Stanley. **The Gold Coast.** TOR, 1988. 389 pp. ISBN 0-312-93050-X. Fiction.

At age twenty-seven, Jim McPherson is still trying to find himself. The would-be poet teaches a night class in basic English and is a part-time word processor for a real estate firm, but neither job holds any interest for him. He can't seem to get along with his father, an aerospace engineer at work on a top secret Pentagon project. What is exciting to Jim is his own fast-paced social life in twenty-first-century Orange County, California—a continuous cycle of parties and designer drugs. When antiwar activist Arthur Bastanchury tells Jim about a secret revolutionary organization that intends to slow down the giant military-industrial complex, this seems like a chance for Jim to act on his beliefs and make a difference in the world. But speeches and demonstrations are not for this group—instead, its members have turned to sabotage. And now Jim is caught up, too.

28.36 Rubinstein, Gillian. **Beyond the Labyrinth.** Orchard Books, 1990. 245 pp. ISBN 0-531-08499-X. Fiction.

Cal, an alien anthropologist on earth to study an aboriginal tribe in Australia, meets fourteen-year-old Brenton. Their friendship is heightened by their desire to save the world. Brenton's dice have always helped him make important decisions for all life's choices. Can they help him now to make decisions that could change everything about his life on earth?

28.37 Sanders, Scott Russell. **The Engineer of Beasts.** Orchard Books, 1988. 258 pp. ISBN 0-531-05783-6. Fiction.

Mooch fixes the robot animals for New Boston Disney and its engineer of beasts, Orlando Spinks. But that's by day. At night she dreams of the wilderness beyond the domes of New Boston, the wilderness where she is sure she was born and raised by bears. Mooch doesn't believe what she's been told all of her life—that she was born from a test tube. Now she plans on reaching that distant wilderness at any cost. Even old and trusted friends like Garrison Rathbone can't stop her, but a dose of Dr. Bob's reality therapy might just bring all of her dreams to an end.

28.38 Shettle, Andrea. **Flute Song Magic.** Avon/Flare Books, 1990. 217 pp. ISBN 0-380-76225-0. Fiction.

There are two distinct classes in the Nelvin society—Flutirr is one of the very highest class. When he hears exceptional music played by someone from the lower class, he could lose everything if he is caught enjoying it. How should Flutirr begin this dangerous quest to find the music?

28.39 Sleator, William. **Singularity.** Bantam/Spectra Books, 1986. 198 pp. ISBN 0-553-25627-0. Fiction.

When their mother inherits a house in rural Illinois, sixteen-year-old twin brothers, Harry and Barry, talk their parents into letting them scout out the house and property. Strange things happen around them, including the deaths of many animals and the strange disappearance of things. They discover a place connecting two different worlds and do not know how to deal with the way it changes Harry; they discover a world they did not know existed. Time and life take on new meanings for them.

28.40 Tepper, Sheri S. **Grass.** Foundation/Doubleday, 1989. 426 pp. ISBN 0-385-26012-1. Fiction.

The galaxy is being ravaged by plague—except for the planet Grass. Marjorie Westriding Yrarier and her family are sent there to discover why Grass seems immune to the plague. Answers are not easy to come by, however, as the humans of Grass are totally preoccupied with "The Hunt," a ritual based on the hunts of Earth—with a couple of dangerous exceptions!

28.41 Thompson, Julian F. **Goofbang Value Daze.** Scholastic, 1989. 261 pp. ISBN 0-590-41946-3. Fiction.

Gabe and Dori are an unlikely pair. Gabe is a tall, skinny, smart-mouthed, manic writer of letters to the editor. Dori is a tall, slender, blonde beauty with an acute intelligence that people, fooled by her looks, don't always give her credit for. They live in a futuristic community under a dome, where strange things are afoot in the high school. As the school administration becomes increasingly authoritarian, Gabe and Dori turn their considerable brain power to finding out what's going on and how to stop it. Of course, their interference leads to some very unexpected results!

28.42 Thompson, Julian F. **Herb Seasoning.** Scholastic/Point, 1990. 280 pp. ISBN 0-590-43024-6. Fiction.

Herbie Hertzman is not sure what he will do when he graduates from high school. When he goes to his school counsellor for help, he receives an address and name which turns out to be life-changing. This place called Castles in the Air, with Sesame DeBarque as proprietor, is a front for a special "career center." Herb blindly selects a profession from the plate and takes a trip into the future. The first of many future work experiences for Herbie is in organized crime, which will bring him money but will leave his other goal, love, unrealized. Herbie plays the game with unusual characters in unusual places throughout his search.

28.43 Vinge, Joan D. **Catspaw.** Popular Library, 1988. 454 pp. ISBN 0-445-20531-8. Fiction.

Cat is a bodyguard, but not by choice. His abilities of telepathy and mind control are extremely valuable to the taMing family, a wealthy, DNA-incestuous clan with so much power that their every move affects the futures of entire worlds. Now one of the taMings, Lady Elnear, is the target of assassination, and Cat is to find out who's behind the previous attempts, stop any future attacks, and protect the taMing family. His hunt will lead Cat to drug kings and religious fanatics, but one thing becomes clear quickly: Cat isn't a bodyguard at all. He's bait.

28.44 Wilhelm, Kate. **The Dark Door.** St. Martin's Press, 1988. 248 pp. ISBN 0-312-02182-8. Fiction.

Extra-terrestrials, devoted to the acquisition of knowledge, developed space probes to search out life in the galaxy while Earth was still in the Ice Age. Unfortunately, one of the probes has malfunctioned; it still seeks out life forms, but it leaves a trail of madness and destruction in its wake. And the aliens that developed it can do nothing to stop it. When the probe comes to Earth, an arsonist begins to pursue it but succeeds only in leaving a trail of fires as he chases it. Finally, two detectives stumble upon the scene, but no one will believe their story. They must rely only upon one another to stop the probe as it continues on its path of destruction across the globe.

28.45 Williamson, Jack. **Mazeway.** Del Rey, 1990. 290 pp. ISBN 0-345-34032-9. Fiction.

Earth manages to repel the attack of the Seeker and her insatiable interstellar brood, but the planet is ravaged and reduced to a state of barbarism from the war. Humankind is doomed if it can't get help. The only hope for salvation is the Eldren, an ancient and peaceful conglomeration of alien races. But the Eldren consider humans too primitive to bother with. Three Earth teenagers set out to prove the worth of humanity to the Eldren by surviving the Mazeway, the testing ground for Eldren youth. To survive, they must fathom alien minds, elude hidden traps, and come to grips with their own motives in making the attempt—but the future of Earth rests with them!

28.46 Wilson, F. Paul. **Dydeetown World.** Baen Books, 1989. 303 pp. ISBN 0-671-69828-1. Fiction.

Imagine being a down-and-out detective hired by an old movie star's clone to find her missing fiancé. Hard-nosed private investigator Sig Dreyer reluctantly agrees to work for Jean Harlow-c, and finds himself tangling with people who have genetically engineered tyrannosauruses for guard dogs, run drugs on an interplanetary scale, and possess limitless creativity and resources to find ways of wiping him and Harlow-c out! In this futuristic adventure, Sig learns to combat his own addictions and prejudices while helping out his client, and finds strength, love, and self-worth through the strangest people and places.

28.47 Wilson, Robert Charles. **Gypsies.** Doubleday/Foundation Books, 1989. 232 pp. ISBN 0-385-24933-0. Fiction.

Karen isn't your typical mom. When she was a child, her younger siblings and she traveled to another dimension. There, they met "The Grey Man," a man she instinctively recognized and feared. Now a grown woman, Karen keeps trying to forget that short trip. However, "The Grey Man" has other plans and starts to appear to her fifteen-year-old son. Mother and son are thrown into an adventure that spans other worlds as they learn about their special gifts and their heritage, and are forced to fight to save their family.

28.48 Womack, Jack. **Terraplane.** TOR, 1988. 227 pp. ISBN 0-812-50623-5. Fiction.

Luther and two of his companions find their aircraft thrown backward through time, from the twenty-first century back to 1939, where history has been mysteriously rewritten. In this new world of the early twentieth century, history books indicate that Abraham Lincoln was assassinated on his way to his inauguration, President Roosevelt was killed even before he took office, and slavery in America never ended. With the help of Doc, a physician from the past, can Luther and his friends figure out how history was changed, return to their own time, and put the world back on its proper course without dying themselves?

28.49 Wu, William F. **Hong on the Range.** Illustrated by Phil Hale, Darrel Anderson, and Richard Berry. Millennium, 1989. 286 pp. ISBN 0-8027-6862-8. Fiction.

Louie Hong, a human cowboy, struggles to make his way in the new Wild West after the old one is destroyed in a series of biological disasters. His life is complicated, however, by the fact that most of the other cowboys have at least one bionic part, and they look down on him. To make things worse, bounty hunters are after him for robbing a bank, and a band of outlaws wants him for the loot. No one seems to care that he didn't do it! Accompanied by his friend, Chuck, one of the mechanical, singing cattle that now roam the range, Hong sets out to clear his name.

29 Short Stories

29.1 Adams, Robert, Martin H. Greenberg, and Pamela Crippen Adams, editors. **Hunger for Horror.** Donald A. Wollheim/DAW Books, 1988. 256 pp. ISBN 0-88677-266-4. Fiction.

This is a collection of fifteen horror stories about food from bizarre modern day vampires to quiet meals served to unsuspecting guests. The commonplace deli becomes a place of death in "The Same Old Grind," and a small studio in the shadow of the village church harbors secret ingredients in a medicinal oil. Included in this collection are Anthony Boucher, Ambrose Bierce, Ramsey Campbell, Stephen V. Benet, Robert Silverberg, and others.

29.2 Aiken, Joan. **Give Yourself a Fright: Thirteen Tales of the Supernatural.** Delacorte Press, 1989. 180 pp. ISBN 0-440-50120-2. Fiction.

In these thirteen stories, bizarre creatures disrupt the lives of ordinary characters. An ancient muse arrives on the doorstep of a sophisticated thief and nags him to write poetry. Twin brothers jealously want a mysterious locket which brings good luck and gives its owner the ability to detect ghosts. Possessed souls, specters, and living talismans prove that the world beyond presents strange phenomena to the unwary and unsuspecting.

29.3 Aronica, Lou, Shawna McCarthy, Amy Stout, and Patrick LoBrutto, compilers. **Full Spectrum 2.** Doubleday, 1989. 464 pp. ISBN 0-385-26019-9. Fiction.

This collection of stories about fantastic other worlds contains tales concerning lethal viruses, alien visitations, and mythical religions. From the mysteries of the mind to worlds on the brink of chaos, the tales gathered here cover the "full spectrum" of science fiction, presented by such names as Patricia A. McKillip, Vonda N. McIntyre, Mike McQuay, and many others.

29.4 Asimov, Isaac. **The Alternate Asimovs.** New American Library, 1988. 316 pp. ISBN 0-451-15370-7. Fiction.

If you are curious about how Isaac Asimov writes his tales of fantasy and science fiction, you will be rewarded here. Asimov presents the original versions of two of his most famous stories with introductions and afterwords for your information. This collection will provide any aspiring young fantasy/science fiction writer a look into how the most accomplished writer in the field does his writing.

29.5 Asimov, Isaac, Martin H. Greenberg, and Charles G. Waugh, editors. **Space Shuttles.** New American Library/Signet, 1987. 384 pp. ISBN 0-451-15017-1. Fiction.

Asimov has assembled a collection of science fiction by well-known authors including Robert Chilson, Timothy Zahn, and Sheila Finch. These stories about future space exploration create suspense and interest.

29.6 Cormier, Robert. **Eight Plus One.** Dell/Laurel-Leaf Books, 1991. 196 pp. ISBN 0-440-20838-6. Fiction.

This compilation of short stories written by Cormier includes notes about what prompted the characters or the plots. Each of the nine stories has a bit of the author because, he says, he has had similar feelings or taken similar actions as those which occur in the stories. The true-to-life depth in each tale is designed to trigger an emotion or memory in the reader.

29.7 Gallo, Donald R. **Connections: Short Stories by Outstanding Writers for Young Adults.** Dell/Laurel-Leaf Books, 1990. 226 pp. ISBN 0-440-20768-1. Fiction.

This collection of seventeen short stories comes from outstanding writers of contemporary young adult literature. Gallo has organized these first-time published stories into four sections: Encounters, Clashes, Surprises, and Insights. More than half of the stories focus on boy-girl relationships in various stages. The teenage characters in the stories experience many of the same problems and triumphs facing young people today. Also included at the end of each selection is a brief biographical sketch of the writer.

29.8 Gallo, Donald R. **Visions: Nineteen Short Stories by Outstanding Writers for Young Adults.** Dell/Laurel-Leaf Books, 1988. 230 pp. ISBN 0-440-20208-6. Fiction.

Nineteen stories have been selected that represent many teenage interests: romance, humor, decisions about friendships and family, ghost stories, science fiction, and the pain inflicted by an often unresponsive society. Many authors are known for their teen novels, such as M. E. Keer, Richard Peck, and Norma Fox Mazer.

29.9 Gingher, Marianne. **Teen Angel, And Other Stories of Young Love.** Atheneum, 1988. 207 pp. ISBN 0-689-11967-4. Fiction.

This collection of ten short stories explores the emotion of love as the teenage characters find themselves on the brink of love and life. In "The Kiss," twelve-year-old Nicodine, a girl of the Carolina hills, eagerly anticipates the unknown handsome stranger with the tall, black silk hat who, she knows, will deliver her first kiss and take her away from her life of caring for an ailing mother. Jennifer, the narrator in "Teen Angel," and her girlfriend Becky are fascinated by the sexual encounters of Rita, Becky's older sister, and witness the explosive reaction of Becky and Rita's volatile father to Rita's escapades. Jennifer prays to experience for herself that same deep love of Rita's. Dobie Rhinehart, the teenage track star in "The Magic Circle," is powerless to resist his love for Meredith MaGraw, even though his parents' disintegrating marriage clearly demonstrates the impermanence of love. And for twelve-year-old Susie, the narrator in "Aurora Island," her first kiss brings her into the world of adult emotions before she is ready to leave childhood behind.

29.10 Haas, Jessie. **The Sixth Sense and Other Stories.** Greenwillow Books, 1988. 180 pp. ISBN 0-688-08129-0. Fiction.

These nine stories explain relationships between humans and animals as they share joy and pain using two main groups of characters. Kris and Aunt Mil learn about each other through two special cats, Puttin and Robert. James MacLiesh will show you how it feels to ride a thoroughbred horse. And Kris returns in one story, taking a stand in an effort to rescue a racing greyhound condemned to die by track operators.

29.11 Jones, Diana Wynne, editor. **Hidden Turnings: A Collection of Stories through Time and Space.** Greenwillow Books, 1990. 192 pp. ISBN 0-688-09163-6. Fiction.

A child dreams of her lover-to-be; a young musician discovers that his mentor is an Irish elf; a great-aunt goes voyaging in the sky; a battle is fought across planes of consciousness, despite changes of shape. These twelve short stories, which deal with possibilities and alternate realities, combine unexpected endings and surprise switches.

29.12 Jordon, Cathleen, and Cynthia Manson, compilers. **Tales from Alfred Hitchcock's Mystery Magazine.** Morrow Junior Books, 1988. 310 pp. ISBN 0-688-08176-2. Fiction.

These are stories about vampires, dragons and wizards, spies, detectives, and teen wargamers, all of which were taken from the issues of *Alfred Hitchcock's Mystery Magazine.* Some of the stories are intriguing puzzles, some are funny, and some bring a touch of terror from the past, from the grave, or from outer space.

29.13 Kingsolver, Barbara. **Homeland and Other Stories.** Harper and Row, 1989. 244 pp. ISBN 0-06-016112-4. Fiction.

Whether they're set in northern California, on the Caribbean island of St. Lucia, or in eastern Kentucky, all of Barbara Kingsolver's tales have a distinctly "Southern" feel to them. In "Homeland," the title story, a young girl tries to hang onto her dying great-grandmother's Cherokee culture, while in "Blueprints," two old people try desperately to reach one another again despite all the odds. These twelve tales explore the relationships of mothers and daughters, husbands and wives, and children and adults.

29.14 La Chapelle, Mary. **House of Heroes and Other Stories.** Crown, 1988. 243 pp. ISBN 0-517-56788-2. Fiction.

The heroes in this collection of short stories, all set in cities and small towns in Minnesota and Wisconsin, are outsiders; they stand out rather than blend in. Among the cast of characters are Anna, the nearly eight-foot-tall woman who yearns for friends and acceptance; Clara and Connie, elderly sisters who flee unhappy marriages and use alcohol to escape from their lives; Ajax, a teenage schizophrenic in a group home for emotionally troubled boys; and Tiffany, a teenage girl trying to cope with a manic-depressive mother and her own emotional instability. Yet the reader may wonder if these heroes are really the outsiders. They seem to have made a brave adjustment to their particular worlds and are in control of their personal lives.

29.15 Mason, Bobbie Ann. **Love Life.** Harper and Row, 1989. 241 pp. ISBN 0-06-016042-X. Fiction.

Though set in Kentucky, these fifteen stories reflect the common bonds of people everywhere. Lost love is the center of "The Secret of the Pyramids," and fantasies of fame and success are the focus of "Piano Fingers." A divorced mother with no idea what she wants out of life is at the center of "Memphis," and a humorous love triangle leads to new bonds of affection in the collection's title story, "Love Life." Each story leads into the next with ease, making fifteen individual tales seem like one complete novel.

29.16 Mazer, Norma Fox. **Dear Bill, Remember Me? And Other Stories.** Dell/Laurel-Leaf Books, 1989. 195 pp. ISBN 0-440-91749-2. Fiction.

Here are eight short stories featuring young women who face life with courage and grace. "Dear Bill, Remember Me?" is a series of letters young Kathy writes to a boy older than herself. "Mimi the Fish" is an insight into Mimi, the girl who doesn't want to have a party because she has no friends. More serious problems face Louise in "Guess Whose Friendly Hands": Louise has terminal cancer and no one wants to talk about it.

29.17 Montgomery, L. M. **Akin to Anne: Tales of Other Orphans.** Edited by Rea Wilmshurst. Bantam Books, 1990. 202 pp. ISBN 0-553-28387-1. Fiction.

Finding love is the goal of each character in this collection of nineteen stories by the author of *Anne of Green Gables.* These stories relate the struggles of others seeking love, such as Charlotte Laurence, who in her desire to escape her critical aunt's supervision, seeks love behind the red door that Witch Penny directs her to. And the two nieces, Marcella and Patty Langley, who are under the care of a grudging aunt—they look for love from their deceased mother's high school friend.

29.18 Montgomery, L. M. **Along the Shore: Tales by the Sea.** Edited by Rea Wilmshurst. Bantam/Starfire Books, 1990. 268 pp. ISBN 0-553-28589-0. Fiction.

Natty's strength of body and character make it possible for his family to remain in the home they love. Uncle Jesse sees and hears his beloved Margaret in the beauty of the morning across the Golden Gate, and Ben loses Mary Stella to a world across the sea. These and more stories portray the rugged and hearty characters of Montgomery's sixteen short stories with one thing in common—their undying love of the sea.

29.19 Montgomery, L. M. **Among the Shadows: Tales from the Darker Side.** Edited by Rea Wilmshurst. Bantam/Starfire Books, 1991. 281 pp. ISBN 0-553-28959-4. Fiction.

A collection of nineteen short stories by L. M. Montgomery includes tales of thieves, drunkards, murderers, and those believing in the supernatural. The editor has chosen short stories never before published. The characters are memorable in these tales of sadness, of evil, and of how justice comes in numerous ways.

29.20 Montgomery, L. M. **Chronicles of Avonlea.** Bantam/Starfire Books, 1988. 183 pp. ISBN 0-553-27534-8. Fiction.

In the tradition of the *Anne of Green Gables* stories, Lucy Maud Montgomery spins twelve tales involving the people of Avonlea, near the sea surrounding Prince Edward Island. Anne Shirley, the now-grown, orphaned redhead with a penchant for trouble and excitement, weaves in and out of these stories of Avonlea's ordinary folk—all of whom experience romance, life, birth, and death. Montgomery's descriptive narrative of the settings is vivid.

29.21 Norton, Andre, compiler, and Martin H. Greenberg. **Catfantastic.** DAW, 1989. 320 pp. ISBN 0-88677-355-5. Fiction.

The most mysterious of all creatures, the cat, is featured here in fifteen tales of wonder. What do cats think of humans? Do they possess higher intelligence? Could they even be an alien species? These short stories explore the magic of cats from ancient times (when they were worshipped by the Egyptians and burned as witches' servants) to the distant future (when they will rule the universe). For anyone who's ever wondered what their cats are thinking when those furry felines are staring off into space, this collection offers some imaginative explanations.

29.22 O'Brien, Tim. **The Things They Carried.** Houghton Mifflin/Seymour Lawrence, 1990. 273 pp. ISBN 0-395-51598-X. Fiction.

The winner of the 1979 National Book Award, Tim O'Brien, has collected together a group of short stories that have appeared in *Esquire, Playboy,* and *Granta.* They are about a group of young footsoldiers in Vietnam. Although each story can stand on its own, as a collective unit they are interwoven together by characters, situations, and memory. This collection's presentation is innovative, and the content, dealing with the "things" we as humans carry with us throughout our lives, is written with wit and style.

29.23 Pettepiece, Thomas, and Anatoly Aleskin, editors. **Face to Face: A Collection of Stories by Celebrated Soviet and American Writers.** Philomel Books, 1990. 233 pp. ISBN 0-399-21951-X. Fiction.

Eighteen of Russia's and America's favorite young adult writers have contributed stories to this collection. The themes are universal: two boys' friendship is tested when one almost drowns; a girl and her father are confronted by a deer too magnificent to shoot while they are out hunting; a boy loses his father's cap and writes such an impassioned letter to the townspeople that he gets a lot more than he had anticipated as a response; a boy visits the Vietnam Memorial to see his father's name. These are touching and funny stories about growing up, no matter where you are.

29.24 Rochman, Hazel, compiler. **Somehow Tenderness Survives: Stories of Southern Africa.** Harper and Row/Charlotte Zolotow Books, 1988. 147 pp. ISBN 0-06-025023-2. Nonfiction.

The Afrikaans word *apartheid* means "separateness" and is pronounced "apart-hate." From these ten stories (some autobiographical) by both black and white authors, you will learn something about what it is like to live in South Africa under apartheid. As Hazel Rochman says, "The stories are grim; but they speak of courage and tenderness in daily life, even where home has become a public toilet or a prison cell."

29.25 Rylant, Cynthia. **A Couple of Kooks and Other Stories about Love.** Orchard Books/Richard Jackson Books, 1990. 104 pp. ISBN 0-531-05900-6. Fiction.

This collection of eight short stories deals with the topic of love. The different characters experience love in various ways, some with gusto, others with reservations and trepidation. All are transformed as they go through the trials of adapting to new experiences and sharing their lives with others.

29.26 Sieruta, Peter D. **Heartbeats and Other Stories.** Harper and Row, 1989. 216 pp. ISBN 0-06-025848-9. Fiction.

Could you deal with a blond, green-eyed, older brother who's built like a bodybuilder, especially when he's dating the woman you love? And you're just a tenth-grade nerd with glasses, a nerd who carries a briefcase and wears a suit to school? Or maybe you're a seventeen-year-old living with twelve siblings, two parents, five animals, and thirty-six fish. You've never had your own room, and now you finally get one. Would you ever come out again? The nine stories in *Heartbeats* concern teenagers dealing with a variety of relationships in funny, sad, and often surprising ways.

29.27 Soto, Gary. **Baseball in April and Other Stories.** Harcourt Brace Jovanovich, 1990. 111 pp. ISBN 0-15-205720-X. Fiction.

Alfonso finally works up the nerve to ask a girl out biking, but then not only breaks his bike chain, but in doing so, hits himself in the face with it, leaving a cut. Not very cool! A little girl gets a "fake Barbie" for her birthday and is devastated. When she finally gets the "real" Barbie with the blond hair, she loses the doll's head within a day. As you will quickly notice in these eleven stories about growing up poor and Hispanic in Fresno, California, the challenges and joys of growing up in the United States are universal. All teens seem to have similar bonds over such things as parents, siblings, romance, baseball, and, of course, school.

29.28 Stevenson, Robert Louis. **The Body Snatcher and Other Stories.** Edited by Jeffrey Meyers. New American Library/Signet Classics, 1988. 350 pp. ISBN 0-451-52153-6. Fiction.

This book presents eight of Robert Louis Stevenson's tales, including "The Sire de Malétroit's Door," "Markheim," and "Olalla." Stories of corrupted native pastors, of ancient ugly secrets newly come to life, and an imp in a bottle all combine to show Stevenson's versatility.

29.29 Vaughn, Stephanie. **Sweet Talk.** Random House, 1990. 194 pp. ISBN 0-394-57605-5. Fiction.

Although most short story collections have little relationship between the stories, the tales in *Sweet Talk* follow the life of one person, Gemma. Although the stories are not organized as a continuous narrative, we get to know Gemma quite well. We first meet her as a young girl, then as a woman, and later we meet her family and friends in these ten stories. Moving through various relationships and the tragic illnesses of both her parents, Gemma is an appealing protagonist whom it is fun to learn so much about.

30 Sports

30.1 Deuker, Carl. **On the Devil's Court.** Little, Brown/Joy Street Books, 1988. 252 pp. ISBN 0-316-18147-1. Fiction.

Joe Faust moves from Boston to Seattle just before his senior year in high school. His parents decide that he should attend a private school—Eastside. Joe's father wants Joe to be a scientist like he is, but all Joe wants to do is play basketball. He's a good player and, after an afternoon shooting baskets by himself in a deserted gym, things begin to go Joe's way. Is it all coincidence, or did he really sell his soul to the devil for a perfect season?

30.2 Dygard, Thomas J. **The Rookie Arrives.** Morrow Junior Books, 1988. 197 pp. ISBN 0-688-07598-3. Fiction.

Drafted into the Kansas City Royals right out of high school, hotshot third baseman Ted Bell expects to be right there in the starting lineup playing ball—as he was hired to do. But thirty games into the season finds Ted still fuming on the sidelines while aging superstar Lou Mills plays the best ball of his career. Then an injury takes Lou out of commission for a month. Will Ted have enough time to prove himself and find a permanent place in the starting lineup?

30.3 Freeman, Mark. **Series Showdown.** Ballantine Books, 1989. 135 pp. ISBN 0-345-35907-0. Fiction.

Former Rosemont, Iowa, high school teammates, David Green and Roberto (Magic) Ramirez, both make the major leagues and, in their rookie year, face each other in the World Series. David is an outfielder for the Red Sox, while Roberto pitches for the Dodgers. This novel is about their confrontations and success in the Series. Will the two rivals remain friends? The author provides the reader with the tense atmosphere and excitement of a dramatic World Series.

30.4 Halberstam, David. **Summer of '49.** William Morrow, 1989. 304 pp. ISBN 0-688-06678-X. Nonfiction.

It was what one sportscaster called the last moment of innocence in sports. The 1949 pennant race between the Boston Red Sox and the

New York Yankees was a shining moment in the baseball era. Legends were being made, legends like Joe DiMaggio, Ted Williams, and Yogi Berra, and the magic of baseball was still an American obsession. This book is an intimate look at not only the exciting winner-take-all final game of the pennant race, but an examination of a very different American society than exists today. There has never been a time since when the baseball player was the hero that he was in 1949, and never was the American pastime more carefully followed than it was during that exciting battle between two legendary teams.

30.5 Honig, Donald. **The Greatest First Basemen of All Time.** Crown, 1988. 148 pp. ISBN 0-517-56842-X. Nonfiction.

Baseball author Donald Honig tackles the question of how to determine the greatest first baseman. Relying on statistics, opinions, memories, and, unavoidably, some bias, he has chosen nineteen players who have dominated this power-hitting position during the twentieth century. Each portrait contains a biography, picture portfolio, and lifetime statistics. Honig starts out with Frank Chance, anchorman on the famous double-play combination of "Tinker to Evers to Chance," and Hal Chase, a dazzling player with a slick glove on the field, but a rough rogue and gambler off the field, and ends with two more recent players, Eddie Murray of the Baltimore Orioles and Don Mattingly of the New York Yankees. In between come the Yankee legend Lou Gehrig, Dodger great Gil Hodges, Giant slugger Orlando Cepeda, and Mets' star Keith Hernandez, among others. Black-and-white photographs, lifetime records, index.

30.6 Klass, David. **A Different Season.** E. P. Dutton, 1988. 199 pp. ISBN 0-525-67237-0. Fiction.

Jim "Streak" Roark is on top of the world. He is the ace pitcher for Oakdale High's top-rated baseball team, major league scouts may check him out if the team has a good season, and he has seen a girl he thinks he likes. But then the object of his interest, Jennifer Douglas, who plays second base on the girls' team, decides that she wants to play on the boys' team! Even though Jenny is the best female athlete at school and the two of them are attracted to each other, Jim just can't accept her playing for the guys' team. As the season progresses, Jim has to sort out his confused feelings about his relationships with a lot of people, including Jenny.

30.7 Klass, David. **Wrestling with Honor.** Lodestar Books, 1989. 200 pp. ISBN 0-525-67268-0. Fiction.

Ron Woods is the best wrestler on his high school team. When the school says that all athletes have to be tested for drug use, Ron feels it is an invasion of privacy, but he goes along with it for the good of the team. His test is positive, even though Ron never uses drugs and his friends and teammates know it. Ron's refusal to take a retest involves his principles, his feelings for his dead father, and his relationships with everyone around him.

30.8 Marshall, Kirk. **Pressure Play.** Ballantine Books, 1989. 134 pp. ISBN 0-345-35913-5. Fiction.

This is the story of the Jefferson High School Patriots' march to the Indiana state basketball championship game. Jefferson's star, 6′8″ junior center Brian Davis, and his teammates overcome numerous obstacles to reach the title game against their arch rival, Gary Tech. The game accounts convey the electric atmosphere of basketball fever, and the Patriots demonstrate what friendship and working together is all about. Will they reach their goal of being state champs?

30.9 Miklowitz, Gloria D. **Anything to Win.** Dell/Laurel-Leaf Books, 1990. 136 pp. ISBN 0-440-20732-0. Fiction.

Cam Potter faces a dilemma: he wants a college scholarship, but he does not want to follow his football coach's suggestion to take steroids. He also faces decisions about his older brother's relationship with their dad and his own with two girls. Laurel, the one he truly likes, doesn't seem to respect him, and Amy, the girl who wants his varsity sweater, pushes him into a relationship. This seventeen-year-old faces decisions not unlike other high school athletes, but his ways of dealing with them are all his own.

30.10 Obojski, Robert. **Baseball Bloopers and Diamond Oddities.** Sterling, 1991. 128 pp. ISBN 0-8069-6982-2. Nonfiction.

George Bush, forty-first President of the United States, captained the Yale varsity baseball team in 1948. Kansas City, Missouri, hosted its first-ever All-Star Game on July 11, 1960. The 101° temperature didn't stop the large group of fans from turning out for the game, though the heat was so fierce that the TV cameras needed to be wrapped in ice. Author Robert Obojski, a former coach, gathers together a collection of fascinating facts and interesting up-to-date information about the exciting and unusual world of baseball.

30.11 Obojski, Robert. **Baseball Memorabilia.** Sterling, 1991. 160 pp. ISBN 0-8069-7290-4. Nonfiction.

Did you know that the Baseball Hall of Fame in Cooperstown, New York, celebrated its fiftieth anniversary on June 10, 1989, by opening the new Fetzer-Yawkey Building, bringing its display area to more than 70,000 square feet? Its annual paid attendance runs to more than 350,000. Or did you know that if a prominent ballplayer of the past or present is spotted in public today, he'll generally be mobbed for his autograph because "Autograph Mania" has now reached almost epidemic proportions? Do you want to begin collecting baseball memorabilia or just know more about it? This book will provide information about the valuable and the not so valuable, as well as lots of trivia for the baseball fan.

30.12 Oldgate, Karl. **Karate.** Illustrated by Bob Williams. Cassell/Ward Lock, 1990. 80 pp. ISBN 0-7063-6857-6. Nonfiction.

This book, an introduction to karate, covers the history and development of that ancient sport. It describes its rules, terminology, and equipment. Through illustrations, diagrams, and action photos, step-by-step self-defense techniques are made easy to understand.

30.13 Paterno, Joe, with Bernard Asbell. **Paterno: By the Book.** Random House, 1989. 287 pp. ISBN 0-394-56501-0. Nonfiction.

Joe Paterno's records in coaching football make him one of the most admired men in America: eighteen bowl games with twelve wins, voted Coach of the Year four times, the only coach ever chosen as *Sport's Illustrated*'s Sportsman of the Year, and numerous other impressive victories. What makes Paterno even more impressive is his commitment to academics—an exceptional graduation rate of those students who have been fortunate enough to have him as a college teacher, including many first-team academic all-Americans. In this book Paterno tells all: how he got where he is today and how his high personal standards helped him achieve his dreams. His story is proof that sports and academics can and should be successfully combined for the best possible results.

30.14 Perry, Frank T. **The Complete Karate Handbook.** Sterling, 1991. 160 pp. ISBN 0-7063-6902-5. Nonfiction.

Writing for beginners in karate, the author begins with a historical view of karate, including its roots in Chinese Buddhism. Step-by-step illustrations (430 black-and-white in all) and instructions take the reader into this physical art. There are chapters for children and women, as well as chapters on kumite and tameshiwari for the more advanced karate enthusiasts. A pronouncing gazeteer of karate words and terms is the final source in this handbook.

30.15 Riddles, Libby, and Tim Jones. **Race across Alaska: First Woman to Win the Iditarod Tells Her Story.** Stackpole Books, 1988. 235 pp. ISBN 0-8117-2253-8. Nonfiction.

Libby Riddles was the first woman to win the Iditarod, Alaska's most famous dogsled race. The trail of the race runs from Anchorage to Nome—twelve hundred miles through winds, snow, wilderness, and below zero temperatures. Inset within Libby's story of her race (including accident, sickness, and storms) are explanations and information about Alaska, the race, and the dogs.

30.16 Simpson, Holly. **To Be the Best.** Fawcett, 1989. 136 pp. ISBN 0-449-14591-3. Fiction.

Jo has a chance to train with the best gymnastic coach in the nation, but she'll have to go to California and leave her family to do it. But she has always dreamed of this opportunity; she finally decides to fly to Malibu. She lives with the Lancaster family, whose daughter, Debbie, is a well-known gymnast. Jo greatly admires Debbie's talents and wonders if she will ever be so skillful. She misses her family, and she must fight her own fears and lack of self-confidence. She knows all her family and hometown friends are counting on her to succeed. From the Perfect 10 series. Easy reading.

30.17 Weesner, Theodore. **Winning The City.** Summit Books, 1990. 208 pp. ISBN 0-671-64241-3. Fiction.

Fifteen-year-old Dale Wheeler is the co-captain of the Whittier Junior High basketball team. He has been practicing all summer, dreaming of winning the City League and turning life around for himself and his alcoholic father. When a former All-American basketball star decides to sponsor the team and then gives Dale's position to his son, Dale can't believe it. Learning the lesson that life is not fair isn't easy, but Dale realizes he can fight back to win, while remembering, "Never to play their game. He was this person. The task was never to be them. Not ever."

31 War

31.1 Amos, James. **The Memorial: A Novel of the Vietnam War.** Crown, 1989. 259 pp. ISBN 0-517-56971-X. Fiction.

Jake Adams, a successful businessman, stands before the Vietnam Memorial in Washington, D.C. He looks through the list chiseled into the stone as he searches for the names he has scribbled on the back of a business message. Jake had gone to Vietnam as a proud Marine, a bit apprehensive and sorry to be leaving his wife and two-week-old daughter, but ready for what he had been trained to do. The memories of those men whose names appear before him flood his mind on the cold winter day, but he does not recall everything of the battles and horrors; he learned while lying wounded in the military hospital in Quang Tri the practice of selective suppression of memories. He also learned while in Vietnam to numb his feelings, but, in this moment, he clearly remembers the people, the courage, the futility, and the events.

31.2 Baklanov, Grigory. **Forever Nineteen.** Translated from Russian by Antonia W. Bouis. J. B. Lippincott, 1989. 168 pp. ISBN 0-397-32296-8. Fiction.

The horrors of war are the same, no matter whose army you're fighting for. Volodya Tretyakov, a nineteen-year-old Russian officer during World War II, discovers how terrible the price can be at the front. It will cost him his youth, his innocence, and his simple concept of life and love. Faces come and go, young men smile and then die, and in the midst of the bombs and the gunfire Tretyakov will learn two horribly contradictory things: that he hates the war but that he wants to fight from a sense of duty. He will fight after he's wounded once; he will fight after he's wounded twice; he will fight to the very end of his life if that's what it takes. And it may.

31.3 Childress, Mark. **V for Victor.** Ballantine Books, 1990. 248 pp. ISBN 0-345-35427-3. Fiction.

Victor goes to the island in Alabama to care for his infirm grandmother and, while there, becomes involved in a war which is related in many ways to the war raging in Europe in 1942. Victor commits brave and not-so-brave deeds as he matures into a different person than he was before being sent to his grandmother's. He learns a great deal about his own family and people in general as he meets murderers and the enemy.

31.4 Courtenay, Bryce. **The Power of One.** Random House, 1989. 513 pp. ISBN 0-394-57520-2. Fiction.

In South Africa during World War II, a pro-Nazi movement exists which young Peekay does not understand and comes to despise. The movement is just one of the strange obstacles which Peekay will try to overcome in his search for his dream: to become a winner. His secret weapon is "the power of one," and he uses it to understand the mystical, sometimes evil, forces which seem aligned against him in a world turned upside down by war, hatred, and suspicion.

31.5 Currey, Richard. **Fatal Light.** E. P. Dutton, 1988. 195 pp. ISBN 0-525-24622-3. Fiction.

The unnamed narrator is hoping for a college football scholarship, but as the war in Vietnam escalates, the draft is stepped up as well. Soon the narrator is drafted and sent to Vietnam as a combat medic. Brief chapters intermix images of the brutality and mindlessness of war with tranquil scenes from the narrator's youth. Vivid images of combat, atrocities, malaria, drugs, Saigon street life, and the difficult reentry into everyday life three years later provide a devastating portrait of the Vietnam War.

31.6 Dolan, Edward F. **America after Vietnam: Legacies of a Hated War.** Franklin Watts, 1989. 160 pp. ISBN 0-531-10793-0. Nonfiction.

Dolan very briefly sketches America's involvement in the Vietnam War, a war that produced 58,000 military casualties, and then identifies five legacies from the war: (1) the legacy of alienation that was caused by the silent, cold, and often angry reception that returning servicemen received; (2) the legacy of psychological trauma from the horror of war, manifested in drug and alcohol abuse, psychological impairment, and criminal activity; (3) the legacy of illness allegedly caused by exposure to the eleven or twelve million gallons of herbicide Agent Orange that were sprayed on Vietnam; (4) the legacy of anguish suffered by the families of the 3,100 American service personnel and civilians listed as missing in action or prisoners of war; and (5) the legacy of thousands of Indochinese refugees trying to make a new life in the United States, including the Amerasian children born of American servicemen and Vietnamese women during the war. Black-and-white photographs, notes, bibliography, index.

31.7 Feldbaum, Carl B., and Ronald J. Bee. **Looking the Tiger in the Eye: Confronting the Nuclear Threat.** Harper and Row, 1988. 286 pp. ISBN 0-06-020415-X. Nonfiction.

A historical perspective of the building and use of the atomic bomb on Hiroshima and Nagasaki is given. Quotes from Oppenheimer, Truman, and other prominent policymakers show the seriousness of the use of any nuclear weapon on the earth and humankind. The authors outline two nuclear races: that of World War II climaxing with Nagasaki, and that with the USSR which rages on, although at a somewhat limited pace. It is the third, the pursuit of human societies to end all nuclear wars, and the author wants people "to look the tiger in the eye" by demanding that world leaders limit all manufacturing of nuclear weapons which can be used by anyone at anytime. The historical view encourages the reader to carefully consider any possible solutions to this large problem.

31.8 Hawks, Robert. **The Twenty-Six Minutes.** Square One Publishers, 1988. 190 pp. ISBN 0-938961-03-9. Fiction.

When Maxwell Neuger asserts, "All of us here in this room are no more than twenty-six minutes away from death," Jenny Westphal figures he is a fanatic. Yet Max is so direct, with blazing, dynamic eyes, that she is intrigued enough to attend a meeting of Max's disarmament group, Stop the Nightmare. There she sees Rich McFadden, an odd boy from her school, Travers Air Force Base High School. Although they are both children of career Air Force officers, Jenny and Rich get swept up by the charismatic Max, and find themselves embroiled in a sequence of events the implications of which they cannot imagine.

31.9 Hayslip, Le Ly, with Jay Wurts. **When Heaven and Earth Changed Places: A Vietnamese Woman's Journey from War to Peace.** Doubleday, 1989. 368 pp. ISBN 0-385-24758-3. Nonfiction.

Alternating between the present and the past, Le Ly tells of her life as a peasant girl in central Vietnam before and after the Americans came to fight in her land. She describes the hunger, the arrests, the torture, the rape, and the desolation that she endured. She interweaves the events of her return to Vietnam in 1986, after living in the United States for sixteen years, with memories of childhood and adolescence in her war-torn homeland. Mature language and situations.

31.10 Hoobler, Dorothy, and Thomas Hoobler. **Vietnam, Why We Fought: An Illustrated History.** Alfred A. Knopf/Borzoi Books, 1990. 196 pp. ISBN 0-394-91943-2. Nonfiction.

This book does a comprehensive job of exploring the causes of the U.S. involvement in Vietnam and tracing the escalation of a war that "claimed thousands of lives, cost billions of dollars, and left an entire generation broken, bitter, and confused." It is effective in providing unbiased answers to the hard and painful questions that persist concerning Vietnam. Divided into three parts, "The Vietnamese and the French," "The United States in Vietnam," and "The End of the Thirty Years' War," it is illustrated with photographs that bring the war and its conflicts to life.

31.11 Johnston, Jennifer. **Fool's Sanctuary.** Hamish Hamilton, 1987. 132 pp. ISBN 0-241-12035-7. Fiction.

World War I has recently ended, but in Ireland the war is just beginning. At first there is no sign of discord at Termon (or "sanctuary"), the farm where eighteen-year-old Miranda Martin lives with her widowed father, though her boyfriend, Cathal, is a student in Dublin and active in the underground movement fighting for Irish independence. But then Miranda's brother, Andrew, appears at Termon with another soldier from his unit in the British army. Conflict encircles all of them, increasing the longstanding personal tensions between father and son, between brother and sister, and between boyhood friends, and emphasizing the political tensions between the IRA and the British Black and Tans sent to quell the revolutionary activity. The resulting tragedy, due both to loyalty and betrayal, is inevitable.

31.12 Katz, William Loren, and Marc Crawford. **The Lincoln Brigade: A Picture of History.** Atheneum, 1989. 84 pp. ISBN 0-689-31408-X. Nonfiction.

In 1936, ninety-six Americans left New York, bound for Spain and the civil war brewing there, a war between the democratic government and a fascist uprising. Over time, 2,800 United States volunteers reached Spain and became the Abraham Lincoln Brigade. They had little military training but all the fervor that they needed to fight "to make Madrid the tomb for world fascism." The Lincoln Brigade came from all walks of life, and those who survived returned to Spain in 1986 for a fiftieth anniversary celebration. The authors traveled with the surviving members of the Lincolns, interviewing them and obtaining never-before published documents and photographs. Index.

31.13 Lopes, Sal. **The Wall: Images and Offerings from the Vietnam Veterans Memorial.** Collins, 1987. 128 pp. ISBN 0-00-217974-1. Nonfiction.

Sal Lopes and sixteen other photojournalists have gone to the Vietnam Veterans Memorial in Washington, D.C. and photographed the wall, the names, the visitors, and the numerous items left at the wall. The photographs are emotion-packed, as is the text which contains excerpts from letters and notes left at the wall. These messages for lost family and friends are interspersed with the photos and prove that the Wall is a permanent shrine to America's lost but not forgotten Vietnam veterans.

31.14 Mansfield, Sue, and Mary Bowen Hall. **Some Reasons for War: How Families, Myths, and Warfare Are Connected.** Crowell, 1988. 218 pp. ISBN 0-690-04664-2. Nonfiction.

Examining warfare from Neolithic times to the present, this book explores what leads us to war and how we could avoid it. How does what our parents teach us to feel about ourselves influence our interests in war or peace? Does society create myths of heroism which suggest that peace can only be achieved through war? While looking at how military objectives have changed over the centuries, this book offers suggestions for how young people can avoid the cycle of war. An appendix of peace organizations is included.

31.15 McPherson, James M. **Battle Cry of Freedom: The Civil War Era.** Oxford University Press, 1988. 904 pp. ISBN 0-19-503863-0. Nonfiction.

The South was fighting to protect traditional rights and state sovereignty. The North was fighting to maintain the Union and, eventually but not initially, to abolish slavery. Both sides took up arms in a "battle cry of freedom," fighting in the bitter war that pitted American against American and that killed more than 600,000 soldiers. James McPherson takes a close look at the events that preceded the Civil War and chronicles the war itself—the battles, the strategic maneuvering, the politics, and the personalities involved. The defeat of the South ended the political power of the South and transformed the United States from a loose union of states to a single nation led by a strong central government, permanently changing American life. Black-and-white photographs, maps, bibliographical note, index. Volume six in the Oxford History of the United States.

31.16 Meltzer, Milton. **Voices from the Civil War: A Documentary History of the Great American Conflict.** Thomas Y. Crowell, 1989. 203 pp. ISBN 0-690-04800-9. Nonfiction.

The voices come from many different sources, including the president, prisoner-of-war camps, battlefields, songs, letters, and diaries. The voices begin in the 1850s, explaining some of the causes of the Civil

War and end after the war is over. A new prisoner at Andersonville asks, "Is this Hell?" The war seems like Hell to many who live through it and share their experiences. Milton Meltzer gives brief explanations and descriptions to put the quotations in perspective.

31.17 Myers, Walter Dean. **Fallen Angels.** Scholastic, 1988. 309 pp. ISBN 0-590-40943-3. Fiction.

Perry, Lobel, Johnson, Brunner, Monaco, and Gates become friends as they fight side by side in the Vietnam War. None of them can say why they are there, fighting a war unrelated to them or their past; yet, each knows he will take care of himself and his friends against the ever-present, elusive Viet Cong. The struggles with the Vietnamese people, the weather, and the horrifying fighting conditions cause young boys to mature into men before their time. Although death is their full-time companion, they work to survive and get back to what they call the "World."

31.18 Nakazawa, Keiji. **Barefoot Gen: The Day After.** Translated from Japanese by Dadakai and Project Gen. New Society Publishers, 1988. 177 pp. ISBN 0-86571-123-2. Fiction.

Considered a classic among Japanese comic books, *Barefoot Gen* is the story of the horrors which befall one family after the bombing of Hiroshima at the end of World War II. The degeneration of others around them, constant hunger, fear, and death lead the family to question and reevaluate their moral positions. Gen, whose name means "roots" or "source" in Japanese, is based on the artist as a young boy, and the terrifying world of life after the bomb is seen through his eyes. Sequel to *Barefoot Gen: A Cartoon Story of Hiroshima* and followed by *Barefoot Gen: Life After the Bomb.* Mature language and situations.

31.19 Noonan, Michael. **McKenzie's Boots.** Orchard Books, 1988. 249 pp. ISBN 0-531-05748-8. Fiction.

Rod Murray is fourteen when he decides to try to join the Australian Army during World War II. He is six feet tall and wears size thirteen boots. On his third try he is mustered in and changes his name to McKenzie (his grandmother's name). Rod is sent to New Guinea where, after months of fighting and killing the enemy, he accidentally encounters a Japanese soldier in the jungle, and his life is suddenly and dramatically changed.

31.20 Reiss, Bob. **Saltmaker.** Viking, 1988. 316 pp. ISBN 0-670-80247-6. Fiction.

General DeLavery is demonstrating to reporters how the mammoth underground NORAD nuclear command center functions when the early warning system indicates numerous Soviet missile launches aimed at the United States. Immediately he is on the phone to President William Madden, informing him that U.S. missiles will have to be launched within the next four minutes, before the Soviet nuclear missiles hit their targets. But the President's decision is not to launch. Over the red hotline phone, Madden announces to the Soviet premier that the United States is surrendering. Thirty seconds later it is discovered that there is no attack—a meteor shower triggered the early warning. A humiliated Madden immediately resigns in disgrace, but his personal and political turmoil only increases. And his attempt at avoiding nuclear confrontation seems to be leading the United States directly to an increased chance of war.

31.21 Safer, Morley. **Flashbacks: On Returning to Vietnam.** Random House, 1990. 206 pp. ISBN 0-394-58374-4. Nonfiction.

In this book, Morley Safer, CBS News correspondent and *60 Minutes* veteran, returns to Vietnam, where his tough reporting in the 1960s won him both acclaim and wrath. Through him, meet General Vo Nguyen Giap, commander of the Vietnamese forces, as he reminisces about the war, speculates on American strategic mistakes, and recalls without regret the hordes of people he sent to certain death. Meet a woman who founded the Vietcong as she remembers the loss of her baby and the loss of her revolution. See Vietnam today and see it as it was, in this precise, insightful, and sometimes even hilarious account of "the war nobody won."

31.22 Sender, Ruth Minsky. **To Life.** Macmillan, 1988. 229 pp. ISBN 0-02-781831-4. Fiction.

Nineteen-year-old Riva Minska walks out of a Nazi labor camp believing that she has finally been freed. In fact, her search for true freedom has just begun. Her return home to Lodz, Poland, in search of any surviving members of her family, is filled with dangers—soldiers, starvation, and fear. When at last she reaches her home, she finds no one. Her family is gone. But she won't give up; she continues on to Wroclaw, Poland, where she hopes to find her older brother and sisters among the refugees from other labor camps. She doesn't find her siblings in Wroclaw; instead, she meets the man she will marry and who will accompany her on her continuing, desperate search for anyone from her family who survived the Nazi horrors. It there anyone left? Has she lost everyone? With her new husband, Riva makes her way across the world, searching for answers and making a new life for herself in the aftermath of the Holocaust that may have cost her everything she ever had.

32 Westerns

32.1 Bass, Milton. **Jory.** New American Library/Signet, 1987. 222 pp. ISBN 0-451-14932-7. Fiction.

After fourteen-year-old Jory sees his alcoholic father beaten to death, his friends, the Jordans, think they're sending him to St. Louis to live with Mr. Jordan's brother; instead, Jory decides to hire on with two Texans on their way back home. One of the Texans, Jocko, discovers Jory is a natural with guns—both in the quickness of his draw and the accuracy of his aim. The trip back to Texas and the Barron ranch is a tough one, and young Jory uses his guns often. After they arrive at the ranch, Jory thinks he's in love with Amy Barron, which leads him to face a difficult decision: stay with Amy and accept the responsibility of the ranch or leave and continue using his guns to survive.

32.2 Bass, Milton. **Mistr Jory.** New American Library/Signet, 1987. 207 pp. ISBN 0-451-14965-3. Fiction.

When Jory takes the job as foreman of the Kingman Spread, he has his work cut out for him: he has to deliver a big herd of cattle to the U.S. Army—fast! Worse, his crew won't take orders without a fight, while cattle rustlers are waiting to ambush him. The teenage foreman has to pull things together, his guns blazing often as he tries to protect his crew and deliver the cattle.

32.3 Carter, Peter. **Borderlands.** Farrar, Straus and Giroux, 1990. 424 pp. ISBN 0-374-30895-0. Fiction.

It is 1871 when thirteen-year-old Ben Curtis and his older brother, Bo, are forced to leave their land in Texas and find work on a cattle drive heading for Abilene. It's a hot and dusty trail, with long hours on horseback and many dangers. But when they reach Abilene, Ben's life is changed forever. Cowboys and settlers, lawmen and outlaws, buffalo hunters, bankruptcy, but most of all the vast, haunting, and haunted Great Plains all feature in this story of how the West really was.

32.4 Hotze, Sollace. **A Circle Unbroken.** Clarion Books, 1988. 202 pp. ISBN 0-89919-733-7. Fiction.

Kata Wi, for seven years raised as an Indian girl, has almost forgotten her white parents and her own name—Rachel. She is brought back to her family and has to relearn their ways. Their fear and hatred of Indians is the toughest problem she has to face. How can she keep both families?

32.5 Schenker, Dona. **Throw a Hungry Loop.** Alfred A. Knopf/Borzoi Books, 1990. 114 pp. ISBN 0-679-90332-1. Fiction.

Thirteen-year-old Tres lives on a ranch with his father and his grandfather. He has a talent for throwing loops and expects to join the rodeo circuit someday, though he desperately yearns for a roping horse, which he needs to fulfill his dream. But Tres encounters family obstacles and small-town prejudices that challenge his commitment to his dream.

Directory of Publishers

Ace Books. Division of Berkley Publishing Group. Orders to: P.O. Box 506, East Rutherford, NJ 07073. 800-631-8571.

Ace/Putnam. See Ace Books.

Algonquin Books of Chapel Hill. Division of Workman Publishing Co., 708 Broadway, New York, NY 10003. 800-722-7202.

Archway Paperbacks. Imprint of Simon and Schuster. Orders to: 200 Old Tappan Road, Old Tappan, NJ 07675. 800-223-2336.

Atheneum. Division of Macmillan. Orders to: 100 Front Street, Riverside, NJ 08075. 800-257-5755.

Atheneum/Jean Karl Books. See Atheneum.

The Atlantic Monthly Press. 19 Union Square W., 11th Floor, New York, NY 10003. 212-645-4462.

Avon Books. Orders to: P.O. Box 767, Dresden, TN 38225. 800-762-0779.

Avon/Camelot Books. Imprint of Avon. See Avon Books.

Avon/Flare Books. Imprint of Avon. See Avon Books.

Baen Books. Division of Baen Publishing Enterprises, P.O. Box 1403, Riverdale, NY 10471. 800-223-2336.

Ballantine Books. Division of Random House. Orders to: 400 Hahn Road, Westminster, MD 21157. 800-733-3000.

Ballantine/Del Rey Books. See Ballantine Books.

Ballantine/Ivy Books. See Ballantine Books.

Bantam Books. Division of Bantam Doubleday Dell, 666 Fifth Avenue, New York, NY 10103. 800-223-6834.

Bantam/Spectra Books. See Bantam Books.

Bantam/Starfire Books. See Bantam Books.

Borzoi Books. Subsidiary of Random House. Orders to: 400 Hahn Road, Westminster, MD 21157. 800-733-3000.

Bradbury Press. Imprint of Macmillan. Orders to: 100 Front Street, Riverside, NJ 08075. 800-257-5755.

Jonathan Cape. Division of Trafalgar Square, P.O. Box 257, North Pomfret, VT 05053. 800-423-4525.

Carroll and Graf. 260 Fifth Avenue, New York, NY 10001. 212-889-8772.

Cassell. Division of Sterling Publishing, 387 Park Avenue, S., New York, NY 10016-8810. 800-367-9692.

Cassell/Blandford. See Cassell.

Cassell/Wardlock. See Cassell.

Celestial Arts. Subsidiary of Ten Speed Press, P.O. Box 7123, Berkeley, CA 94707. 800-841-2665.

Clarion Books. Division of Houghton Mifflin. Orders to: Wayside Road, Burlington, MA 01803. 800-225-3362. Call for school ordering information.

Cobblehill Books. Division of Penguin USA. Orders to: 120 Woodbine Street, Bergenfield, NJ 07621. 800-253-6476.

Collins. Division of HarperCollins. Orders to: 1000 Keystone Industrial Park, Scranton, PA 18512. 800-242-7737.

William Collins and Sons. Division of Penguin USA. Orders to: 120 Woodbine Street, Bergenfield, NJ 07621. 800-253-6476.

The Countryman Press. P.O. Box 175, Woodstock, VT 05091-0175. 800-245-4151.

Thomas Y. Crowell. Distributed by HarperCollins. Orders to: 1000 Keystone Industrial Park, Scranton, PA 18512. 800-242-7737.

Crown/Harmony Books. See Crown Publishers.

Crown Publishers. Division of Random House. Orders to: 400 Hahn Road, Westminster, MD 21157. 800-733-3000.

DAW Books. Distributed by Penguin USA. Orders to: 120 Woodbine Street, Bergenfield, NJ 07621. 800-253-6476.

Del Rey. Division of Random House. Orders to: 400 Hahn Road, Westminster, MD 21157. 800-733-3000.

Delacorte Press. Division of Bantam Doubleday Dell. Orders to: 666 Fifth Avenue, New York, NY 10103. 800-223-6834.

Dell. Division of Bantam Doubleday Dell, 666 Fifth Avenue, New York, NY 10103. 800-223-6834.

Dell/Laurel-Leaf Books. See Dell.

Dembner Books. Division of Barricade Books, 61 Fourth Avenue, New York, NY 10003. 212-228-8828.

Dial Books. Division of Penguin USA. Orders to: 120 Woodbine Street, Bergenfield, NJ 07621. 800-253-6476.

Dial Books for Young Readers. See Dial Books.

Tom Doherty Associates. Distributed by St. Martin's Press, 175 Fifth Avenue, New York, NY 10019. 800-221-7945.

Tom Doherty Associates/Tor Fantasy. See Tom Doherty Associates.

Donning Company. 184 Business Park Drive, Suite 106, Virginia Beach, VA 23462-6533. 800-446-8572.

Doubleday. Division of Bantam Doubleday Dell, 666 Fifth Avenue, New York, NY 10103. 800-223-6834.

Doubleday/Foundation Books. See Doubleday.

E. P. Dutton. Division of Penguin USA. Orders to: 120 Woodbine Street, Bergenfield, NJ 07621. 800-253-6476.

Dutton Children's Books. See Dutton.

Enslow Publishers. Bloy Street and Ramsey Avenue, Box 777, Hillside, NJ 07205. 908-964-4116.

M. Evans. 216 E. 49th Street, New York, NY 10017. 800-462-6420 (schools) or 212-688-2810 (individuals).

Facts on File. Subsidiary of Commerce Clearing House, 460 Park Avenue, S., New York, NY 10016. 800-322-8755.

Farrar, Straus and Giroux. 390 Murray Hill Parkway, East Rutherford, NJ 07073. ATTN: Dept. B. 800-631-8571.

Fawcett. Division of Ballantine Books. Orders to: 400 Hahn Road, Westminster, MD 21157. 800-733-3000.

Fawcett Crest. See Fawcett.

Fawcett/Gold Medal Books. See Fawcett.

Fawcett/Juniper Books. See Fawcett.

Donald I. Fine. Distributed by Penguin USA. Orders to: 120 Woodbine Street, Bergenfield, NJ 07621. 800-526-0275.

Firebird Books. Distributed by Sterling Publishing, 387 Park Avenue, S., New York, NY 10016-8810. 800-367-9692.

Fireside Books. Division of Warren H. Green, 8356 Olive Boulevard, St. Louis, MO 63132. 800-537-0655.

Gallery Books. Division of Smithmark Publishers. Orders to: 80 Distribution Boulevard, Edison, NJ 08817. 800-932-0070.

Graywolf Press. 2402 University Avenue, Suite 203, St. Paul, MN 55114. 612-641-0077.

Greenwillow Books. Division of William Morrow. Orders to: 39 Plymouth Street, Fairfield, NJ 07004. 800-843-9389.

Grove Press. Division of Wheatland Corp., 841 Broadway, New York, NY 10003-4793. 212-614-7850.

Hamish Hamilton. Imprint of Penguin USA. Orders to: 120 Woodbine Street, Bergenfield, NJ 07621. 800-253-6476.

Harcourt Brace Jovanovich. 6277 Sea Harbor Drive, Orlando, FL 32887. 800-225-5425.

Harcourt Brace Jovanovich/Jane Yolen Books. See Harcourt Brace Jovanovich.

Harmony Books. Division of Random House. Orders to: 400 Hahn Road, Westminster, MD 21157. 800-733-3000.

Harper and Row. Division of HarperCollins. Orders to: 1000 Keystone Industrial Park, Scranton, PA 18512. 800-242-7737.

Harper and Row/Charlotte Zolotow Books. See Harper and Row.

Harper and Row/Perennial Library. See Harper and Row.

HarperCollins. Orders to: 1000 Keystone Industrial Park, Scranton, PA 18512. 800-242-7737.

Hill and Company. 754 Main Street, Presque Isle, ME 04769. 800-462-6420.

Hill and Wang. Division of Farrar, Straus and Giroux. Orders to: 390 Murray Hill Parkway, East Rutherford, NJ 07073. ATTN: Dept. B. 800-631-8571.

Hodder and Stoughton. Division of Lubrecht and Cramer, R.D. 1, Box 244, 38 County Road 48, Forestburgh, NY 12777. 914-794-8539.

Holiday House. 425 Madison Avenue, New York, NY 10017. 212-688-0085.

Henry Holt. Orders to: 4375 W. 1980 S., Salt Lake City, UT 84104. 800-488-5233.

Henry Holt/Donald Hutter Books. See Henry Holt.

Henry Holt/Owl Books. See Henry Holt.

Houghton Mifflin. Orders to: Wayside Road, Burlington, MA 01803. 800-225-3362.

Houghton Mifflin/Seymour Lawrence. See Houghton Mifflin.

Alfred A. Knopf. Subsidiary of Random House. Orders to: 400 Hahn Road, Westminster, MD 21157. 800-733-3000.

Alfred A. Knopf/Borzoi Books. See Alfred A. Knopf.

Alfred A. Knopf/Borzoi Sprinters. See Alfred A. Knopf.

Lerner. 241 First Avenue, N., Minneapolis, MN 55401. 800-328-4929.

J. B. Lippincott. 227 E. Washington Square, Philadelphia, PA 19106-3780. 800-638-3030.

Little, Brown. Division of Time Warner Publishing. Orders to: 200 West Street, Waltham, MA 02254. 800-343-9204.

Little, Brown/Joy Street Books. See Little, Brown.

Lodestar Books. Division of Dutton Children's Books. Orders to: Penguin USA, 120 Woodbine Street, Bergenfield, NJ 07621. 800-253-6476.

Lothrop, Lee and Shepard Books. Division of William Morrow. Orders to: 39 Plymouth Street, Fairfield, NJ 07004. 800-843-9389.

Macmillan. Orders to: 100 Front Street, Riverside, NJ 08075. 800-257-5755.

Macmillan/Collier Books. See Macmillan.

McClelland-Bantam/Seal Books. 105 Bond Street, Toronto, ON M5B 1Y3, Canada. 416-340-0777.

Margaret K. McElderry Books. Division of Macmillan Children's Books Group. See Macmillan.

Julian Messner. Division of Silver Burdett Press. Orders to: P.O. Box 1226, Westwood, NJ 07675-1226. 800-843-3464.

Millennium. Orders to: Walker and Company, 720 Fifth Avenue, New York, NY 10019. 800-289-2553.

Minstrel Books. Division of Simon and Schuster. Orders to: 200 Old Tappan Road, Old Tappan, NJ 07675. 800-223-2336.

Morrow Junior Books. See William Morrow.

William Morrow. Orders to: 39 Plymouth Street, Fairfield, NJ 07004. 800-843-9389.

New American Library. Division of Penguin USA. Orders to: 120 Woodbine Street, Bergenfield, NJ 07621. 800-253-6476.

New American Library/Mentor. See New American Library.

New American Library/Signet. See New American Library.

New American Library/Signet Classics. See New American Library.

New Society Publishers. 4527 Springfield Avenue, Philadelphia, PA 19143. 800-333-9093.

Newmarket Press. Division of Newmarket Publishing and Communications. Distributed by Random House. Orders to: 400 Hahn Road, Westminster, MD 21157. 800-733-3000.

NewSage Press. P.O. Box 41029, Pasadena, CA 91104. 818-795-0266.

North Point Press. Distributed by Farrar, Straus and Giroux. Orders to: 390 Murray Hill Parkway, East Rutherford, NJ 07073. ATTN: Dept. B. 800-631-8571.

W. W. Norton. 500 Fifth Avenue, New York, NY 10110. 800-233-4830.

Orchard Books. Division of Franklin Watts. 387 Park Avenue, S., New York, NY 10016. 800-672-6672.

Orchard Books/Richard Jackson Books. See Orchard Books.

Oxford University Press. Orders to: ATTN: Order Department, 2001 Evans Road, Cary, NC 27513. 800-451-7556.

Pantheon Books. Division of Random House. Orders to: 400 Hahn Road, Westminster, MD 21157. 800-733-3000.

Pfeifer-Hamilton. Division of Whole Person Associates. P.O. Box 3151, Duluth, MN 55803. 800-247-6789.

Philomel Books. Imprint of The Putnam Berkley Group. Orders to: 390 Murray Hill Parkway, East Rutherford, NJ 07073. 800-631-8571.

Pineapple Press. P.O. Drawer 16008, Southside Station, Sarasota, FL 34239. 813-952-1085.

Plume Books. Imprint of Penguin USA. Orders to: 120 Woodbine Street, Bergenfield, NJ 07621. 800-526-0275.

Pocket Books. Division of Simon and Schuster. Orders to: 200 Old Tappan Road, Old Tappan, NJ 07675. 800-223-2336.

Popular Library. Imprint of Warner Books, 1271 Sixth Avenue, New York, NY 10020. 212-484-2900.

Poseidon Press. Unit of Simon and Schuster Trade Division. Orders to: 200 Old Tappan Road, Old Tappan, NJ 07675. 800-223-2336.

G. P. Putnam's Sons. Imprint of The Putnam Berkley Group. Orders to: 390 Murray Hill Parkway, East Rutherford, NJ 07073. 800-631-8571.

Random House. Orders to: 400 Hahn Road, Westminster, MD 21157. 800-733-3000.

Real Comet Press. Subsidiary of Such a Deal Corp. Distributed by Inland Book Company, 140 Commerce Street, East Haven, CT 06512. 800-243-0138.

ROC Books. Imprint of Penguin USA. Orders to: 120 Woodbine Street, Bergenfield, NJ 07621. 800-526-0275.

Rosen Publishing Group. 29 E. 21st Street, New York, NY 10010. 800-237-9932.

St. Martin's Press. 175 Fifth Avenue, New York, NY 10010. 800-221-7945.

Scholastic. Orders to: 2931 E. McCarty Street, Jefferson City, MO 65102. 800-325-6149.

Scholastic Hardcovers. See Scholastic.

Scholastic/Point. See Scholastic.

Scott, Foresman and Company. Division of HarperCollins. Orders to: 1900 E. Lake Avenue, Glenview, IL 60025. 800-554-4411.

Charles Scribner's Sons. Division of Macmillan. Orders to: 100 Front Street, Riverside, NJ 08075. 800-257-5755.

Seal Press. 3131 Western Avenue, Suite 410, Seattle, WA 98121. 206-283-7844.

Signet. Imprint of Penguin USA. Orders to: 120 Woodbine Street, Bergenfield, NJ 07621. 800-526-0275.

Silver Burdett Press. Subsidiary of Simon and Schuster. Orders to: P.O. Box 1226, Westwood, NJ 07675-1226. 800-843-3464.

Simon and Schuster. Orders to: 200 Old Tappan Road, Old Tappan, NJ 07675. 800-223-2336.

Soho Press. Orders to: The Putnam Publishing Group, 1 Grosset Drive, Kirkwood, NY 13795. 800-631-8571; in New Jersey, call 201-933-9292.

Spectra Books. See Bantam Books.

Square One Publishers. 6 Birch Hill Road, Ballston Lake, NY 12019. 508-877-4946.

Stackpole Books. Division of Commonwealth Communications Services, P.O. Box 1831, Cameron and Kelker Streets, Harrisburg, PA 17105. 800-732-3669.

Sterling. 387 Park Avenue, S., New York, NY 10016-8810. 800-367-9692.

Stewart, Tabori and Chang. Distributed by Workman Publishing, 708 Broadway, New York, NY 10003. 800-722-7202.

Summit Books. Unit of Simon and Schuster Trade Division. Orders to: 200 Old Tappan Road, Old Tappan, NJ 07675. 800-223-2336.

Tessera Publishing. 9561 Woodridge Circle, Eden Prairie, MN 55347. 612-941-5053.

Thorndike Press. P.O. Box 159, Thorndike, ME 04986. 207-948-2962.

Times Books. Division of Random House. Orders to: 400 Hahn Road, Westminster, MD 21157. 800-733-3000.

Tor. Division of Tom Doherty Associates. Distributed by St. Martin's Press, 175 Fifth Avenue, New York, NY 10019. 800-221-7945.

Troll Associates/Watermill Press. Subsidiary of Educational Reading Services, 100 Corporate Drive, Mahwah, NJ 07430. 800-526-5289.

Turman Publishing. 1319 Dexter Avenue, N., Suite 30, Seattle, WA 98109. 206-282-6900.

University of Nevada Press. MS 166, UNR, Reno, NV 89577. 702-784-6573.

University Press of New England/Wesleyan University Press. 23 S. Main Street, Hanover, NH 03755. 800-421-1561.

Viking Kestrel. Division of Penguin USA. Orders to: 120 Woodbine Street, Bergenfield, NJ 07621. 800-253-6476.

Viking Penguin. Division of Penguin USA. Orders to: 120 Woodbine Street, Bergenfield, NJ 07621. 800-253-6476.

Villard Books. Division of Random House. Orders to: 400 Hahn Road, Westminster, MD 21157. 800-733-3000.

Walker and Company. Division of Walker Publishing, 720 Fifth Avenue, New York, NY 10019. 800-289-2553.

Warner Books. 1271 Sixth Avenue, New York, NY 10020. 212-484-2900.

Franklin Watts. Subsidiary of Grolier, 387 Park Avenue, S., 4th Floor, New York, NY 10016. 800-672-6672.

Wesleyan University Press. Distributed by University Press of New England, 23 S. Main Street, Hanover, NH 03755. 800-421-1561.

John Wiley & Sons. Orders to: 1 Wiley Drive, Somerset, NJ 08875. 908-469-4400.

Workman Publishing. 708 Broadway, New York, NY 10003. 800-722-7202.

Yankee Publishing. *Winter Wolves* is no longer available. Other orders to: Rodale Press, 33 East Minor Street, Emmaus, PA 18098. 800-441-7761.

Charlotte Zolotow. Imprint of HarperCollins. Orders to: 1000 Keystone Industrial Park, Scranton, PA 18512. 800-242-7737.

Author Index

Title Index

Subject Index

Editor

Shirley Wurth is Coordinator of Public Information for the Raytown School District in Raytown, Missouri. She has taught at both the elementary and secondary levels and has been active in a number of professional organizations, including both the Missouri and National School Public Relations Associations, the Missouri Association of Teachers of English, and the National Council of Teachers of English. In addition to these and other scholarly affiliations, she serves her community through a wide variety of organizations.